'It's time, HR people! It's time for us to be brave and to boldly and finally step into the next generation of HR that the world of work is eagerly looking on at us for. This book hands us this beautifully on a plate, giving us the key ingredients of an operating model of spirit and flow, human centredness and engineering, and readies us to supercharge the human and digital age in the workplace. I was propelled with spark and inspiration throughout and cannot wait to get started. This is a must read for anyone in HR who knows that in our world, our operating model, that it is time, HR 3.0 is finally here.'
Michelle Clark, Executive Director of People, Culture and Transformation, The Children's Society

'This book is all you need to know about operating models and the ultimate solution, HR 3.0. Perry Timms is exactly the people scientist, Futures Thinker, HR trend setter and legendary thought leader that this book needed and he has delivered with a unique masterpiece that will stand the test of time for many years to come.'
Idris Arshad, Head of People, Asthma + Lung UK

'I see this book as a catalyst for progression with the introduction of a modernized HR operating model. This book is a call to action; it is time for us to think differently. Whether you are someone who is currently operating in a more traditional HR space or already a progressive people professional who is ambitiously carving out new ways of working, you will glean all the inspiration you need, through Perry Timms' work, along with a plethora of recommended books and resources to delve deeper into the science.'
Nebel Crowhurst, Chief People Officer, Reward Gateway

'Perry Timms reframes the HR function as a designer of systems that generate energy – the fuel for people, performance and progress. This book helped me see that energy is always a system's outcome, and that HR 3.0 shows us how to design for the kind of energy that sustains people and drives value.'
Chris Metcalfe, Founder, Red Oak Agency

'So many talk about changing the system – Perry Timms has actually built something that can. In a world of continuous disruption, *The HR Operating Model* offers more than a blueprint: it's an anchor. It supports organizations as they undertake transformation and organizational design, offering a people function that truly aligns with business outcomes and stakeholder value. For anyone serious about building a world-class people function that delivers competitive advantage, this book is essential reading.'
Louise Brown, Board Chair, City HR Association

'*The HR Operating Model* is a significant guide to HR Professionals, and their C suite collaborators, enabling them to co-build the people system for the next decade.

'Perry Timms is both professionally and soulfully diligent as he guides the reader through the evolutions of HR models, aiming at presenting a Systems Thinking model for the modern, Futures-Thinking HR professional. In parallel, he highlights the identity shift in HR towards shaping the ecosystem rather than solving problems; towards forward thinking rather than responding.

'*Using the future to make decisions today* is a mantra among futurists and Futures Thinkers, and this is just what Perry Timms does: using the ideas, trends, movements and disruptions that currently shape the business world to imagine scenarios and futures for the HR function. From that, his HR 3.0 Operating Model emerges, as an enabler for the futures-ready organization.'
Erik Korsvik Østergaard, futurist, author and leadership adviser

'Perry Timms has always had the ability to influence HR professionals, but this book takes it to a new level – redefining how our profession could be organized in order to have impact, on a global scale, into the future. Perry has given us the tool to seize the moment and turn the HR function on its head – together. By the final page, you'll not only believe in the need for change – you'll be equipped, inspired and ready to lead it with confidence and purpose.'
Alex Bibby, Director of HR, The Guide Dogs for the Blind Association

'Perry Timms' HR 3.0 model represents a progressive evolution of the people function, one that resonates strongly with the postmodern paradigm. It challenges the traditional, linear models of HR by embracing a more fluid, participatory and systemic approach. Reimagining HR roles as Relationship Brokers, Systems Designers, Product Managers and Meaning Makers, the model places emphasis on people, processes, systems and products – not as silos, but as interconnected elements of organizational vitality.'
David Liddle, CEO, TCM Group, and author of *Managing Conflict* and *Transformational Conflict*

The HR Operating Model

Designing a people function that supports the workforce and the business

Perry Timms

KoganPage

First published in Great Britain and the United States in 2025 by Kogan Page Limited

Kogan Page

Kogan Page Ltd, 2nd Floor, 45 Gee Street, London EC1V 3RS, United Kingdom
Kogan Page Inc, 8 W 38th Street, Suite 902, New York, NY 10018, USA
www.koganpage.com

EU Representative (GPSR)

Authorised Rep Compliance Ltd, Ground Floor, 71 Baggot Street Lower, Dublin D02 P593, Ireland
www.arccompliance.com

Kogan Page books are printed on paper from sustainable forests.

ISBNs

Hardback   978 1 3986 2239 5
Paperback   978 1 3986 2237 1
Ebook   978 1 3986 2238 8

British Library Cataloguing-in-Publication Data

A CIP record for this book is available from the British Library.

Library of Congress Control Number

2025938722

Typeset by Integra Software Services, Pondicherry
Printed and bound by CPI Group (UK) Ltd, Croydon CR0 4YY

CONTENTS

Foreword xi

Acknowledgements, appreciation and thanks xiii

1 **Introduction to HR operating models** 1

Operating models – engineering on display 1
Work is engineering 2
What is an operating model? 5
Operating models and business models 7
OD – going beyond the operating model 8
In closing 15
References and further reading 17

2 **The emerging future of work and its catalytic changes for HR** 18

Introduction 18
Futures Thinking 20
Systems in OD and the HR Operating Model 23
OD as the 'HR superpower' 26
Science in OD and the HR Operating Model 26
How does this all link to Futures Thinking? 30
An HR scenario using the four elements of Lindkvist's futurist
    framework 33
Theories of human-centred evolution of work 34
Audacious futures 36
In summary 40
References and further reading 41
Expanded references for Table 2.1 41

3 **The evolution of HR Operating Models** 44

Five words to frame the importance of an optimized HR operating
    model 46
The HR Operating Model evolution 49
Is there a more criticized function in the corporate world than HR? 52
The nobility in work we should never overlook 55

The significance of your HR Operating Model 57
Overview of the HR Business Partner-based operating model 58
21st-century impacts on the HR Business Partner model 60
References and Further Reading 66

4   Additional perspectives on HR Operating Models 68

Introduction 68
Gartner's view 69
McKinsey's view 70
Deloitte's view 72
The Talent Strategy Group 74
Mercer's Target Integration Model 77
EY's People Value Chain Model 79
The Chartered Institute of Personnel and Development (CIPD) 81
CIPD HR Operating Models Review 2024 83
The 'father' of modern HR and his take on an evolved model 88
Josh Bersin's vision for the future of HR 93
References and further reading 98

5   HR 3.0: The genesis, Systems and People Operations 99

Introduction 99
The genesis of a new operating model for HR 100
Using this model (influenced by the 42@Work model) 104
How I see the HR 3.0 model working 108
HR 3.0 – elevating People Operations 113
HR 3.0 – focusing on Systems 114
References and further reading 119

6   Core principles of HR 3.0: Products and Science 121

Products: a shift from compliance to value 122
HR product management in action: three scenarios 126
Agility and product management in HR 3.0 128
Progressive approaches to data and analytics in HR 131
Predictive and prescriptive analytics: from insight to action 133
People and performance analysts: the new data translators in HR 133
Ethical considerations in HR data and analytics 135
The role of science in HR 3.0 135

Technology integration in HR 3.0: digital tools and platforms for a smarter workforce 140
References and further reading 147

7 **Implementing and transitioning to HR 3.0** 148

Getting started 149
Exploring and capturing the essence of vibrant culture 155
Into operational mode – our delivery agenda 157
Creating a transition plan 161
People, planet and prosperity-centric design: HR 3.0's role in shaping additional forms of value 166
Implementing HR 3.0: practical strategies 168
References and further reading 170

8 **Real-world applications influencing HR 3.0** 171

Introduction 171
Diverse industry examples: HR teams who have influenced HR 3.0 172
An operating model built for change *and* stability 180
An operating model built to flex 181
References and further reading 184

9 **Overcoming challenges in HR Operating Model transformation** 186

Introduction 186
Identifying barriers: why HR hasn't shifted its operating model in 25+ years 187
Strategic solutions: moving towards a new HR Operating Model 192
Developing new HR capabilities in systems, products, analytics, digital and science 197
Potential business resistance to HR 3.0: organizational barriers to transformation 199
Overcoming barriers: experimentation, iteration and adaptive change 203
The future of HR's Operating Model: sustaining long-term evolution 206
References and further reading 209

10   Insights from thought leaders 211

Introduction: the new frontiers of HR 211

Key components of HR 3.0 as a progressive operating model:
  HR's shift to dynamic, iterative ways of working 213

Science and data-driven HR: transforming HR into an evidence-based
  discipline 217

Systems Thinking and organizational complexity: rethinking HR as an
  adaptive system 222

Process and product mindset: reimagining HR as a design-driven
  discipline 227

Cultural sensitivity, inclusion and intersectionality as strategic
  imperatives 232

HR 3.0 in practice: transforming the people function 239

References and further reading 242

11   HR 3.0 and organizational culture 245

Introduction 245

Culture transformation: HR 3.0 as a catalyst for change 245

Shaping culture through behaviour and mindsets 251

References and further reading 255

12   Conclusion and call to action 257

Introduction 257

Changing change management: a theory of evolutionary change 258

The HR 3.0 playbook: a step-by-step guide 263

References and further reading 269

Index 270

FOREWORD

HR doesn't need another book full of abstract models or empty buzzwords. What it needs, what we need, is clarity, courage and a new operating logic that cuts through the chaos, unpredictability and contradiction of today's workplaces.

There are moments in every profession when the stars align, and we're presented with an opportunity to redefine the future. For HR, that moment is most certainly now, and the potential to shape the next era of work is within our reach. We must transform in order to remain relevant, respected and trusted, because without that transformation, we risk becoming obsolete in a world that demands more of us in the HR profession than ever before.

When Perry and I met seven years ago, we clicked immediately. Kindred spirits. I will always be grateful for that day, as it ignited a partnership that has shaped so much of my thinking. We shared the same fire: restless about the state of our profession, hungry for meaningful change and fiercely committed to making HR not just relevant but transformative. Both of us brought a shared understanding of Systems Thinking and design principles, which shaped how we view the interconnectedness of people, processes, technology and outcomes. Our conversations have always cut deep into capability, culture, purpose, performance, and how we shift from theory to action in ways that matter for real people in real organisations.

The HR profession already owes a great deal to Perry's thinking and unwavering commitment to pushing us forward. His relentless dedication to evolving our field has sparked new ideas, fostered bold conversations and helped countless leaders rethink their roles in a rapidly changing world. And now, with this book, he's tipping the scales even further, offering a roadmap that could genuinely redefine how we operate as a profession.

This seminal book is built from that kind of thinking. It doesn't romanticise the past or recycle old frameworks. Instead, it critically examines the operating models that have dominated the HR landscape for decades, starting with Ulrich's foundational work and extending to those put forward by McKinsey, Harvard, and others. Perry doesn't just highlight their strengths; he digs into their weaknesses and asks the tough questions: where have these models fallen short, and how can we break free from outdated assumptions to create something that truly works for today's organisations?

What Perry calls **HR Operating Model 3.0** is not just a tweak to what's gone before, it's a provocation. A sharp, informed, and necessary redefinition of how HR delivers value in organisations that are messy, dynamic, and constantly evolving.

So let me be clear: this book isn't comfortable reading, and it's not meant to be.

Perry doesn't offer neat answers or polished models that fit conveniently onto a slide. What he offers is far more valuable: a provocation, a framework for action, and a deep respect for the complexity of the real-world HR leaders are navigating every day.

He's done the hard thinking, the kind that makes you stop mid-sentence and reflect, not just on the design of your function, but on the impact you're really having. It's rigorous, practical, and full of hard-won insight from someone who has lived this work, not just studied it.

This is the model for those who are tired of defending HR, and ready to redefine it.

It's for those who believe our job isn't to mirror the business, but to challenge it, evolve it, and shape it to be more human, more intentional, and more capable of delivering sustainable performance.

It's for those who know that purpose and profit aren't at odds, but that unlocking both demands better systems, braver decisions, and a total rethink of how we show up as a profession.

You don't need to agree with everything in this book. But you do need to engage with it, because what's laid out here will provoke you, push you, and pull you forward. In years to come, I am certain we will all look back at this work and think 'this was the one that changed the game'.

I would argue that right now, that is exactly what is needed. The world doesn't need incremental change, it needs an HR that is bold, unflinching, and unafraid to reshape itself to meet the demands of tomorrow. This is the moment to take the leap, to challenge the norms, and to step into a future where HR is not just a function, but an enabling force that drives extraordinary value, purpose, and performance. The question is: are you ready to lead the charge?

Bertie Tonks

ACKNOWLEDGEMENTS, APPRECIATION AND THANKS

Writing a book – let alone a third one – is because you have people with you, who back you, inspire you and share with you. This long list is those who've done at least one of these things, if not all four.

First, as this is a book about HR Operating Models, a very special acknowledgement and thanks to Professor Dave Ulrich. You've championed, researched, and enlightened the HR and People Profession for decades. Without your work from the 1990s and on, HR would probably not exist. We owe you so much gratitude, and this book is as much a tribute to continuing your work as my own labour of love.

To the team I've come to bond, bind and believe in more than any other group of people I've ever worked with. Agnè Chmyznikova, Catalina Ticau, Hannah Rogers, Katy Stanley, Kirsten Buck and Maddy Woodman are the most special people. Riding the waves and choppy waters of PTHR's operating world, you've helped me see how mighty an adaptive and effective Operating Model is in helping build the relationships and systems for another labour of love – our enterprise. This is for all of you and your futures.

A close group of People Professionals whom I've come to call my HR/OD Heroes: Bertie Tonks (and thanks for the outstanding foreword, my friend), Gill Morris, Michelle Clark, C-J Green, Sarah Eglin (your initial critiques of my thinking helped shape it into this body of work), Nebel Crowhurst, Idris Arshad, Louise Brown, Siobhan Sheridan, Teresa Gould, Lucy Tobin, Julie Griggs, Vikki Matthews, Kate Jansen, Rob Neil, Janice Keyes, Shakil Butt (who is an HR Hero for hire), Meg Cox, Woosh Raza, Jenna Blood, Emma Parry, Paul Taylor-Pitt, Gail Hatfield, Jo Pick; Katy Lumsden, Estelle Hollingsworth, Robert Ordever, Sarah Hayes, Vilma Nikolaidou, Vickie Lee, Gail Atkins, Kate Clay, Michelle Reid, Angela Newman, Samantha Betts, Kerry Smith, Kirsty Lister, Martyn Dicker, Michelle Fellows, Peter Reeve, Deborah Lee, Anouska Ramsey, Sue Swanborough and David Frost.

People who trust me to chair, curate and speak at their events. Christian Milam at Working Futures, Jane Barry at Liberty HR, Mihaly Nagy at the HR World Congress/Summit, Meena Anand and Andrea Eccles at City HR, Jeannine Mortlock at Hult International Business School and Steve Benfield at the OD Academy.

A fellow author who made such a magnanimous gesture to postpone his own publication and is a standout dedicated professional in People and Culture, David Liddle.

Erik Korsvik Østergaard, who is not only a decade-long friend and fellow 'new work' warrior and author, but whose work on Futures Thinking inspired me to include it in this book.

HR journalists who've given me airtime, column space and believed in my messages: Jo Gallacher (then *HR Magazine* Editor who afforded me a six-part serialization that was the prologue for this book), Becky Norman at HR Zone and lately Charissa King at *HR Magazine*. Plus, a special non-journalist mention to Research Lead at the CIPD, Rebecca Peters, for featuring my work in your review of HR Operating Models.

And outlying thinkers and doers in the world of work who've given me belief and backing: Gareth Jones, Eva Morales, Amy King, Nick Court, Gethin Nadin, Sarah-Jane Last, Rob Baker, Rob Robson, Nial Cluley, Tomas Chamorro-Premuzic; Chris Metcalfe; Neil Usher; Megan Reitz, Atif Choudhary, Hung Lee, Rich Sheridan, Bruce Daisley, Alex Edmans, Jaideep Prabhu, Rajeeb Dey, Margaret Heffernan, Rachel Pendered, Alexandra Couzens, Sophie Lovejoy, Helen Scott, William Murtha, Sarah Andrews, Dave Wynn, Michelle Minnikin, Lisa Gill, Helen Sanderson, Karen Tenelius, Jorge Silva, Christiaan Grové, Daphne Van Beek, Traci Fenton, Arko Van Brakel, Farouk El-Kodady, Pim de Morree, Joost Minnaar, Yvonne Verwohlt Hansen, Matteo Violi, Camilla Miehs, Ciprian Arhire, Obi Abuchi, Simone Fenton-Jarvis, Sasi Venables, Joanne Lockwood, Vicky O'Farrell, Vicky Campbell, Miranda Ash, Ray Pendleton, Nicky Hoyland, Luke O'Mahoney, Yetunde Hoffman, Chris Shambrook, Matthew Ash, Lizzie Benton, Sharon Aneja, Vikram Jain, Timm Urschinger, Danny Seals, Nina Pozderec, Jaka Kladnik, Kim Atherton, Porteur Keene, Jon Stanners, Nathan Ott, Amachree Isoboye Afanyaa, Harley Kisberg, Rbb Ashcroft, Tom Paisley, Martin Baker, Sonia Mooney, Robbie Jones, Neil Andrew, Conor Moss, Jana Ceklanovic, Andreea Runceanu, Cristina Riesen, Philippe Pinault, Angelique Slob, Gary Butterfield, Bill Banham, Jo Burrell, Penny Pullan, John Boudreau, Ravin Jesuthasan, Michele Zanini, Gary Hamel, Sergio Carredda, Otti Vogt, Antoinette Weibel, Natal Dank, John Stepper, Julie Turney, Andy Spence, Steven D'Souza, Toby Kheng, Heather McGowan, Saurav Chopra, Steven Frost, Danny Hodgson, Tim Littlehales, Helena Clayton, Tom Nixon, Garry Turner, Tom Levitt, Alex Sooyung-Kim Pang, Linda Holbeche, Naomi Stanford, Paul Tolchinsky and Dan Pontefract.

To a host of others who've inspired me and continue to do so along the way: Carina Sebastiao, Damiana Casile, Ana Marica, Maryanne Raasch, Michelle Parry-Slater, Chris Britten, Andy Lancaster, Evelina Dzimanaviciute, Danny Saadu, Cat Barnard, Claire Cathcart, Deborah Onbashi, Dafydd Sion, Julij Fischer, Ana Gabrscek, Kath Ennis, Holly Smith, Ulrika Brunner, Su Sehmer, Barbara Thompson, Nate Harwood, Donna Standing, Jessica Cooper, Charlotte Neil, Lee Avery, Laura Dawson, Nathalie Nahai, Alessia Mevoli, Aimee Haynes, Katie Marlow, Lynne Booth, Sharon Tan, Ainsley McLeod, Jo Wright, Agatha Fox, Tom Robinson, Milly Richardson, Katie Franklin-Thorpe, Tamasin Sutton, Natasa Tovornik, Arti Pun, Barry Cranford, Maureen Sandbach, Jacqui Findlay, Lisa Tomlinson, Teresa Wilkins, Sarah Giles, Kym Lovett, Ed Curley, Kerry Eldridge, Margaret Burnside, Shelley Measures, Nic Elliott, Sile O'Donnell, Nikki Keable, Emma-Jayne Perez-Chies, Marguerite Ulrich, Rochelle Haynes, Fiona Evans, Hilary Pearl, Desiré Saffer, Jane Rawden, Steve Othen, Dan Lucy, Zofia Bajorek Ryan Cheyne, Deborah Hartung, Duncan Ledger, Emma Djemil, Laura Weaving, Jenny Streeter, Liz Tolcher, Thomas Schilling, Helen Attia-Tolken, Emma Bridger, Belinda Gannaway, Gary Cookson, Garin Rouch, Dani Bacon, Halima Sacranie, Laura Weaving and Louise Dillon.

I did my best to recall those who've supported the things I do in the world that I love so much, whether that's supportive messages, LinkedIn likes and comments, sharing stages, working together, or kicking around thoughts on this crazy world.

This book is my ultimate labour of love. I care about what I do to help people experience a flourishing sense of life *and* their work. I have come to treasure and value the People Profession and HR practice field I'm a part of. This book – I hope – ushers in a new era for the profession and work.

My penultimate thanks are perhaps the biggest – to two people who are no longer in the world of work, through age or illness: my dad, Terry, and my wife (aka Mrs T), Teresa. They both know how devoted I am to the work that I do, and I hope I show a similar level of devotion in caring for, about and with you through the challenges of life you now have.

Lastly, thank you to the team at Kogan Page because you believed in me enough to put this book into the world. To Lucy, Joe, Susi and Helen – heartfelt thanks for being the platform to continue telling my story about this profession. One that suffers misunderstanding and criticism, but has the opportunity to turn things around and help people and organizations have that flourishing experience of work.

If no one's talking about HR Operating Models until this book, I hope we've all combined to give them something of a different perspective and talking point: to change the game and make the meaning of work something genuinely worthwhile.

Post script: One more poignant note of appreciation and gratitude is to the dearly departed Roxana Mocanu. Roxana did so much for me in my early days of independent practice and took me to Romania, where I met so many friends and learned so much. Rest in Power, Rocs. You'd have loved this book, so it's also a big tribute to you.

1

Introduction to HR operating models

A bad system will beat a good person every time.
W EDWARDS DEMING, ENGINEER, STATISTICIAN AND SYSTEMS THINKER

WHAT'S COVERED IN THIS CHAPTER

- **Overview and definitions:** Defining HR operating models and explaining their significance in organizational success.

- **HR operating models – the story so far:** A brief history of HR practices and how operating models have been shaped up to now.

- **The stimulators for change:** Why an evolved HR operating model is essential in a rapidly changing, turbulent, uncertain business environment.

Operating models – engineering on display

Engineering has given the human race a competitive edge on planet Earth, from the earliest forms of tool-making to the multifaceted sophistication of digitized tools and platforms of the virtual world we've created on top of the physical spaces we operate within.

Engineering is perhaps a bizarre starting point for a book about the Human Resources – or now more often called the People – profession. It is bizarre because whilst engineering is a feat of human endeavour, it is associated with mechanics and automation more than things like spirit, motivation and feelings. Machines and machinery. Construction and constructs. Powered and powerful.

Engineering has seen the human race tame the world. Dams, ploughs and furnaces use natural elements (water, earth and fire) as assets to channel, grow and create things to improve our lives, solve problems and develop production systems that sustain an ever-complex form of life.

Human beings are engineers – all of us. The HR profession is really an engineering function in the world of work without ever being decreed as such.

Why is this corporate bureaucratic function deemed worthy of this engineer accolade? Let's take a somewhat philosophical look at how this form of engineering shapes people's work. All life on the planet 'does' work. Whether surviving predation, shaping a safer environment, foraging or hunting for food, territorial battling with rivals of the same (and different) species, or traversing the world in pursuit of survival, all living things work in some shape or form.

Only with the human race's advent of trade, mercantilism and commerce has it become a 'corporate' – or entrepreneurial – pursuit.

We now associate much of our work as a form of labour in return for tokens (aka money) that help us live a safe, satisfying and abundant life. And that work we do is now part of a complex series of systems we have engineered as the dominant force on the planet.

The HR profession – and work more widely – operates in economic, social, militaristic, religious, scientific and consumerist systems.

The Industrial Revolution of the 18th and 19th centuries created monolithic corporations working through controlling governmental, dictatorial and, in some cases, tribal or monarchical systems that channelled human labour (work) through pioneering individuals. This would result in enterprises (investors/inventors) using natural and synthesized resources (materials) assembled into products and sold to those labouring humans for economic gain (profit), eventually spreading to our systems of life in health, education, law and what governments provide.

And those moving parts of financing, materials, production and the graft of human beings had to come together in coordination, utilization and distribution systems. This brought into being the 'science' of management and, eventually, the role of the Human Resource management profession.

Work is engineering

If you have read Yuval Noah Harari's seminal work in his book *Sapiens*, or Dave Graeber's final published piece before his sad passing, *The Dawn of Everything*, you will know that both our social structures and our production systems have evolved through the advent of work and management of that work.

HR has a primary 'engineering' role in creating coordination systems to ensure that the organization is fair, legal, compliant, optimized and effective in supporting and enabling people to deliver their purpose and mission.

Within that economic transactional exchange also lies a sense of worth and value many people derive from their work – an increasingly powerful driver and differentiator for the world's most enduring and inspiring organizations. Flourishing people equate to a flourishing enterprise.

In doing that work, HR has crafted (or helped craft) systems, an environment, protective (and in some cases punitive) measures and processes. HR has been an essential component of well-governed enterprises that perform sustainably as a collection of people and systems.

It could be argued that if an organization is fortunate enough to have a compassionate and commercially brilliant leader, they are likely to have an organization to be proud of and that does the right thing by its obligations to not only customers and shareholders but also to its stakeholders, the communities that businesses operate in, the ecosystems of life and, of course, its own employees and colleagues.

Sadly, that's not always the case and HR's role, with either more benevolent leaders or hard-nosed capitalists, is to create the best systems where people are appreciated, rewarded and cared for, and performance now and in the future is optimized.

HR is, therefore, an engineer of people and systems at work. And neither are simple, easily replicable and scalable, and certainly not as predictable as we might like them to be:

- Think for a moment about how your mood and energy fluctuate. Sometimes, you find yourself incredibly motivated to do your best work and, at other times, incredibly jaded, distracted or even angry about your work.

- Think about how you respond to other people's behaviours. You might find comfort in being told what to do or resent it so much that you rebel and protest.

- Think about how the human ego, a desire for greed and power, prevails in some, whilst in others there is a strong sense of service, the pursuit of noble outcomes and helping other people without a thought to material gains for themselves.

Such polarity and variability in why people work, how much they enjoy it and are committed to the company and their team, and how satisfied they are with their reward and benefits, are the chaotic and complex elements for which the HR profession is tasked with engineering solutions.

Now think about how you may have experienced the HR profession in your time at work (or have read in the media).

- Bureaucrats
- The 'fun' police
- Policy creators
- On the side of poor managers
- Risk-averse administrators
- Tribunal avoiders
- Secretive
- Don't understand the business
- Overly representative of 'the people' and their whims/demands
- Locking horns with union leaders
- Always saying 'no' to inventive or alternative approaches

Now, think again about these experiences and set them against the multiple layers, interactions and unpredictability of those complex and chaotic systems of people, work and any form of enterprising organization.

Is it any wonder it's difficult and that consistent and repeatedly successful HR is a tough ask? To plot, develop, deliver and achieve consistently and in a standardized format is largely enigmatic.

Engineering aims to manage complexity and devise solutions that are as straightforward and practical as possible. In my 20+ years in HR, I would argue that even the volatility of chemicals is more definable (and therefore manageable) than people in organizations at work.

HR is undeniably one of the most complex functions within the world of work, given its unique intersection of human behaviour, strategic alignment and regulatory demands. However, functions like Finance, IT and Supply Chain Management also contend, with significant complexities, particularly in highly dynamic and regulated environments.

The difference between those functions and HR is that they still rely on, need and use HR. HR has to rely on itself. There's rarely 'HR for HR'.

HR navigates an increasingly broader range of macro complexities – such as emerging sciences, shifting human behaviours, complex strategic alignment, rapid technological innovation and increasingly demanding regulatory changes – to design effective solutions and scalable systems that address business-specific challenges while maintaining consistency across the organization.

This book is not, though, about glorifying HR over other corporate functions. It is to demonstrate how significantly challenging HR is and dispel the myth that it is an 'overlord bureaucrat' that adds no value to an enterprise. HR is perhaps under-credited with the engineering element of its function in that chaotic environment of people and systems of work, commerce, legal and production. Therefore, an operating model for HR is arguably not an easy one to conceive and continually adapt.

Understanding HR's complex and ever-shifting operating landscape may offer valuable context if you're **sceptical** of HR's performance and impact. If you're **neutral**, recognizing the intricate systems, sciences and challenges at play might deepen your appreciation of the function. And if you're pro-HR – or work within it – you may find a helpful reminder of the difficult conditions that make excellence in the field so demanding. Perhaps, too, this brings a newfound respect for the often-overlooked engineering behind the People profession.

This leads us to the importance and growth of the concept of operating models.

What is an operating model?

The last 10 years have seen even more focus on operating models – particularly through the phrase 'Target Operating Model'. Before we explore why this is suddenly *en vogue*, it is worth reminding ourselves what we mean by an operating model and how they are useful and create value.

We have perhaps always had them, but now we are more clearly articulating **models** for our businesses and enterprises. To understand why, here is a ridiculously short look at the history of business and operational organizations.

Pre-industrialized work (outside of the monarchy, religions, scholars and the military) was often on a smaller scale: family-run businesses and craftspeople like stone masons, blacksmiths, carpenters and some bureaucrats like tax collectors.

As the **Industrial Revolution** took hold worldwide, more complex businesses were created and machinery and efficiency systems were introduced to aggregate this form of labour in fields, mills and factories. This required mapping work and production flow to handle complex tasks like delivering materials and distributing goods for sale. We saw things like the first hierarchy-based organization charts and roles introduced, such as supervisor and quality checking.

These early forms of operating models weren't necessarily called that, but schemas, flows, process charts, manuals, guides and more were all introduced as 'intellectual' assets to the (primarily) mechanical production. Ironically, smaller-scale models were built and used to test some early production prototypes, but that is a very different form of operating model!

As we moved into the **Knowledge Economy** of the mid-20th century, we started to see a more sophisticated understanding of additional areas such as psychology and behavioural science, motivation and incentives and, of course, worker representation, voice and protection through unionization (particularly in the now more efficient industrial and manufacturing enterprises).

Because much of this was challenging to define in production manuals, we started to see more policies and specified assets, such as competency profiles that described behaviours and skills alongside tasks and accountabilities. We also saw more focus on culture and values as statements of intent and on framing those behaviours, goals and how values were manifested.

This is also where we started to see the emergence of the Organizational Development (OD) practice, roles and accountabilities that diagnose, design, develop and deploy systems of work that were not just about mechanical processes and compliance. They addressed the complex arrangements of all the moving parts of an organization and were not just limited to physical assets and workflows.

The OD profession is often a subset of the HR function, with specialists who are usually described as systems thinkers, organizational psychologists, business analysts and designers.

So, back to our engineering frame for this opening chapter, this shows we are beyond mechanical engineering and into more complexities around social and psychological systems and the behavioural aspects of work. The organization may be metaphorically a machine, but with people involved, emotions and behaviours are interwoven with the mechanics. The threads of human behaviour flow through the harder machine elements of the tapestry that is the organizational system.

Operating models and business models

An effective metaphor for understanding an operating model is to compare it to a **building's blueprint.**

Just as a blueprint provides a detailed plan of a structure's layout, dimensions and internal wiring, an operating model maps out the organization's constructs, key components and how each element is interconnected to function effectively. It illustrates the operational foundation that supports an organization in delivering value, encompassing its processes, governance, technology and workforce alignment.

This is distinct from an organization's **business model.** Suppose the operating model is akin to the blueprint of a house, illustrating the design and functionality. In that case, the business model is like the developers' aspirations and the real estate agent's property description, highlighting its features, cost and how it will have value for buyers.

The business model explains *what* the organization offers and *why* it's valuable, while the operating model details *how* those offerings are executed and sustained.

To recap on models, so far, we have:

TABLE 1.1 Types of model and OD practice

Business model	Why an organization exists (Purpose) and what it does to deliver that purpose (Products and Services).
Operating model	How the business model is actioned into operating and through functions and flow.
Organization Design and Development (OD)	The strategic process of shaping and evolving the organization's structure, roles and culture to align with its goals and ensure sustainable performance. While Organization Design focuses on structuring teams, roles and workflows for optimal efficiency, organization development emphasizes the nurturing of capabilities, resilience and growth through continuous improvement and adaptation.

OD – going beyond the operating model

Organization Design, Development and Effectiveness (OD/D/E, referred to by many as just OD) plays a critical role in translating the business model into actionable structures by defining how the organization's people and processes should be organized.

It supports the operating model by ensuring that the organizational structure, leadership and culture are equipped to carry out operations effectively.

In essence, OD provides the adaptive framework and human capital strategies that bring the business and operating models to life and sustain them as market conditions evolve.

If you are an HR practitioner of some experience, you may – like me more recently – be now thinking, 'Why haven't I been more involved in the business model and operating model conversations before?' If you're an OD professional you may be saying, 'Of course, the business model and operating model are important, but they're only parts of the equation for us as dynamic practitioners helping to bring things from the purpose and principles through the blueprints into ongoing and sustainable operation, change, performance and learning.'

There is undoubtedly an increased focus on the work and certainly use of the phrases 'business model' and 'operating model'. Why is that now more prevalent to a wider audience than just OD practitioners and Strategic Leaders?

From OD to D&D

The answer to our questions on why business models and operating models are now so readily used and deployed lies in two words: **Disruption** and **Digitization**.

Disruption – and the more acutely defined term Disruptive Innovation – has been a feature of enterprise thinking and doing since (at least but probably before) the advent of the internet.

What online commerce, information, transactions and access to the world gave the business and working world was a hugely disruptive force. No longer were business ventures (and government administration and more) confined to brick-and-mortar outlets (and paper catalogue-based mail-order).

The internet explosion allowed smaller enterprises to market and compete with gargantuan incumbents and disrupt such market dominance, which was previously based on scale and capitalization.

Mobile technologies and the advent of the smartphone and app stores further exploded this market into accessible, real-time, choice-based purchasing and interactions to the world's connected population.

And with over 30 years of internet use, whole generations of humans have known nothing but the ability to connect, share, learn, buy and interact this way.

This disruptive force came into being because of the increased capability to digitize.

Digitization grew from the miniaturization and abundance of computational power making personalized computing available at an affordable price. Which of course led to the disruptions and the entire Silicon Valley-led surge we know today. Of course there were technology giants before this. However, many of those have been disrupted and are unrecognizable, if they are still operating, or no longer exist (perhaps having been acquired or dissolved).

Much was reported on the 'half-life' of businesses now being much shorter on the higher echelons of Stock Value exchanges and it gave rise to not just multi-billion-dollar industries, but the world's first trillion-dollar valuations.

Not all of this disruption and digitization was good. This concentration of wealth has been the subject of economist debates and World Economic Forum agitation, but that's where we've got to when it comes to business and commerce. We are all completely dependent on the digital world and the digital economy we've created. Yet many organizations were not built for this and that's caused a rise in adaptations to the business models for those companies and the use of target operating models (TOMs) as a 'silver bullet' for a transformed enterprise.

The proliferation of operating models

This is where the operating model comes into being. Once the business model has been reviewed and set up, a trigger will be used to review how the organization responds to that demand and operational need.

An operating model provides the framework for translating strategic aspirations into practical, day-to-day operations. It acts as the playbook for how resources – people, technology, processes and governance – are configured and deployed to deliver value efficiently and effectively.

To break it down further, an operating model involves several key dimensions (see Table 1.2).

TABLE 1.2 Operating model dimensions

Processes and workflows	This is the engine room of the organization, detailing how work gets done, from the flow of tasks and services to the integration of activities across departments. Streamlined processes ensure consistency, quality and speed in meeting customer and business requirements.
Organizational structure	This aspect defines how teams and functions are arranged and may include some of the OD elements of delineating roles and responsibilities to promote collaboration and look at the optimized state of resourcing from a people, capabilities and managerial sense. Whether through centralized, decentralized or hybrid structures, the operating model shapes the balance between autonomy and oversight.
Technology and systems	In today's digitally driven world, technology is the backbone that supports operations. The operating model identifies what tools, platforms and systems are necessary for seamless work, data management and real-time decision making.
Governance and decision making	Effective governance is about having clear pathways for decision making that align with strategic priorities. The operating model specifies who makes which decisions, how those decisions are made and how risks are managed to maintain coherence across operations.
Culture and behaviours	Although less tangible, the way people interact, communicate and adhere to shared values is crucial. The Operating Model embeds practices that align the organizational culture with the strategic aims, ensuring that employees are motivated and empowered to execute their roles with purpose. In a way that's distinct from OD, this is likely to be aspirational, desired and potentially different from the prevailing culture of now. For example, it could be that the operating model calls for more customer loyalty than hunting down more customers and having very casual but voluminous customer churn, which would change attitudes, behaviours and protocols.
Performance metrics	Measurable performance indicators are embedded to gauge how well the operating model is functioning. These metrics track efficiency, output quality and the alignment between operational execution and strategic objectives, enabling continuous improvement.

An effective operating model doesn't just meet *today's* operational needs; it anticipates *future changes*. It has built-in adaptability to respond to shifts in market demands, technological advancements or competitive pressures. In this way, it sets the organization up not just to survive but to thrive amid change.

By fully understanding and harnessing the operating model, organizations can create an ecosystem where strategic intent and operational reality are seamlessly connected, driving not just efficiency but also innovation and resilience.

For the sake of clarity, it is worth addressing how these interplay with the OD function found in many larger HR teams/functions.

The distinction between an *operating model* and *Organization Design* lies in their scope and focus, though they are closely related and often intertwined.

TABLE 1.3 Operating model – Organization Design comparison

Operating model	Organization Design
Definition and focus	
An operating model is a high-level representation of how an organization is structured to deliver its strategy. It focuses on the practical, interconnected systems of processes, roles, governance, technology and metrics that align resources to execute strategic goals. It's essentially the 'how' of translating strategy into action.	Organization Design is more specifically the process of shaping the organization's structure and roles to optimize efficiency and effectiveness. It deals with 'who' does what, how authority flows and how teams and functions interact. While an operating model provides the overall framework, Organization Design drills down into the details of reporting lines, job roles and team structures.
This distinction will be important when we work specifically on our HR Operating Model – it's not about team constructs and an organization chart. Instead it is more about the flow and interactions of work and tools that we map into the operating model. The Organization Design for the operating model will be more specific on roles, spans of control, decision making and governance, capabilities and skills people will need and the allocation of resources, assets and materials.	
Scope and application	
Encompasses a broader view that integrates various components like processes, technology and performance metrics with organizational structure. It addresses how these components interact and operate together to achieve strategic objectives.	Primarily concentrates on the internal configuration of an organization's people and roles, deciding how tasks and responsibilities are distributed. It also determines how communication and coordination occur between different functions and levels within the organization.
Again, an important distinction here: an HR Operating Model will base itself on the use of systems, science, data, technology and processes and not on the specifics of roles that sit inside it and align to people's capabilities.	

(continued)

TABLE 1.3 (Continued)

Operating model	Organization Design
Relationship and overlap	
The operating model can be seen as the overarching guide that defines the necessary components for strategy execution, while Organization Design provides the specific framework for structuring the human element within that model. For instance, if an operating model dictates the need for greater cross-functional collaboration to foster innovation, Organization Design might address this need by establishing matrix teams or agile project groups.	Increasingly, we see organizations have to make adaptations to their HR Operating Model without perhaps knowing or sensing that's what they're doing. Bringing more cross-functional teams together on projects is an Organization Design and development process, yet if this is proving to be more of a constant (as it appears to be for many HR teams I am working with and experiencing) then perhaps the operating model needs to be adjusted to cater for specific shifts of this nature.
Example comparison	
The operating model will see a company shifting from a traditional product-centric model to a customer-centric approach that would develop an operating model that redefines processes, integrates new technologies and adjusts workflows to ensure customer insights are central to decision making.	Organization Design will support this new operating model and would specify changes such as creating a dedicated customer experience (CX) team, redefining reporting structures or redistributing roles to break down silos between sales, marketing and product development.
Outcomes and intentions	
The operating model aims for comprehensive alignment between strategy and execution, ensuring that all parts of the organization work cohesively to produce the desired outcomes.	Organization Design seeks to optimize the way human resources are organized and managed for efficiency, productivity and adaptability to align with the overall operating model.

Conclusion: While an operating model provides the 'big picture' of how an organization operates to deliver on its strategic goals, Organization Design is a key component within that picture, explicitly focused on shaping the human structure to support the operating model. The two work in concert: the operating model provides the guiding framework and Organization Design fleshes out the details of how the organization's people will function within that framework.

Distinguishing between operating models and OD

It's not that essential to do so, but there are plenty of ways to look at the differences, intersections and similarities between operating models and OD. The language and scope may even appear to be the same. But Table 1.4 helps set out what we mean by each one and the components/elements they somewhat share.

TABLE 1.4 Aspects of operating model and Organization Design contrasts and links

Aspect	Operating model	Organization Design
Definition	A comprehensive framework that translates strategy into action by defining how processes, technology, people and governance interact to deliver value.	The process of shaping the structure and roles within an organization to optimize efficiency, communication and effectiveness.
Focus	The *how* of executing strategy, involving processes, technology, roles and governance.	The *who* does what; focuses on defining job roles, reporting structures and team interactions.
Scope	Broad, encompassing all operational elements (processes, technology, people, metrics) needed for strategic alignment.	Narrower, centred on internal configuration, hierarchy and workflow between individuals and teams.
Components	Includes processes, technology, roles, governance structures and performance metrics.	Involves job roles, reporting lines, team structures and decision-making frameworks.
Primary goal	To create a unified system that ensures strategic goals are met efficiently and effectively.	To optimize organizational structure for better coordination, communication and performance.
Outcome	A functional blueprint that ensures all elements of the organization work in harmony to deliver on strategy.	A detailed layout of how human resources are structured to support the operating model and strategic objectives.
Relationships	An overarching guide that includes Organization Design as one of its components.	A subset or element of the operating model, focusing on the human aspect of the organization.
Example application	Developing an operating model to support a shift to a customer-centric business approach, integrating new technologies and cross-functional processes.	Redesigning the organization to create cross-functional teams or flatten hierarchies to support a customer-centric operating model.
Adaptability	Focuses on overall adaptability to align with strategic goals and changes in the market or industry.	Emphasizes adaptability within human resources and team structures to respond to changes in strategy or operations.

REAL-WORLD EXAMPLE
Unilever's agile operating model transformation

Unilever, a global leader in consumer goods, is often cited as an exemplary case of how a well-defined operating model can drive strategic success and operational excellence. Facing mounting competitive pressures, rapid market changes and the need for greater customer-centricity, Unilever embarked on a transformation to revamp its operating model in the late 2010s.

The challenge

Unilever's traditional operating model, while successful for decades, was increasingly seen as too rigid for the fast-paced demands of the modern consumer landscape. The company needed to adopt a more agile and responsive approach to maintain its market leadership and respond to new consumer behaviours, sustainability expectations and digital disruptions.

The transformation

Unilever set out to redesign its operating model with a focus on greater flexibility, decentralization and digital integration. Key elements of this transformation included:

1 **Decentralized decision making:** The company shifted decision-making authority closer to local markets. This enabled regional teams to respond swiftly to consumer trends and regulatory changes, fostering a more adaptive approach to market needs.

2 **Digital integration:** Unilever invested heavily in digital tools and platforms, integrating technology across supply chain management, marketing and consumer data analytics. This enabled real-time data flow and enhanced collaboration across functions.

3 **Streamlined processes:** The company re-engineered its workflows to reduce silos and improve cross-functional communication. Agile methodologies were introduced in project management and product development to increase speed and adaptability.

4 **Sustainability at the core:** Reflecting its Sustainable Living Plan, Unilever embedded sustainability into its operating model. This ensured that operational processes aligned with the company's commitment to reducing environmental impact and promoting social responsibility.

5 **Performance metrics and continuous improvement:** Unilever implemented
   KPIs that tracked not just financial performance, but also sustainability metrics
   and consumer engagement levels. These measures allowed for real-time
   adjustments and promoted a culture of continuous improvement.

Results

The transformation yielded significant benefits. Unilever reported higher levels of
innovation and market responsiveness, which helped the company launch new
products more efficiently and tailor offerings to local tastes. For instance, Unilever's
quick adaptation during the Covid-19 pandemic demonstrated the strength of its
revamped operating model, allowing it to pivot supply chains and respond to spikes
in demand for hygiene products.

This approach not only improved operational agility but also strengthened
Unilever's reputation as a purpose-driven company committed to sustainability and
social impact. The operating model transformation played a key role in enabling
Unilever to align its strategic vision with daily operations, creating a more resilient
and customer-focused organization.

In closing

As the business model changes, so does the operating model, thereby calling
upon OD to reshape all the 'moving parts' of the organization.

The Unilever example shows us that a business 'pivot' is more than a
temporary project – it is a fundamental shift in why, what, how, where and
by whom work gets done. The operating model therefore needs to shift into
a new version.

Taking another metaphor, if the organization were a digital platform,
introducing new features and functionality changes what it can do for its
users. We see this in operating systems for digital platforms – from Version
10 to Version 11.

Keeping with that metaphor, were HR a digital platform, the current
operating system is likely V2.0. (V1.0 was the move from Personnel
Administration into Human Resources in the later 1980s.) And yet in 2025,
HR is still operating with V2.0 despite a more complex and uncertain world.

In later chapters, we will explore the prevailing HR V2.0 in much more
detail and, of course, explore HR V3.0 – the next iteration to a new 'platform'
with additional and revised features, functions and applications.

A new operating model for HR would need to be:

- a flexible and contextually adaptive approach mirroring how Digital, Customer Service, Product Development, Supply Chain, Research and Marketing functions now operate;

- pliable enough so that the size and scope of your organization would shape an HR Operating Model that would see you through constant change and adaptation and grow with you as you scale, diversify and transform;

- able to cater to multi-disciplinary and complex HR functions in huge global conglomerates and comprehensive but compact teams in smaller enterprises.

That's the challenge a new operating model for HR has to contend with – flexible over prescriptive and comprehensive yet simple enough to allow it to be contextualized for HR functions of all sectors and scales.

In over 20 years of being an HR practitioner, I've seen an evolved profession with more sophisticated and aspirational tendencies. What's lacking is the 'engineering' we opened this chapter with.

A new operating model is not just to keep in step with Digital, Product and Operations – it is about HR engineering its systems to adapt and enhance its service and value proposition.

It will need:

- enhanced capabilities in its practitioner community;

- better use of evidence – science and data;

- more accessible and efficient processes (especially tapping into the growing fields of artificial intelligence and automation); and

- the creation of enhanced products that create more value for people and the organization.

So engineering – not a term associated with the HR/People profession much – is perhaps our next frontier, via an operating model that balances and handles ever-more complex demands and navigates the evolution of work to ensure more flourishing experiences for people driving successful enterprises forward.

Links and flows, ones and zeros, hearts and minds – paradoxes and complementary energies and systems.

WHAT WE'VE COVERED IN THIS CHAPTER

1 **Embracing the engineering mindset:** Reposition HR as engineering complex systems of work. Shift your perspective to see HR as an enabler of progressive systems and structures that capitalize on more innovative ways to create value across your organization.

2 **Agitating in strategic conversations:** Kick off more active reviews and progressive responses to shifts in your organization's business model and operating model. Understand how these frameworks function so that you can engineer HR practices to more clearly drive value through supporting strategic and operational goals.

3 **Considering a more flexible HR Operating Model:** Develop an HR Operating Model that is adaptable and impactful, allowing it to fit your unique business context. This ensures your HR function remains relevant and responsive in an ever-changing environment.

4 **Championing Organization Design and Development:** Utilize your OD skills to translate the business model into actionable structures. Support your organization by crafting systems that align with the operating model, facilitating seamless operations and ensuring sustainable performance.

5 **Rethinking and innovating:** Be prepared to challenge established practices and explore new models that better serve your HR function. Drive innovation by integrating product management, Systems Thinking and design principles into HR operations.

6 **Preparing for future disruption:** Equip your HR team with the skills and processes needed to respond effectively to future disruption and change. Build resilience into your operating model so that it survives and thrives amid change.

References and further reading

Danoesastro, M and Zeggers, M (2023) How Unilever elevated Agile, www.bcg.com/publications/2023/elevating-agile-principles-to-help-enterprise-sized-companies (archived at https://perma.cc/7JU8-FGHC)

Deming, W E (1986) *Out of the Crisis*, Cambridge, MA: MIT Press

Graeber, D and Wengrow, D (2021) *The Dawn of Everything: A new history of humanity*, New York: Farrar, Straus and Giroux

Harari, Y N (2014) *Sapiens: A brief history of humankind*, London: Harvill Secker

Unilever (n.d.) Sustainable Living Plan, www.unilever.com/our-company/our-history-and-archives/2010-2020/ (archived at https://perma.cc/J9RQ-D2SJ)

2

The emerging future of work and its catalytic changes for HR

The future is always stranger than we imagine.
MAGNUS LINDKVIST, FUTURIST, TRENDSPOTTER AND POSSIBILIST

WHAT'S COVERED IN THIS CHAPTER

- **Futures Thinking and trends shaping HR:** Exploring the probes, forecasts and trends defining the next phase of the Future of Work – from the Knowledge Economy through the Automation Era into the Regenerative Age. This will be brought to life with illustrative examples of some of the leading organizations and People teams' practices and methods of working.

- **Impact on HR models:** Analysis of how these trends affect HR operations and strategies.

- **Preparing for the future:** A deep dive into the skills and capabilities HR professionals will need in the coming years (based on validated research and example pioneering practices in play already).

Introduction

In Chapter 1, we left you with these headlines.

1 Embracing the engineering mindset
2 Agitating in strategic conversations

3 Considering a more flexible HR operating model

4 Championing Organization Design and Development

5 Rethinking and innovating

6 Preparing for future disruption

And that all sounds (hopefully) plausible, if not ambitious, set against what I've called *the turbulent twenties*. Or, as the World Economic Forum calls it, a *polycrisis world*.

In my 50+ years on the planet, the majority of which have been in the world of work, I don't think I've seen such:

---

a unprecedented use of the word *unprecedented*

b pace of change and volatility of it all

c clustering and simultaneous challenges all at once, and

d a challenging time for HR teams, having to do (as the motion picture goes) *everything, everywhere, all at once.*

It's not just HR, clearly, but I've never seen the workloads currently stacking up in the HR backlog so significant, complex and important.

Much of this is under the banner of 'The Future of Work' – a pseudo-strategic agenda that encompasses everything from:

a hybrid working, office returns and remote/work from anywhere, to

b AI and automation technologies that will revolutionize work and shift work from people to machines (mostly digital applications but some robotic), removing a whole swathe of jobs.

The Future of Work as an agenda intends to be helpful but ends up being a vague quasi-paradigm shift for which we all need to plan but in a very random and non-specific fashion.

This chapter – and in somewhat of a time capsule, as formally published content is these days – is setting out many of the things we should consider in the turbulent twenties, particularly from an HR practice field lens and on people, culture, learning, Organization Design and Development, talent, inclusion, wellness and performance perspectives.

In doing so, this chapter will use – and spotlight – an emerging field of practice which by its nature might jar with what we've traditionally known as jobs, roles and expertise.

Futures Thinking

You may have heard of this term; you may now be thinking about two other forms of thinking (design and Systems Thinking) and you may be feeling it's another 'not real thing' dreamed up by someone.

What is Futures Thinking? I am fortunate enough to be connected to someone who is a leading light in this field – and at the intersection of things like Business Strategy and Operational Excellence. **Erik Korsvik Østergaard** from Denmark is that leading light, so it is with a very respectful and honourable homage to him that this chapter features his work, brought to my attention through his book *Anticipatory Leadership* (Korsvik Østergaard, 2023).

So what is Futures Thinking?

Futures Thinking is often connected to strategic foresight, innovation, business development, market adaptation, competitor moves and shifts in customer preferences. However, applying Futures Thinking inside an organization has different uses:

- as a change management tool for engaging the managers in shaping their role in the organization;
- scenarios for global and local HR initiatives, adapting to a shift in society and demographics over the coming five years;
- workforce planning, considering the rapid advancements within technology, especially AI;
- scenarios for investments in R&D in emerging scientific domains (high risk, high potential), also to investigate the alternative futures for Organization Design and decision governance;
- building change management storylines for the roll-out of new ways of working across several different countries;
- investigating the possible futures for a sales department, given the potentially disruptive changes in global politics.

'*Using the future to make decisions about today*' is the mantra.

So, imagination, storytelling and prototyping are vital components of what is referred to as anticipatory leadership in an organization. Therefore, we can use Future Thinking as a 'methodology' to implement this.

Using 'the future' can be described in two key elements, of which Futures Thinking is the second element, and also gives it that title.

Firstly, **Futures Literacy**: the ability and capacity to think critically and abstractly about the future. Key building blocks are the understanding of anticipation and assumptions.

Secondly, **Futures Thinking**: the creative and investigative process of exploring and evaluating what affects us to describe scenarios for the future. And notice the use of the pluralized form (describing multiple futures) and not the singular version: the future. Futures Thinking has to consider the variety of possibilities in something that has yet to happen.

And in this, there are three aspects:

1 **Possible futures:** These may include outrageous and hugely imaginative versions of the future. Would the Victorian industrialists have predicted we would have a pocket-sized device to speak to others and access the world's information? Unlikely – they would have deemed it viable but dreamt of the possibilities.

2 **Plausible futures:** At the outset of understanding how the miniaturization of computer processors was accelerating, a portable version of a mainframe computer was plausible based on trends, analysis and engineering know-how at that time.

3 **Preferable futures:** Knowing what we now know about smartphone addictions, we may have preferred a more controlled version of ourselves and our information at the outset of a pocket-sized device at the advent of the internet.

In this, my friend Erik's work has found two aspects of this work having discernible impact:

1 **Anticipatory leadership.** The title of his third book in a series around work, leadership and creating thriving organizations. In this paradigm, leaders who are forward-looking use a Futures Thinking approach to navigate uncertainty, anticipate emerging trends and signals, and effectively explore and evaluate *alternative* futures and scenarios in order to drive transformation through a mindset, methodology and approach that uses the future to make decisions about today.

2 **Participatory organizations.** Structures, governance and cultures that enable organizational adaptability, sensing and sense-making, with widespread colleague involvement and shared decision making. A management style that actively engages and involves people in the exploration and direction-setting process.

Futures Thinking is typically applied in one of these situations:

1 as an alternative to transformation planning

2 as a supplement to transformation planning

3 in strategy projects

4 in a change management project

Indeed, all of those four areas are increasingly part of what organizational leadership is focused on, whilst short-term profit acquisition/reporting, stock market value and shareholder demands compete for the attention and decisions of leaders.

Of course, the here and now is vitally important, but overlooking a significant shift that could secure the longer-term future (a 'heads up' approach) for the enterprise is somewhat sacrificed by this 'heads down' approach. So, when leaders get their 'heads together', they are near-sighted, obsessed about short-termism and less about their true future potential.

Futures Thinking and Futures Literacy address this and ensure that 'heads together' and 'heads up' give more alertness, readiness and deliberate ways to head into a possible, plausible and preferred future.

In bringing this to HR's 'jurisdiction', how might Futures Thinking be of use? After all, isn't HR often the backstop for *harder* principles around employment law and other legislative 'here and nows'?

In the grey areas

More often than some people realize, HR operates between black and white, thereby in the grey areas. There are potential policy breaches where there is a real ambiguity at play and divisive misunderstanding of intent, mitigating circumstances behind someone's level of performance, and the unique, individualized human need that may not be as clear-cut as some might prefer it to be when reaching decisions on promotability, performance or reward.

However, outside of the day-to-day, HR is a future-looking function, recruiting people, developing them based on their potential, looking ahead to market competition for key roles and enabling leaders to match their strategic direction with compliant and enabling support for their people, processes and performance.

My 20+ years of experience in HR lead me to say this: **We (HR) are often brought into future-focused conversations at too late a juncture.** We are not invited in – or considered to be useful enough – to cast those future trajectories. On rarer occasions, HR leaders have been catalytic in crafting those future trajectories, where a talent, people, culture and learning agenda is at the forefront of product, service and business model shifts for the better.

So, with HR either not being in those shaping conversations, or only engaged at a later point in their development and delivery, how might Futures Thinking boost not only HR's credibility, but, more so, its capability in being at the forefront of those decisions of possible, plausible or preferred futures?

The answer to this lies in the importance placed on two key areas: **Systems** and **Science**.

Systems in OD and the HR Operating Model

Starting with systems. All work – and thereby organizations doing the work – is made up of a multiplicity of layered, interconnected and, in some cases independent, systems.

Of course, businesses operate in the wider systems of life: societal, economic, political, legal and transportation systems.

Linking, utilizing and strengthening compliance within these systems is, of course, vital to operations.

Not only does each organization operate in those systems, it is a system in its own right.

Research, innovation, production, supply, service, financial, intellectual property, real estate, partnerships, employment, performance, development, adaptation, change, culture and, of course, leadership: many moving parts link to the broader systems of the world and are systems created to deliver and realize why the organization exists – its purpose.

In mapping out how these systems interact, influence and shape each other, we are attempting to define the conditions and actions taken to bring as much coherence, cohesion and harmony to those systems as possible. We might call that efficiency and, through productivity, the harnessing of the energies in those systems.

When we are operating in those systems we may not always be aware of the multiple layers at play and influencing the things we do. However, if we are an administrator securing a transaction in compliance with our financial system, we are also invoking our production, supply, delivery and customer service systems. Which in turn creates data about all of those elements so that we might track and optimize all the processes in those systems and, where there are deviances, misfires and failings, know how to put them right and correct the system in (sometimes) more than one place.

In defining this, we have a simplified – but still complex – map of how all the systems of work come together and where Organization Design, Development and the Operating Model intersect, interact and create what we need to deliver on the purpose.

FIGURE 2.1 Flow and spans of Organization Design, Development and the target operating model

Organization Design, Development, effectiveness and operating model

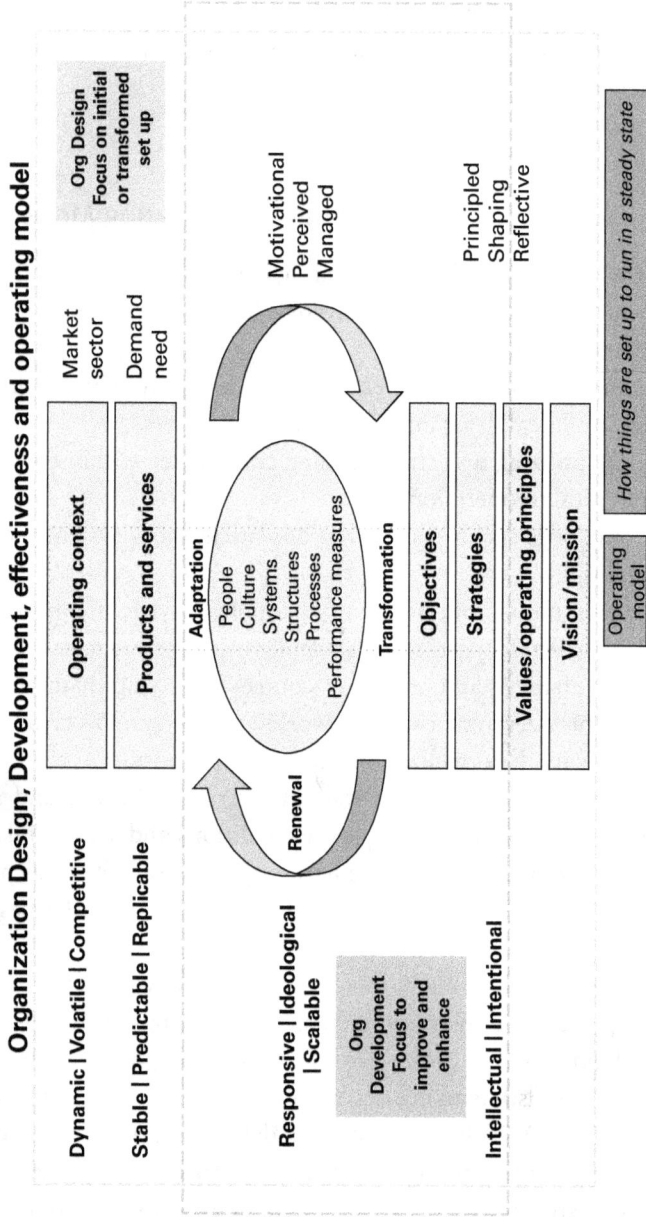

Dynamic | Volatile | Competitive

Stable | Predictable | Replicable

Operating context

Products and services

Market sector

Demand need

Org Design Focus on initial or transformed set up

Adaptation

People
Culture
Systems
Structures
Processes
Performance measures

Motivational
Perceived
Managed

Transformation

Renewal

Responsive | Ideological | Scalable

Org Development Focus to improve and enhance

Intellectual | Intentional

Objectives

Strategies

Values/operating principles

Vision/mission

Principled
Shaping
Reflective

Operating model

How things are set up to run in a steady state

Underpinning the entire model is the reason the company/enterprise exists, framed by its vision and mission. And this, of course, links to the top of this model – the market/sector and where the organization will operate and deliver its products and/or services.

This model captures all of a business's intellectual and practical aspects:

- **Why** it exists is to serve a mission or vision (its purpose for being) at the very base of this model.

- **Where** it exists is the operating context (markets and sectors) elements at the top, serving a demand and need in those markets/sectors.

- **What** it exists to deliver is in the products and services aspects that meet demand and need through the market/sector it operates in.

- **How** it turns that into an enterprise is the four boxes at the bottom and through the centre of the model: objectives, strategies, values/operating principles and vision/mission, then people, culture, systems (like decision making, governance and legal, learning and developing, hiring and promoting people, rewarding and looking after people), the structures people are organized into, processes and the measures of performance that determine success.

On the model's left are phenomena, sensations, conditions and factors to account for. For example, at the top left of the model, markets can be dynamic, volatile and competitive as can consumer/service user needs and demands. Just below that, operating conditions need to be stable, predictable and replicable to service demand, to provide quality of product and to deliver those efficiently and, therefore, be economically viable.

At the centre level are the enabling conditions for operations and these are described as responsive (to increased or adaptive need or demand), ideological (tending to be the most optimized, contextual and adapted to the nature of the enterprise you are operating in) and scalable (great ideas like flexible working, dynamic resource allocation to account for surge capacity and hiring practices at times of growth).

The lower part of the model is more philosophical and of the mind and heart combined. Values, principles, mission and strategy are intellectual and intentional constructs that inform the enabling conditions and shape the operation to deliver in its markets and sectors through the products and services people want and need.

The middle dotted section is the **operating model** for the entire organization, not just for a function or part. in Chapter 1 we defined the operating model within the business model and as a part of the Organization Design process thus:

- A business model – what and why an organization exists.

- An operating model – how the business model is actioned into operating and through functions and flow.
- Organization Design and Development (OD) – the strategic process of shaping and evolving the organization's structure, roles and culture to align with its goals and ensure sustainable performance. While Organization Design focuses on structuring teams, roles and workflows for optimal efficiency, development emphasizes nurturing capabilities, resilience and growth through continuous improvement and adaptation.

This leads us to a crucial element within the HR professional field and a key element of how we need to create the HR Operating Model to take advantage of this strategic and tactical element in our arena: OD

OD as the 'HR superpower'

Since the 1950s and 1960s, when OD became a specified practice field, and into the 1990s and with the advent of HR, OD has been seen as part of the HR portfolio. Whilst some OD work is undoubtedly carried out by the executive team operations and more likely strategy (and performance) teams, OD – in all the academic teaching you'll find on it – is considered a part of HR.

Therefore, the operating model for the entire business/enterprise is a hugely important factor in HR, taking that into account in the organization's design.

The systems of work are a huge part of what HR is there to deliver. And imagining – through Futures Thinking – a different set of scenarios is absolutely something HR, Culture, Learning and, of course, OD and Change professionals should be a part of and, if anything, own. Own, convene, curate, compile, craft and apply.

OD is not just an efficient and optimized design within complex systems. It is also framed and supported by science – our next topic.

Science in OD and the HR Operating Model

Science here comes in a range of some areas we may be familiar with and some less so (but may be aware of).

Firstly, there's science in the systems – much research, evidence, data and know-how that uses a science-backed approach. Table 2.1 explores key areas of business operations, some references from academics and researchers and how this is applied through HR interventions, products and services.

There are lots of sciences at play in work, not always obviously.

OD practice is founded in much of the sciences of not just workflow and performance optimization but also mainly in the way people behave – the links between individualized psychology and that of groups and social settings and into things like power, persuasion, collegiality, what we believe in, how we channel innovative thoughts and ideas, how we respond to crises and challenges and how we get the best from our combined skills, values and effort.

TABLE 2.1 Operating model links to sciences and HR practices

Behavioural Science		
Key areas: decision making (e.g. biases, heuristics); behavioural economics in workplace design; nudging and behavioural interventions	References: *Daniel Kahneman: Thinking, Fast and Slow [decision making and biases]* *Richard Thaler and Cass Sunstein: Nudge [applying nudges to HR practices]*	HR application: structuring performance reviews to counter biases; using nudges in employee engagement or learning programmes; behavioural nudging for diversity and inclusion efforts
Occupational Psychology		
Key areas: job satisfaction and its impact on performance; employee well-being frameworks (e.g. Job Demands-Resources model); psychological contract theory	References: *Arnold Bakker and Evangelia Demerouti: Job Demands-Resources Model* *Denise Rousseau: Psychological Contracts in Organizations*	HR application: creating well-being programmes to overcome burnout; tailoring career development paths based on intrinsic motivators; addressing unspoken psychological contracts in employee retention
Data Science		
Key areas: predictive analytics in workforce planning; advanced analytics for skills mapping; use of AI and machine learning for HR decision making	References: *Josh Bersin: work on people analytics and AI in HR* *David Green: Data-driven HR and people analytics thought leader*	HR application: predicting future skill gaps with AI; real-time dashboards for people performance and well-being metrics; using network analysis to understand collaboration patterns

(continued)

TABLE 2.1 (Continued)

People and Performance Analytics		
Key areas: employee lifecycle analytics (recruitment, onboarding, attrition); linking HR metrics to business outcomes; social network analysis (e.g. collaboration effectiveness)	**References:** *Ben Waber: work on organizational network analysis* *Tomas Chamorro-Premuzic: Predictive Analytics For Talent Management*	**HR application:** identifying underperforming teams through engagement data; linking leadership behaviours to team performance analytics; proactive measures for retention based on turnover predictors
Organizational Psychology		
Key areas: change management and resistance; organizational culture and its impact on innovation; group dynamics and team cohesion	**References:** *Edgar Schein: Organizational Culture and Leadership* *John Kotter: change management frameworks*	**HR application:** leading culture transformations aligned with strategy; building resilience in times of organizational change; strengthening psychological safety within teams
Team Psychology		
Key areas: groupthink and cognitive diversity; high-performing team frameworks; psychological safety in teams	**References:** *Amy Edmondson: The Fearless Organization [psychological safety]* *Patrick Lencioni: The Five Dysfunctions of a Team*	**HR application:** facilitating interventions that continually improve team dynamics; designing interventions to foster diversity of thought; coaching leaders to build trust and collaboration
Science on Leadership		
Key areas: adaptive and situational leadership; servant leadership and its impact on engagement; neuroscience of leadership and emotional intelligence	**References:** *Daniel Goleman: Emotional Intelligence [leadership and EQ]* *Ronald Heifetz and Marty Linsky: The Practice of Adaptive Leadership*	**HR application:** leadership development grounded in neuroscience; using EQ to enhance leader impact in hybrid work models; helping leaders manage their levels of stress and lead more empathetically and therefore sustainably

(continued)

TABLE 2.1 (Continued)

Science on Motivation		
Key areas: intrinsic vs extrinsic motivation; self-determination theory (SDT); behavioural incentives	**References:** *Edward Deci and Richard Ryan: self-determination theory* *Daniel Pink: Drive: The surprising truth about what motivates us*	**HR application:** designing for autonomy, mastery and purpose; aligning incentives with intrinsic motivators; personalizing learning through choice and agency
Science on Sustainable Performance		
Key areas: burnout prevention and recovery; long-term productivity vs short-term gains; work-life integration frameworks	*Christina Maslach: burnout research* *Tony Schwartz: The Energy Project [managing energy for sustainable performance]*	**HR application:** shifting away from 'peak work' towards sustainable productivity; integrating well-being into performance metrics; encouraging regenerative practices (breaks, reflection, learning) and more use of agile, iterative and adaptive approaches that punctuate relentless demands
Science on Work-Based Organizations		
Key areas: agility and adaptive organizations; sociotechnical systems theory; new models for distributed work	*Frederic Laloux: Reinventing Organizations [Teal organizations]* *Margaret Wheatley: Systems Thinking in work organizations*	**HR application:** designing sociotechnical systems for hybrid working; leading agile transitions with a science-backed framework; embedding purpose as a driver of organizational cohesion

Scenario planning: Using behavioural science to understand how cognitive biases might affect scenario development.

Adaptive strategies: Drawing on organizational psychology to prepare for change management in complex futures.

Analytics for future-readiness: Using predictive analytics to map skills and trends needed for future scenarios.

Motivation for future-readiness: Leveraging motivation science to align future strategies with purpose and the meaning people attach to their work and their place in it.

How does this all link to Futures Thinking?

A Futures Thinking approach will help HR complement the engineering essence outlined in Chapter 1, with leading professionals in HR acting as architects of scientifically grounded, future-ready organizations.

Whilst Futures Thinking might seem abstract to the point of being dismissed as a nebulous concept, it is actually aligned with lots of proven science in how people are and how their work and their future in it has strength and commitment that forges a stronger connection to it. And a possible, plausible and preferred future does that. It allows people to project ahead to something desirable and thereby mapped and achievable – all alongside a more effective, adaptive and achievable business proposition.

So where strategy might seem like a really corporate, necessary thing to do that appeases investors, consumers, shareholders or trustees, it can – and should – appeal to the very people who will deliver it beyond merely mechanical and somewhat dry business forecasting.

> A strategy should excite people – especially those willing and active in it and delivering it.

The co-creation, story-based approach *coupled with* science, data, evidence and analysed elements is what Futures Thinking helps us to do. And that HR should be such a big part of that approach is, to me, undeniable. The future of any enterprise has to be about people – those there now and those who will come to be part of it. And not just the consumers, service users, shareholders, trustees or investors. They are undeniably important but the colleagues, partners and employees are absolutely critical shapers and developers of that future vision and actions to achieve it.

My possible, plausible and preferable futures

As the author of this book, it would be wrong of me to lay out a process for Futures Thinking without actually doing my version. So here goes.

Navigating the future requires mapping and determining where your business's main catalyst for evolution will come from. As a starting point, *the signals from the future* may well be in one or more of a series of paradigms, disruptive innovations and opportunities to leverage capabilities, product and market experiences and bold aspirations.

I've analysed many future trends and distilled them into four main areas of response to those changes (Figure 2.2). I've also playfully given them Latin labels as an homage to the past.

Ex Machina – from machines. Advancing digital technologies, robotics, automation, artificial intelligence, Web 3.0, extended, augmented and virtual reality, quantum computing and continued exploration of blockchain technology and even crypto-currencies.

Ex Peritus – from skills. As we see reports of the 'half-life' of skills being reduced by up to 50 per cent, we are at an inflexion point regarding what is required from people (especially when machines are taking the load from certain work-related transactional activities). Many predictions say we need to be more empathetic towards our fellow humans and capitalize

FIGURE 2.2 Four domains of futures paradigms

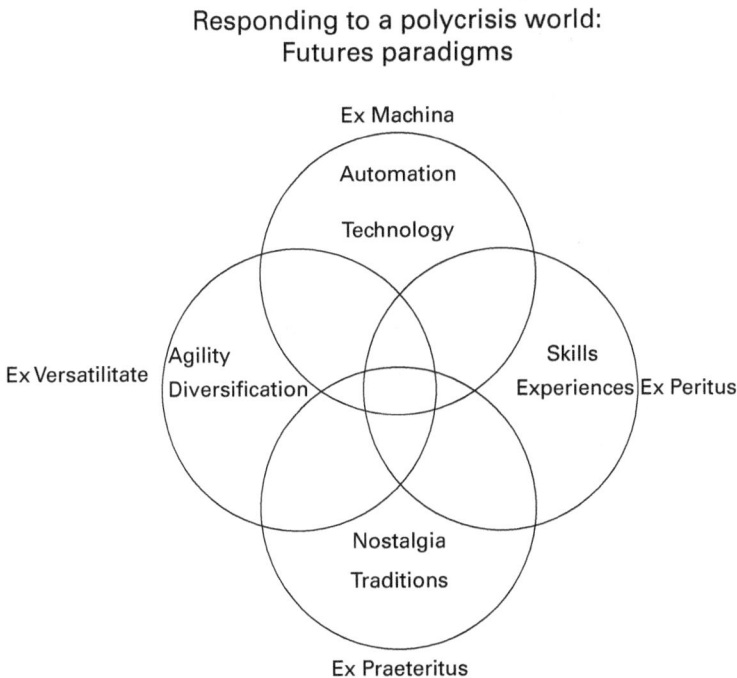

Responding to a polycrisis world:
Futures paradigms

Ex Machina

Automation

Technology

Ex Versatilitate

Agility

Diversification

Skills

Experiences Ex Peritus

Nostalgia

Traditions

Ex Praeteritus

on imagination, creativity and analytical and critical thinking skills – all of these will likely be more in demand in the near future, alongside technological literacy to make the most of the machines we will increasingly rely on to perform programming tasks, ourselves interacting with machines in a different form of symbiosis.

Ex Versatilitate – from agility. The era of rigid five-year plans is over. Organizations must adopt iterative, adaptive approaches that respond to emerging changes in technology, attitudes and the environment. Success now depends on anti-fragility, agility and diversification, enabling pivots even in unpredictable circumstances.

Ex Praeteritus – from tradition. Nostalgia can anchor us, offering a platform to build on reputation, culture and heritage. While clinging to stasis or backwards-looking tendencies hinders growth, leveraging tradition with purpose and clarity can create a stabilizing force amid change.

Future gazing – looking into possibilities and their interconnection

There is a form of future gazing from our opening quote maker, Magnus Lindkvist, and his theory that futurology has four key elements (some of which match my four paradigms): data, scenarios, heritage and asymmetries (Lindkvist, 2013).

These four areas give us a chance to think about the future through the lenses of information (data), projected possibilities (scenarios), what's happened before (heritage) and a combined state of both future and present (asymmetries). Let's look at each in turn.

Data: The obvious one – trends in information that signal what the future will likely be based on analysis and projecting past patterns into the future.

Scenarios, like Futures Thinking, involve imaginative, narrated versions of what might be. These scenarios are played through in a simulation to see how they might pan out.

Heritage is the past that shows us how the future can be a looping series of recurrences. William Strauss and Neil Howe's *Four Turnings* (Howe and Strauss, 1997) map major economic, societal and worldly events that occur every generation or so.

Asymmetries – someone's version of the future is the reality of someone else's present. Think of a farmer in rural China untouched by modern technology who is whisked to Shanghai – he may think he's travelled in time, having never seen a skyscraper, a mobile phone, monorails, drones or neon lights. In reality, this is where the author William Gibson's quote comes in: 'The future is already here; it's just unevenly distributed.'

An HR scenario using the four elements of Lindkvist's futurist framework

The HR version of the four elements from Lindkvist's take on the future can be described in a new form of employment contract, onboarding, learning and innovation:

Data: Most 16–20 year olds who are not yet employed declare an interest in working shorter weeks. This would allow them to build side hustles and entrepreneurial ventures and not be beholden to one employer.

Scenarios: An organization experiments with shorter weeks and allows people to work on side hustles that build their capabilities, skills, perspectives on the world and overall maturity and growth.

Heritage: Within the experiment, and with automation stripping out entry-level jobs, instead of giving graduates and new hires jobs, they are paired up with a more experienced colleague and a pooled workload is created. With an apprentice/master craftsman feel, part of the job of the experienced colleague is to share institutional knowledge and awareness of how pre-automation work happened. This gives the new entrant vital insight into the past and strengthens their understanding of the commitment clients and customers have based on personalized, attentive management and handling of their accounts. This relationship-based approach is then passed on and integrated with the new automation and technology-fuelled approaches to serve them better in the future.

Asymmetries: The incoming new entrant – having already shown entrepreneurial spirit outside of their employ – brings their side hustle findings into the mix for the enterprise to learn from and exploit with mutual consent and gain. A *marketplace* for innovation so that future possibilities sit alongside adapted traditional processes. The future and the now co-exist in pockets of exploration and discovery.

That is one area of a potential, plausible future. In my small consulting venture (People and Transformational HR Ltd) we:

- Adopt shorter working weeks (to handle caring responsibilities, life pursuits and general energy).

- Encourage our team members to create side hustles (or 'spin-outs', as we call them). We already have one successful, revenue-generating spin-out in Sustainability and B Corp Certification – not our core proposition, but adjacent to it.

- Offer an incubator approach to our team and people in our network. We already have one hugely successful entrepreneur who is now a leading expert in digitized, short-form and flowing learning content creation, which we incubated on the initial concept.

We made no revenue from this venture, but the point isn't to do that. The point is to create a space where expertise, experience, tools and shaping can happen to help people flourish through their work – part of our mission to create better business for a better world.

So, we are the future compared to organizations that may be attracted to this kind of employment 'deal' but have yet to experiment with or experience this way of working.

Our approach to *adjacency* – not just core operations – symbolizes possible, plausible and preferred futures.

Theories of human-centred evolution of work

Indeed, let's look at the work of **Professor Clare Graves** (1974) (who created the Emergent Cyclical Levels Of Existence), which inspired Ken Wilbur, Don Beck and Christopher Cowan (*AQAL* and *Spiral Dynamics*), which in turn inspired Frederic Laloux (2014) and the manifestation of a *Teal organization*. We see a future of more human-centred, autonomously self-managed, non-hierarchical purpose-led enterprises.

Futures Thinking may use much of this body of work and contextualize it to the organization you are a part of, for a version of this thinking in how you operate as a corporation.

From an HR perspective, this represents a significant departure from leadership control, hierarchical structures, roles and rewards, performance measures and recruiting practices that are based more on values, culture, mission alignment, potential and a sense of self than purely on academic attainment, experience and validated capabilities.

This is another reason why HR cannot be late to (or worse, excluded from) any conversations about Futures Thinking exercises and attention to that adaptive, shaping and aspirational way of being and becoming.

If anything is emerging from the *Future of Work* expositions, human centricity is a more compassionate and considerate way to lead and work with others, showing stronger empathy, creativity and relational ways of being. The powerful force of a purpose that forges connection to other people and a sense of belief, worth and virtue, gives HR more licence to lead Futures Thinking exercises.

It's not just for the operational engineers, the technologists or the business strategists – it has to be a combination of those and the People, Culture, Learning, Design, Behavioural and Talent professionals to ensure Futures Thinking is a comprehensive, adaptive and centrifugal force for a more prosperous future for all.

YOUR FUTURE EMPLOYEE USING A FUTURES THINKING APPROACH

It's 2029 and the lead on People and Culture at the Decarbon Alliance (DA) – a global prosperity-based enterprise – needs some fresh thinking in the Analyst Capability Pool.

Through the DA Work Community Portal, Ayisha Lato's Skills Passport has come up as a good match for what you're looking for. You moved to being a skills-based (not job-based) organization in 2027.

The company always runs an initial 'chemistry' call, which *Eden*, your workforce bot, has handled. Ayisha is based in Manchester, and Eden connected the company to Ayisha and six of the current members of the Analyst Pool, plus colleagues on a UN-sponsored project spanning the globe.

After having the initial conversation and Ayisha's conversations with two former members of the Analyst Capability Pool, Ayisha offered her services for a six-week paid trial with the company. This was approved, and the contracting was instigated by Eden and set up through DA's Blockchain contract workflow.

During her first four weeks, Ayisha saw the potential for a new venture using Protein Folding Biotech to generate soil nutrients from genetically modified algae. She presented her findings to the Incubation Squad, which approved her proposal. Ayisha's contract was immediately revised to a six-month sponsorship and a Squad to work with her on this project.

Ayisha used the Eden bot to help assemble a team, and whilst she was based in Manchester, her Squad colleagues were in Mali and Burkina Faso.

> Having worked virtually to run digital simulator scenarios, the Squad could then agree on how to work together on this project over the coming months – crafting their culture, governance and learning plan. The team's networks and previous experience meant they could bring in additional skilled people and accelerate their first production cycle to start work into the delivery sprints.
>
> Ayisha and some of the team visited their production site with representatives from each of the Mali and Burkina Faso Agricultural Ministries. With successful installation and two proofs of concept, the project was in its operational stages to test production capabilities and capacity.
>
> DA worked on an agreement to provide the two ministries with 100 algae production sites across the two countries that turned the algae's consumption of waste materials into soil nutrients that can turn desert land into arable farming.
>
> As a result of the value created by this venture and the working chemistry, Ayisha was invited to join the Biotech Incubation Team for three days per week into the foreseeable future and to continue to lead the Algae Ponds venture.

There are existing and realistic attributes of Ayisha's story.

It's not so much *science fiction* as this is a very plausible future. Many elements of this projected future story are based on things 'in play' now: '... already here, just unevenly distributed.'

Audacious futures

Being bolder and more imaginative, though, here are some future projections I will make. I will call them my **10×BHAGs** – Big, Hairy, Audacious Goals x10:

1 **Sustainable and Earth-pro operations not only limiting harm to the environment but also repairing our ecosystems of life.**
   Increasingly, governments fail to introduce more approaches to regenerative practices through COP gatherings and Davos-like forums. It's on the business world to act in a more regenerative way. As consumers, investors, workers and citizens, the consequences of planetary ill-health will hit value chains and profit margins, so the commercial and moral imperative will combine to create a new era in the world of work – the Regenerative Era. Advances in science and technology will help us address global warming and combat freak climate shifts. More work will be found in these areas with both a moral and a commercial imperative.

TABLE 2.2 Existing approaches to a futures story

HR/work area	Use cases/examples
Strategic workforce planning	Skills-based hiring, working and delivering on projects
Project work	Work as project-based and innovation-led approaches
Automation	AI-enabled administration/governance with automation in identifying prospective new team members and the formalization of the contract of work
Agile and Sprint-based working	Agile approaches to working in iterative sprints, with prototyping and value creation along the chain of production
Leading for innovation	Leadership that is more about incubation than control and work allocation
Participatory teams	Team constructs and agreements that help individuals align to each other's expertise, availability and in making decisions and prioritization of work
Flexible working	Virtual, synchronous/asynchronous working via digital platforms and applications
Augmentation	Capacity managed through AI workflow assistance and automated time/space creation in schedules and deadline management
Scenario planning	Business simulators which help people learn and explore possibilities before committing to real-world work and potential investment

2 **Education shifts to good citizenship and volatile world readiness.**

Going beyond core curricula, helping young people learn their way into not just being activists on conscience but being equipped for a world that is turbulent by default will advance the education agenda and not only make a more successful transition from education into work, but prepare people for what life really is like beyond the teach-test-awards model. All forms of health – physical, human, mental, financial, societal and planetary – will rebase the education proposition and allow children to enjoy the intellectual enrichment from education, equipping them for a more complex and chaotic world.

3 **The dissolution of many jobs as we know them has resulted in the division of work into different forms.**

Yes, we'll still have surgeons, aeroplane pilots, firefighters and chefs, but digital technologies and robotics will significantly augment all of those jobs. Where such jobs are critical to the safety and security of others, human expertise, intervention and capability will have to be more reliable, comforting and only achieved through that human intervention. We know that the emerging use of robotics and digital technologies can link a surgeon based in the UK to a *da Vinci* robot operating on a patient in Singapore. All other work outside of ultra-core professional, legal and safety-type work will likely be set into projects and formulations of people will assemble and disassemble into project teams from their capability pools and domain hubs. Flexible ways of working – not just in-office or remotely, but the very nature of working in states of fluidity – will become the increasing norm.

4 **People experience and dynamic workforce planning will reshape and drive new forms of productivity.**
Key performance indicators (KPIs) and even gross domestic product (GDP) are no longer sufficient ways to frame what is a successful, good, enduring, sustainable and likeable form of work. To be successful, the measures need to shift to be more about wider forms of prosperity. Prosperity comes in a range of forms covering human, social, intellectual, material, natural and, of course, financial value. To facilitate this, how people are treated and feel about their work has been proven through studies to correlate with high performance at an organizational level. Employee engagement will be a nullified measure replaced with voice, influence, participation, sentiment, intent and overall sense of the experience of work.

5 **Digital integration, not just digital transformation.**
Sequencing and splicing artificial intelligence (AI – generative AI and increasingly soon agentic AI) into work is not just about what can be automated – huge though the potential and 'gold-rush' mentality we see in the mid-2020s is. It's more about 'outsourcing' to machines combined with augmentation and assimilation of the use of advancing technologies with people, their capabilities, imagination and relational skills in the work they do.

6 **Inclusivity, personalization and the uniqueness of people as a default for consumers, partners and colleagues.**
Far from the backlash to the so-called *woke* agenda, advanced systems design will be driven by data sets, digital augmentation and integration, and allow for individuality to be part of the design of services, products, experiences and participation, not an adjustment post-design. What's

most important is the commercial, moral and societal edge this brings and how it liberates and enables participation aligned to key strategic aims, creating more innovative approaches naturally through connected systems of data capture and analysis into the flow of work. This will see people driving their own career paths using their organization's mission and systems to have impact in a way they desire that ultimately creates a stronger, high-performing overall enterprise.

7 **Intelligence and fast strategy will become the hallmarks of 21st-century organizational success and effectiveness.**

Strategy playbooks built on five-year plans are already nullified by volatile and turbulent conditions in the world. And yet, to abandon them in favour of constant, tiring and confusing chaos would be equally pointless. Faster ways to get, analyse and use intelligence into more rapid forms of flowing strategy will be the key role of leaders. They will need to set ambitious and alluring visions, to engage and inspire their people and consumers, investors and stakeholders, and to plot courses with as much certainty as can be mustered, and readiness for constant iterative and adaptive approaches to being successful.

8 **Culture will be even more important in determining how successful any enterprise can be.**

Already inclusive cultures are more desirable and positive, participatory forms of culture are showing how rapidly scaling and already huge organizations can create the environment for success. For too long, culture has been set by the leaders and a trickle-through form determines how people are expected to deliver and behave. With a more centre-out (not even bottom-up) form, the best of what creates the most appropriate and sustainable culture needs to come from all of those invested in any organization's mission and successfully delivering it. Culture can give meaning, purpose, belonging, becoming, maturing and evolving when allowed to blossom and grow as the 'spiritual' centre of the organizational 'machine'.

9 **A total reinvention of the role of managers.**

As it stands, the team leader, supervisory role of a manager is a continuing hangover of the industrial age – someone to check up on the work of team members, allocate work, direct prioritization and handle exceptions. In the more complex and adaptive work of the 2020s and beyond, the manager role will morph into one of either a technical expert (unlikely to have a team to manage and lead but will form into project squads as appropriate) or an enterprising leader who coaches, develops, guides and supports other people who are working on projects.

10 **There is a resurgence and restoration of the concept of work as craft.**
Call it a work renaissance, if you will. With robotics, automation and AI
taking some 'heavy lifting' (literally in many cases) away from humans,
work as craft will become increasingly important in our search for
meaningful and purposeful living. Viewing ourselves as craftspeople will
bring us back to pre-commercial times when we mastered, engaged in
and felt good about doing something other than just for economic
tokens – a sense of worth, self, fulfilment and joy. That it also ties into
economic and environmental stability will mean we have a work
platform that is desirable and helps people – and the planet – flourish.

In summary

On reading these 10 things, you may feel this is wildly ambitious, utopian or
even ridiculously naïve and optimistic. Yet the signals have already formed
in the future and are casting back to us that this is possible, plausible and
preferable.

Without Futures Thinking and a future-casting HR function, some of this
might happen. With a more applied, exuberant and determined future-
focused HR function, it becomes more likely and more desirable as we truly
unlock the potential in systems, science and the spirit of our people.

As Pablo Picasso said, 'Everything you can imagine is real.'

WHAT WE'VE COVERED IN THIS CHAPTER

1 **The nature of Futures Thinking:** Defined as a method to explore multiple
potential, plausible and preferable futures, highlighting its use in strategy,
change management and Organization Design.

2 **The role of HR in Futures Thinking:** Advocated for HR as a proactive
participant in shaping future trajectories, integrating anticipatory leadership
and participatory organizational practices.

3 **Integration of systems and science:** Explored how Systems Thinking and
scientific disciplines (e.g. behavioural science, data science and
organizational psychology) support Futures Thinking in HR.

4 **Application of scenario planning:** Introduced scenario planning as a tool
to help HR evaluate potential outcomes and adapt strategies for emerging
trends and disruptions.

5 **Shift towards skills-based organizations:** Highlighted the transition from job-based to skills-based models, emphasizing adaptability and agility in workforce planning.

6 **The impact of digital transformation:** Addressed the integration of AI and advanced technologies to reshape work processes, governance and organizational operations.

7 **Cultural and managerial evolution:** Discussed the importance of inclusive, participatory cultures and the redefined role of managers as coaches and guides in adaptive, project-based environments.

8 **The concept of work as craft:** Reintroduced the idea of meaningful work rooted in mastery and fulfilment, enabled by automation and AI reducing transactional tasks.

9 **Future-ready operating models:** Explained the connection between operating models, Organization Design and Development to prepare for dynamic and regenerative business landscapes.

References and further reading

Graves, C W (1974) Human nature prepares for a momentous leap, *The Futurist*, 8 (2), pp 72–87

Howe, N and Strauss, W (1997) *The Fourth Turning: An American prophecy*, New York: Broadway Books

Korsvik Østergaard, E (2023) *Anticipatory Leadership: Navigating complexity and uncertainty in a fast-changing world*, Denmark: Publishare, https://lidpublishing.com/books/anticipatory-leadershp/ (archived at https://perma.cc/P4EM-J4QG)

Laloux, F (2014) *Reinventing Organizations: A guide to creating organizations inspired by the next stage of human consciousness*, Brussels: Nelson Parker

Lindkvist, M (2013) *When the Future Begins: A guide to long-term thinking*, London: Marshall Cavendish

Expanded references for Table 2.1

Behavioural science

Kahneman, D (2011) *Thinking, Fast and Slow*, London: Penguin

Thaler, R and Sunstein, C (2008) *Nudge: Improving decisions about health, wealth, and happiness*, New Haven, CT: Yale University Press

Occupational psychology

Bakker, A B and Demerouti, E (2007) The Job Demands-Resources Model: State of the art, *Journal of Managerial Psychology*, 22 (3), pp. 309–28

Rousseau, D M (1995) *Psychological Contracts in Organizations: Understanding written and unwritten agreements*, Thousand Oaks, CA: Sage

Data science and people analytics

Bersin, J (2018) *HR Technology Market Disruptions*, Oakland, CA: Bersin by Deloitte

Green, D (2021) *Excellence in People Analytics: How to use workforce data to create business value*, London: Kogan Page

People and performance analytics

Chamorro-Premuzic, T (2017) *The Talent Delusion: Why data, not intuition, is the key to unlocking human potential*, London: Piatkus

Waber, B (2013) *People Analytics: How social sensing technology will transform business and what it tells us about the future of work*, Upper Saddle River, NJ: FT Press

Organizational psychology

Kotter, J P (1996) *Leading Change*, Boston: Harvard Business Review Press

Schein, E H (2017) *Organizational Culture and Leadership*, 5th edn. Hoboken, NJ: Wiley

Team psychology

Edmondson, A (2019) *The Fearless Organization: Creating psychological safety in the workplace for learning, innovation, and growth*, Hoboken, NJ: Wiley

Lencioni, P (2002) *The Five Dysfunctions of a Team: A leadership fable*, San Francisco, CA: Jossey-Bass

Science on leadership

Goleman, D (1995) *Emotional Intelligence: Why it can matter more than IQ*, New York: Bantam Books

Heifetz, R and Linsky, M (2009) *The Practice of Adaptive Leadership: Tools and tactics for changing your organization and the world*, Boston: Harvard Business Review Press

Science on motivation

Deci, E L and Ryan, R M (1985) *Intrinsic Motivation and Self-Determination in Human Behavior*, New York: Springer

Pink, D H (2009) *Drive: The surprising truth about what motivates us*, New York: Riverhead Books

Science on sustainable performance

Maslach, C and Leiter, M P (2016) *Burnout: The cost of caring*, New York: Malor Books

Schwartz, T (2010) *The Way We're Working Isn't Working: The four forgotten needs that energize great performance*, New York: Free Press

Science on work-based organizations

Laloux, F (2014) *Reinventing Organizations: A guide to creating organizations inspired by the next stage of human consciousness*, Brussels: Nelson Parker

Wheatley, M (2006) *Leadership and the New Science: Discovering order in a chaotic world*, San Francisco, CA: Berrett-Koehler

3

The evolution of
HR Operating Models

The business that we're in must include the future.
W EDWARDS DEMING, QUALITY VISIONARY AND SYSTEMS THINKER

WHAT'S COVERED IN THIS CHAPTER

- **Traditional to modern models:** Transition from traditional HR structures to more agile, responsive models.

- **Technology's role:** The increasing technology shifts that are shaping modern HR practice, especially Generative AI and automation tools.

- **Globalization and diversity:** Examining how global and diverse workforces have changed HR approaches.

I'll start this chapter with a provocative response to the Deming quote:

As a profession and a practice field, HR is too much a *here-and-now* function and barely grasps or grips onto the future.

In Chapters 1 and 2 we described the changing world (and of work) and how a Futures Thinking approach is needed for anyone trying to navigate the increased complexities of the world. We will need a more capable way of approaching the future and therefore our options, not to the detriment of the here and now but to enhance the next iteration of what here and now could become – more impactful, positive and fruitful. Short-termism is not what we need. Current and future states are now constantly intertwined.

Some might say that being fixated on what's happening right now is enough. Fixing employment law issues (HR's *industrial relations* heritage) and personnel matters of a transactional, administrative nature is where it should be.

Some might say that's grossly unfair, as talent, workforce planning and Organization Design are future-proofing the organization. And they are, or at least have greater potential to be, more *future-ready*.

Taking one of the most important decisions any business makes – recruitment and hiring – is a good place to start. And sadly, in my experience, recruitment is convulsive 'vacancy filling'; workforce planning is not sufficiently or strongly enough done (not all HR's fault – I'm aware of its immaturity in business leaders, and sympathetic that HR pushes as hard as it can to get this on the business agenda). Organization Design, similarly, is taken over by strategist leaders keeping HR on the fringes and late to the game. So this isn't HR bashing – there's enough of that out there.

But in an increasingly complex and chaotic world, being *future-mute* is being too low down the value chain, boxing this profession in when it could and should be a leading thinker, strategist and practitioner of more future-focused activity.

So, this book, partly about the 'blueprint' aspect of HR's Operating Model, is also a call for business leaders (operational, executive, customer, marketing, financial and otherwise) to coalesce and have HR lead and drive *much* more of the future agenda.

Chapter 2's Futures Thinking is part of that. With so much of the future being about systems and science (not just operational cadence or product development), HR must be *let in* and *step up*.

Much of that starts with a compelling vision for people, culture, learning, talent, workforce planning, compliance, performance and effectiveness, especially when so many people are looking for their work to go way beyond the economic transactional elements of the industrial age. Meaningful, good work is open for all with the intent and skill to create value.

But then it must also be set against a believable, inspiring and impact-driven operating model.

This book sets out to make the *entire* organization interested in the HR Operating Model. But why is such a bold claim from an oft-maligned professional function so important?

Five words to frame the importance of an optimized HR operating model

People. Culture. Learning. Performance. Purpose.

The demands and aspirations for HR of the 21st century are way beyond compliance administration and employment market operations. What is often cited in case studies, articles and even research is that purpose – the reason the organization exists, the meaning that people derive from their work – is ever more crucial. People make the organization what it is and how it can be. Culture, learning and performance are the systems and energy forces that connect purpose to people.

It's a balance and a recipe for success that is not just the engineering we opened this book with but also the spirit, the soul and the sense of doing something worthwhile.

When highly capitalized businesses can pay for the most lucrative talent on the market, what helps them retain their spot as highly successful businesses is not simply a 'blank chequebook' but a spirit and a sense of *doing and being*.

And of course, those less capitalized but 'challenger' organizations that double down on how it feels to work for an enterprise need to be competitive and have an efficient, effective value proposition and business operation, or else they become well-intended social constructs that the market may even admire but chews them up and spits them out in the name of raging capitalism.

Back to the 'exam question' – why would the HR Operating Model be so worthy of the attention and support, enablement and respect of the value chain, supply and partnerships, customer insight, financial investment and acquisition and product/service differentiation?

People. Culture. Learning. Performance. Purpose.

It is a mantra worth repeating. Of course, these factors also matter:

Product. Service. Financialization. Reputation. Diligence.

A brilliant product and a fantastic service proposition lead to stabilized financialization and build a strong reputation of a trusted and admired brand that is diligent in its place in the market and to its customers, investors and the planet, community and society it is a part of.

And all of those success factors can only come into maximum overdrive with people (who are creative, committed and inventive in building the product and service proposition). The organization's culture is attractive to the most dedicated and talented people and their construct into high-achieving and sustainable teams and functions, who focus on learning (to be and do more than they ever thought possible) and, of course, how that translates into meaningful, fulfilling performance.

Much of what we know about people science has given us deeper insight into the working systems and relationships through a business and operations lens. Motivation, compliance, decision making, innovation, overcoming challenges, improving systems, building trusted relationships and creating a sense of being together in pursuit of the business goals has given us a different form of evidence. Such sciences are known and used, but perhaps not as prominently or regularly as they could. The evidence is compelling, though (Table 3.1).

TABLE 3.1 Narrative descriptors of sciences and phenomena in work

Organizational psychology	This field offers insights into motivation, team dynamics and leadership styles. Deci and Ryan's self-determination theory (popularized in Daniel Pink's work on autonomy, mastery and purpose – *Drive: The surprising truth about what motivates us*) reveals how intrinsic motivation is more powerful than simply external rewards in creating enduring engagement and performance in people at work.
Behavioural economics	From the studies of Daniel Kahneman (*Thinking, Fast and Slow*) and Richard Thaler and Cass Sunstein (*Nudge*), we understand how biases influence decision making and how small changes in choice architecture can have outsized impacts on positive and sustainable employee behaviour and organizational culture.
Cognitive neuroscience	Research into how the brain learns and adapts, such as by Dr John Medina in *Brain Rules*, explains how learning environments can be optimized for better retention and application of knowledge. This is critical for organizations focused on continuous improvement and innovation.
Sociology	Studies of social capital and network effects (like those by Robert Putnam in *Bowling Alone*) emphasize the importance of connections and community in creating a collaborative and resilient organizational culture.

(continued)

TABLE 3.1 (Continued)

Performance science	Work by Marc Effron and Miriam Ort in *One Page Talent Management* shows how simplifying and focusing on core performance drivers creates clarity and accountability in performance systems.
Self-worth	Performance is deeply tied to a sense of self-worth and esteem. Abraham Maslow's Hierarchy of Needs places esteem – the recognition and respect of others – just below self-actualization. When employees feel valued and see their contributions making an impact, their performance often reaches new heights. This sense of self-worth becomes a virtuous cycle, reinforcing confidence, engagement and a willingness to innovate. Organizations that recognize and nurture this link between performance and esteem cultivate an environment where individuals perform and thrive.
Purpose and meaning	The power of purpose and meaning cannot be overstated. Viktor Frankl's seminal work *Man's Search for Meaning* highlights the human need for purpose as a driving force in life. In organizations, purpose aligns individual goals with a greater mission, providing a sense of significance and belonging. When employees see their work as meaningful – contributing to something bigger than themselves – they engage more deeply, bring their best selves to work and persist even in the face of challenges. Purpose transforms tasks into vocations and workplaces into communities.

These sciences offer HR practitioners the frameworks and tools to build organizations where people thrive, cultures flourish, learning is pervasive, performance excels and purpose resonates deeply.

The resources mentioned above provide foundational and advanced understanding for those who wish to delve deeper into these topics. This intersection of people sciences with HR operating models ensures that what we build is not only operationally sound but also deeply human and impactful.

In the next section, we will explore integrating these sciences into practical HR frameworks that can be adapted and scaled to diverse organizational needs.

This chapter also addresses the evolution of the HR function – understandably in many more forward-aspiring organizations called People (and

Culture), headed by a Chief People Officer or Director of People – and why it is yet to truly ascend to its rightful place as the key determinant in the ongoing success of any enterprise. And why science – not just information derived from data (surveys, sentiment analysis and performance statistics) – is a crucial leverage to why the rest of the organization should become more attuned to both responding to, and shaping, a more progressive HR Operating Model.

In essence, this entire book is a declaration:

> Overlook, underplay and ignore the power in a progressive HR operating model at your peril.

Are we making HR operating models 'sexy'? Not so much that. It's beyond marketing hype, relabelling and tinkering.

We're making the HR Operating Model the *fusion core* of energy, power and momentum that will see organizations successfully reengineer and reimagine their HR, People, Culture, Learning, Performance and Purpose into the sustainable powerhouses of a better future.

People-centric operations with strong and adaptable systems, leading to enhanced products and powering processes, result in a future-ready HR operating model.

Within that are a raft of changes to roles, enhanced capabilities and strengthening what HR already has in its ranks – a renaissance for HR into a reimagined and recalibrated function driving organizational success and prosperous ways of operating.

Before we look further ahead, we'll take a look at the past and explore some of the reasons HR might be undervalued, underachieving and under-appreciated.

The HR Operating Model evolution

Before operating models were really a *thing*, there was a growing need for some parts of (particularly large) industrial and institutional organizations to organize their 'human resources'. Materials, stock, financial capital and legal governance were all advancing as more organizations became more efficient in how they created products and served their markets.

The term 'operating model' appears to have its origins in management and organizational theory, likely gaining prominence in the mid-20th century as businesses began formalizing their strategic and operational frameworks. It became more explicitly used during the rise of management consulting firms like McKinsey & Company and Boston Consulting Group in the 1970s and 1980s. These firms focused on helping organizations align their operations with strategic goals, introducing structured approaches to understanding and improving business processes, systems and Organization Design.

The concept gained further traction with the popularization of frameworks like Michael Porter's value chain (1985) and Peter Drucker's focus on organizational effectiveness. By the early 2000s, with the advent of digital transformation and complex global supply chains, the term became firmly embedded in the business lexicon, particularly as organizations sought clarity in adapting their operations for agility, scalability and efficiency.

Until this point, no one was talking about 'models' other than the classic organization organogram/chart and the construct of the business to generate profit or serve a need.

The shift from personnel to human resources and beyond

In a compressed timeline of the last 8–10 generations, Table 3.2 plots the shift for a function ordained to address the 'people' elements of enterprises and organizations.

Human Resources became a label to move the function of Personnel Administration (arguably an institutional/militaristic term) into this more sophisticated realm of understanding all the moving parts of a business and its system or operation.

The 1920s and 1930s brought the *Hawthorne Studies* by Elton Mayo (1933) and others, highlighting the importance of employee welfare,

TABLE 3.2 Function timeline

1850s–1900s	1900s–1950s	1950s–1980s	1980s–2000s	2000s–to date
Early Industrial Era	WWI/II, Cold War + Rebuild	Post-war Industrial boom	The Knowledge Economy	Digitization + Industry 4.0
Worker Welfare	Industrial Relations	Personnel	Human Resources	People and Culture

motivation and social dynamics in productivity. These studies laid the groundwork for considering workers as individuals with psychological and social needs.

Through the mid- and post-World War II world, more theoretical foundations emerged. The term *Industrial Relations* became a key function as more unionization and representation of employee voice and influence came alongside the boom in capitalist wealth after the devastation of the War. Conditions of employ – the advent of more laws around equality, workplace and employment conditions – were state-introduced frameworks and legislature that forced employers into more ethical, legalized and considerate terms of employ.

In the early 1950s, Personnel Management focused on administrative functions like payroll, compliance and employee record-keeping.

Much of this occurred alongside scholarly research, and (now) renowned figures like Kurt Lewin and Abraham Maslow introduced theories such as the Hierarchy of Needs and Change Management and Group Dynamics.

Lewin's foundational work in change management introduced the concept of unfreezing, changing and refreezing – a vital process in helping organizations navigate transformation. His theories on group dynamics emphasized the importance of understanding how groups influence individual behaviour, shaping team culture and effectiveness. Lewin's *Force Field Analysis* (1951) also provides a practical tool for identifying forces that drive or resist organizational change, making it invaluable for HR practitioners designing adaptable and resilient workplaces.

Maslow's *Hierarchy of Needs* (1943) brought a much-needed emphasis on human self-actualization and people's basic life needs, communal, social and psychological factors and their aspirational and developmental potential.

Douglas McGregor's *Theory X and Theory Y* (1960) contrasted autocratic and participative management styles, further advancing the view of employees as active contributors rather than passive subordinates.

In the 1960s, the term 'Human Resource Management' gained traction. Economists like Gary Becker introduced the concept of Human Capital in the 1960s, emphasizing investment in education, training and skills development as key economic drivers (Becker, 1964).

Moving into the 1970s–1980s we saw the formalization of HR as a practice field and/or discipline. The term *Human Resources* was popularized through books like Peter Drucker's *Management: Tasks, responsibilities, practices* (1973) and writings by thought leaders who emphasized the strategic importance of people management in achieving business goals.

Large corporations such as IBM and General Electric began adopting the term 'Human Resources' to reflect a shift towards integrating personnel functions with broader organizational strategy.

Key pioneers in HR Thinking emerged during this period. Peter Drucker advocated for treating people as central to organizational success.

In the 1990s, Dave Ulrich introduced the *HR Business Partner model*, which reframed HR as a strategic partner in business operations rather than a purely administrative function.

Early adopters of this evolved HR approach were, again, major corporations like Procter & Gamble and General Electric, which were among the first to institutionalize the term and approach, leveraging HR as a strategic function to build organizational capability and competitive advantage.

Government and nonprofit sectors also began adopting the term in alignment with broader workforce management strategies.

The evolution of 'Human Resources' marks a significant shift in viewing employees as a vital resource, embedding the function within the strategic fabric of organizations rather than limiting it to operational tasks. This approach has continued to evolve, with modern HR focusing on areas like Organization Design, employee experience (EX), diversity, equity, inclusion (DEI) and aligning people strategies with organizational purpose.

However...

Is there a more criticized function in the corporate world than HR?

A 2015 article called 'Why we love to hate HR' (Cappelli, 2015) somewhat blew this up into a full-scale debate and self-appraisal and has often been quoted back.

HR has become a tainted and tarnished phrase and the profession finds itself on the backfoot a lot to justify its products and services and, in some cases, its very existence.

Scholars and business leaders alike both openly call for reform, reinvention and reimagining of what this function should do more of, less of and generally be called upon to do and create value.

Is this without justification and simply an 'easy target' for organizational woes? Perhaps.

This targeting often comes at times of great shifts (increased reliance on and utilization of digital capabilities being just one) and the need for more skilled, adaptable, aligned and performance-enhancing human effort.

Isn't this a more widespread *leadership and management failure*, and not simply because of HR policies, somewhat tame interventions and an inability to cater to an ever-expanding remit given to HR?

Why leaders and managers face criticism

1 Accountability for organizational outcomes
Leaders are held responsible for the success or failure of their organizations. When things go wrong – be it financial performance, employee engagement or public reputation – they are the first to face blame. Examples of criticism include poor strategic decisions (e.g. blockbuster failures or poorly timed expansions) or unethical practices (e.g. high-profile corporate scandals – fraud and unethical practices).

2 Failure to inspire or engage employees
According to Gallup research, up to 70 per cent of variance in team engagement is attributable to managers (Royal, 2019). When employees feel disengaged, the criticism often falls on leaders for failing to provide vision, purpose or connection. A lack of emotional intelligence or micromanagement often compounds these criticisms.

3 Unrealistic expectations of leadership
Leaders are expected to possess a wide array of capabilities – vision, decisiveness, empathy, adaptability and innovation – all of which are difficult to master simultaneously. This gap between expectations and reality often fuels disenchantment.

4 Toxic leadership and power dynamics
Workplace toxicity – ranging from overt bullying to subtle favouritism – is frequently attributed to poor leadership. Studies on toxic leadership highlight its damaging effects on morale and retention.

5 Lack of managerial skills
Many organizations promote high-performing employees into management roles without providing adequate training in leadership. As a result, managers may struggle with basic tasks like delegation, feedback and team-building.

6 Economic and social context
During crises like layoffs, recessions or organizational restructures, leaders are often seen as prioritizing profits or shareholders over employees. This perception reinforces broader societal critiques of corporate leadership.

The scale of criticism for leaders and managers

Empirical evidence:

Edelman Trust Barometer (2023) found that trust in CEOs remains fragile, with 63 per cent of respondents globally saying CEOs are 'out of touch' with employees and societal issues.

Gallup's State of the Global Workplace (2022) reports that poor leadership accounts for 85 per cent of disengaged employees, with criticism falling heavily on frontline managers.

Leadership is one of the most written-about elements of the world of work. Many books highlight leadership failings and better ways to lead others:

Simon Sinek's *Leaders Eat Last* (2014) emphasizes how leaders' inability to foster trust damages team cohesion.

Barbara Kellerman's *The End of Leadership* (2012) critiques the modern cult of leadership and the gap between leaders' promises and their actions.

Why leaders may face more criticism than HR

- **Visibility and power**
  Leaders are public-facing figures and their decisions are directly tied to the organization's trajectory, making them obvious targets for blame.

- **Cultural ripple effects**
  Toxic cultures are often traced back to leadership, with 'tone at the top' cited as a key driver of employee dissatisfaction.

- **Moral failures**
  Failures in ethics or integrity (e.g. overpaid CEOs during layoffs) are widely criticized because they reflect poorly on the entire organization.

In conclusion

While HR is a common scapegoat for organizational shortcomings, leaders and managers arguably face greater scrutiny because their influence is more visible and far-reaching. When leadership fails, the resulting dismay and disenchantment ripple throughout the organization, often with lasting consequences. If anything, any criticisms of HR and leadership are inextricably interconnected and aimed at both aspects, as HR is often having to act as both the enabler and the 'watchdog' of leadership capability and behaviours.

So if you DO find yourself (as a leader or otherwise) criticizing HR, you're probably also projecting somewhat broader leadership failures, not just some HR inefficiency.

Finger-pointing and point-scoring are pretty futile; instead, a more collegiate approach to improving things regarding People, Culture, Learning, Performance and Purpose is a shared endeavour by everyone in an organization with HR as stewards, value creators, arbitrators and agitators for the best possible outcomes, however smooth or bumpy the ride that is organizational operation.

This is why the HR Operating Model is more important than it is currently viewed, especially considering shifts in the business and overall operating model that are cast once the product and service (value) propositions have been decided upon. The next logical sequence is that the HR Operating Model helps as a primary consideration for things like:

1 **Organization Design** (and no, not just the restructured organization chart) – a broad and all-encompassing design that links purpose, culture, values, learning, performance, decision making, compliance/standards, governance and...

2 **Workflow** – balanced and loaded fairly across the organization, including a hard and deep look at capabilities, skills, behaviours, inclusivity, fairness, equity, adaptability and versatility, which needs...

3 **Talent** – how we use those skills we have, grow or acquire those we don't and build a more sustainable people proposition, which leads to a more flourishing and renewable...

4 **People proposition** – not just the Terms and Conditions but the sense of belonging, psychological contract, safety and strength of conviction and a belief that the work people do and the organization they do it for is good for them and for other people (consumers/clients, partners, communities, society and the planet).

The nobility in work we should never overlook

Whilst some of this may sound incredibly grandiose and noble, I doubt anyone goes into work and the feat of business of any sort wishing for it to be mediocre, tolerable and inconsequential to their life or the lives of others.

We may be receptionists, teaching assistants, bricklayers or lorry drivers in job title, but we're doing this work not only to earn a living but to make a difference somehow and do something worthwhile.

We can talk about glamorous strategies and feats of superhuman endeavour in sports or the military and link them to business, but the reality is that we spend:

- over 86,000 hours of our life at work (equivalent to 10 years);
- 34,000 hours (four years) in some form of commuting – work and life;
- 17,000 hours (or two years) on personal learning and development.

So, working is linked to *16 years of our time* on the planet. Not 40–50 years, as we may think (from education to retirement). This way of thinking (a three-stage life: education/school – work – retirement) has us somewhat resentful of spending so much time at work, when in reality, the rest of our life (65 years) is made up of:

- more than 233,000 hours of our lives asleep (27 years);
- 129,000 hours of leisure and recreation (15 years, although it might not seem it);
- and then things like family time, volunteering, household chores and self-care, totting up to 197,000 hours (23 years).

This 20 per cent of our life (connected to work) is undeniably what helps us with that quality of leisure, family and self-care time (the 80 per cent that admittedly includes sleep as a form of self-care).

It has become (understandably) reductive that we have to tolerate the 20 per cent (work time) to enable the other 80 per cent of our lives. Yet in that 20 per cent, we can be so much more fulfilled if our work experiences are positive and enable a truly flourishing life.

It's where the focus (of late, post-Covid, perhaps enhancing the feeling somewhat) comes from that we strive for more from our 20 per cent time at work. And why a strong, purposeful working proposition is so important.

It isn't just the domain of white-collar, knowledge workers to pursue more purpose in work; it's on all of us that what we do in that 20 per cent of our lives is as purposeful as the 80 per cent spent on family, leisure, sleep, self-care and more.

So the days of 'any conditions at work are OK as long as you're getting paid' are no longer viable, feasible or desired. Whether we say we're only doing the work we do because we get paid for it or not, we *want* to feel that what we do has value and is valued; we *need* to feel like we make a difference with what we do because we have pride, esteem and worth; and we *like* to feel a sense of connection, purpose and meaning from what we do as a form of discovery of self – who we are and what we're here to do.

Any leaders who still think people will come to work for you *solely* for the money, best think again. It's way more than that which will get you the most dedicated, creative, applied and talented people. Time and again we see studies that point to salary and benefits as being important (the 20 per cent that enables the 80 per cent) but in reality, when people give their best, it's because they feel they are valued, what they do creates value and it is done in a values-based way towards something worthwhile.

People. Culture. Learning. Performance. Purpose.

The significance of your HR Operating Model

Like an infinity loop, a great purpose attracts good people who will help create a positive and vibrant culture. Who will learn with you and help you as an organization learn to adapt and keep pace with change. Who want to perform and whose performance helps the organization thrive and be a differentiator around its product, service and supply propositions that create financial value and prosperous ways of operating, aligned to that very purpose that attracted people to you in the first place. And so it continues.

And again, this is why an HR Operating Model that accentuates, amplifies and accelerates the positive experiences of those five core elements is important and will deliver positive impacts to and for people at work and, ultimately, the entire enterprise.

It's not a question of 'Is the HR Operating Model more important than the Business or Enterprise Operating Model?' It's more this: 'What good are those two (Business and Operating Models) without a dynamic, progressive and impactful HR Operating Model?'

And this question – in my experience and view of the world over 20 years in the HR profession – is not asked enough, if at all.

It's why an HR Operating Model should demand more focus, input and attention and why this book will help go beyond being simply a reinvented, reimagined and realigned People profession.

It's about ushering in a refreshed, reinvigorated proposition and, without hyperbole, a renaissance of the experience of work for people.

And we need to start that renaissance from where we are now regarding HR Operating Models. The dominant one is the focus for the rest of this chapter: the HR Business Partner model (sometimes called the Ulrich Model, after the work of Dave Ulrich, Professor at the Ross School of Business, University of Michigan, and Partner at The RBL Group).

Overview of the HR Business Partner-based operating model

The model, outlined in Dave Ulrich's book *Human Resource Champions* (1997), redefined HR's role, emphasizing its strategic contribution to organizational success. Ulrich proposed that HR should move beyond administrative tasks and adopt roles that add value to the business.

Key components of the HRBP model

Sometimes simplified as the *Three-Legged Stool model*, Ulrich's model also led to the structural redesign of HR into three core components:

- **HR Business Partners:** Embedded within business units to provide strategic support and tailor HR solutions.
- **Centres of Excellence (CoEs):** Specialized teams that focus on areas like talent management, compensation, and learning and development.
- **Shared Services:** Centralized operations handling transactional and administrative tasks, such as payroll and benefits.

FIGURE 3.1 A paradigm evolution of the HR and People profession

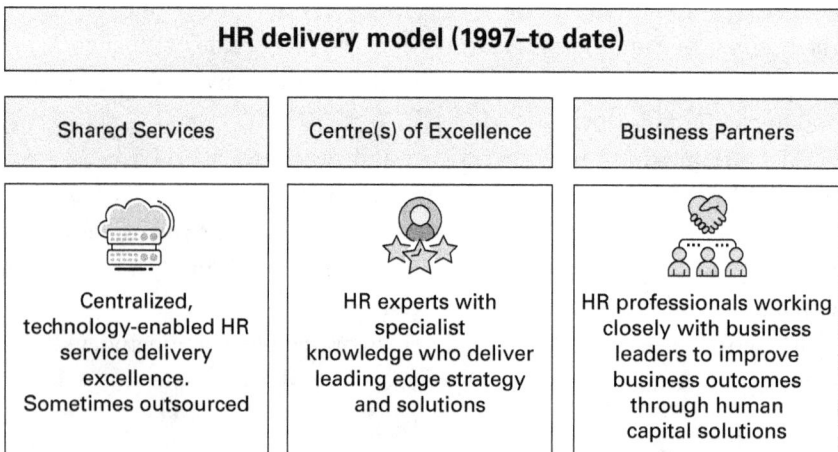

HR delivery model (1997–to date)		
Shared Services	Centre(s) of Excellence	Business Partners
Centralized, technology-enabled HR service delivery excellence. Sometimes outsourced	HR experts with specialist knowledge who deliver leading edge strategy and solutions	HR professionals working closely with business leaders to improve business outcomes through human capital solutions

The model focuses on delivering value in three key areas:

- **For the business:** Aligning HR with organizational strategy.
- **For employees:** Enhancing engagement, satisfaction and productivity.
- **For customers:** Creating a workforce that delivers better products and services.

Ulrich identified four roles that HR must play to be effective:

- **Strategic partner:** Align HR practices with business strategy to drive organizational success.
- **Change agent:** Lead and manage organizational transformation and culture shifts.
- **Administrative expert:** Ensure operational efficiency by improving processes and using technology to manage administrative tasks.
- **Employee champion:** Advocate for employees, ensuring engagement, well-being and capability development

At the time of introduction, the model was considered a revolutionary shift for HR from personnel administration and employee/industrial relations to a more strategic focus.

The model elevated the perspective (and performance arena) for HR from a back-office function to a strategic partner, tying people management directly to business outcomes.

FIGURE 3.2 The HR Business Partner or Ulrich Model for HR

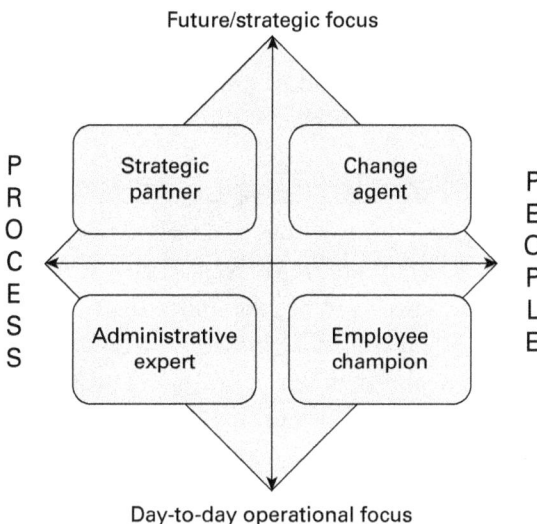

Future/strategic focus

P R O C E S S

Strategic partner

Change agent

Administrative expert

Employee champion

P E O P L E

Day-to-day operational focus

It advocated for specialization and efficiency by dividing HR responsibilities into distinct areas (business partners, CoEs and Shared Services), and improved HR's ability to handle both strategic and operational tasks effectively.

It recognized the importance of HR in shaping organizational culture and enabling change and has become the default for any HR team of more than a handful of practitioners. Although there are still outsourced, fractional/part-time and generalist roles in HR that cover a multitude of people-related services in smaller enterprises, most HR teams operate some form of this business partnering model.

While transformative at the time, the Ulrich model has faced criticism and adaptation in light of modern challenges:

- **Overcomplication:** Critics argue that the three-legged stool structure can be bureaucratic, creating silos and inefficiencies if not implemented effectively.

- **Limited adaptability:** Some organizations, especially smaller ones, find implementation and utilization of this model challenging due to resource constraints.

- **Evolving workforce needs:** The model was developed in a pre-digital, hierarchical era. Today's agile, skills-based and hybrid work environments demand more flexible and integrated approaches.

21st-century impacts on the HR Business Partner model

Advances in digital technologies

Automation, machine learning and AI are transforming access to information and services normally delivered through a shared service centre, enabling HR to focus more on strategic and human-centric work.

We are seemingly at the beginning of a significant shift to more *white-collar* automation, service propositions and technological advances beyond the robotics in manufacturing we've seen since the 1990s and 2000s. Quantum computing power and agentic and artificial general intelligence are still in their early experimental phase but promise much in terms of advanced abilities to deploy digital technologies in protein folding, genome sequencing and advancing science and medicine research.

The advent of a people/employee experience (PX/EX) focus

Increased utilization of design thinking and behavioural science can create more meaningful experiences for people at work, going beyond traditional HR boundaries of compliance and legislative updates.

This largely came about as we realized more of the sciences of attraction, persuasion, loyalty and reputation that came from customer experience (CX) and how human-centred design has become a crucial shaper of how services are delivered to meet people's spoken and unspoken needs.

The climate emergency and eco-system sustainability

Arguably, this is the biggest challenge of our times – the extractive and polluting damage done by our industrialization and the need to arrest rising sea levels, deforestation, species loss and freak weather conditions.

Whilst ESG (environmental, social and governance) is not specifically an HR discipline in itself, as more organizations pursue net-zero targets and more sustainable operations (and indeed, new industries emerge in carbon sequestration and alternative energy sources to fossil fuels) HR is involved in the Organization Design, skills and capabilities and the reputational impact of being a pro-planet enterprise.

Ageing populations and declining birthrates

As quality of life improves globally and science pushes further on the boundaries of medicinal and remedial treatment, we are living longer. Yet paradoxically, much of the Western world is seeing population decline through lower birth rates. A skills and labour force challenge is already looming, and this is set against the rising tide of anti-immigration sentiment in much of the right-wing political world.

Integration with skills-based organizations and contingent workforce models

Modern adaptations align with skills-based operating models emphasizing workforce agility and continuous learning over static divisional, hierarchical constructs.

Occasional and additional models for workers through gig and contingent models have ushered in a work proposition vastly different from that of permanent contracted employees.

Arguably the education system – still based on the industrial economy model – is slow to react to shifts in needs for greater interpersonal and relational skills, creativity and the arts, sciences and the known psychological impacts of a challenging and shifting economic system which is consistently fragile and in need of reinvention.

There are many factors rendering business models and thereby operating models nearly (or fully) obsolete and long-standing enterprises are failing and being closed down in favour of those organizations that read the signs and indeed disrupt markets and create new ones.

All of these call for people, culture, learning, performance and purpose factors to have increased focus and an HR Operating Model derived in the 1990s knowledge economy boom is stuttering and showing signs of no longer being the viable approach to take.

Adaptations and increments

Of course, it would be wrong to say that the entire HR profession is stuck in a 1997 time capsule and operating exactly how the original HR Business Partner/Ulrich model was conceived at that time.

And Dave Ulrich himself has consistently adapted his thinking and shaping to provide evidenced insight to HR practitioners to evolve and iterate on the original concept. Some examples are shown in Table 3.3.

TABLE 3.3 Types of model in the HR and People profession domain

People and Organization Development (OD)	Specific shifts to elevate the continuous improvement and adaptation, performance and effectiveness from a Centre of Excellence (CoE) specialism to an all-pervasive and change-oriented approach to 'doing' HR.
Tiered service model	Levels 1–3 or 4 – where HR teams are assembled according to complexity and specific services. Where Tier 1 is foundational compliance and administration, through Tier 2 and 3 being more complex operational challenges and Tier 4 is more strategic and leadership interventions.
Levelled expertise and pooled capabilities	HR Business Partners, HR Operations and CoE teams that consist of Heads of, Lead Roles and teams working on both Business-As-Usual support and project enablement.

(continued)

TABLE 3.3 (Continued)

Embedded additionality and out/insourcing	Recruitment in particular with RPO (Recruitment Process Outsourcing) as embedded agencies, specialists and contingent colleagues often used in scaling and shifting enterprises. Similarly with Pay and Reward Modelling, Learning and Development, and Change and Leadership Capability. HR teams working in partnership with solution-providing vendors who have multi-disciplinary teams to act as additional to a core HR team.
Talent and workforce planning models	HR teams deploy internal talent marketplaces to optimize workforce agility and enhance employee development.CoEs for talent management create systems where employees can take on stretch assignments, short-term gigs or projects across the organization, breaking down silos and promoting skill mobility. HRBPs and CoEs collaborate on long-term workforce planning, focusing on skills-based approaches rather than traditional job descriptions. CoEs develop skill taxonomies and identify critical capabilities, while HRBPs work with business leaders to align workforce strategies with organizational goals, ensuring agility in responding to future challenges.
Agile HR, HR as Product Managers and people/ employee experience (P/ EX) focused models	HR functions are adopting Agile methodologies to become more flexible and responsive to organizational needs. Example: CoE teams collaborate with HRBPs in cross-functional Agile squads to work on high-priority projects such as DEI initiatives, leadership development and digital transformation. This reduces siloing and improves delivery speed. HR teams adopt a product management mindset, treating HR initiatives (e.g. onboarding programmes, benefits systems) as 'products' to be designed, tested and iterated upon. HRBPs and CoEs collaborate to develop and refine 'HR products' based on employee feedback, ensuring continuous improvement. And moving beyond traditional HR metrics, teams are now tasked with improving the holistic employee experience (EX), integrating areas like well-being, workplace design and career growth. Example: HR Operations teams incorporate feedback loops (e.g. pulse surveys) into service delivery. CoEs focus on creating personalized employee journeys, leveraging technology and design thinking.

(continued)

TABLE 3.3 (Continued)

Technology-enhanced self-service models, data-driven decision making and people analytics	HR Shared Services have evolved into self-service portals powered by AI and automation, allowing employees to resolve queries without human intervention.
	Chatbots and virtual assistants handle Tier 1 inquiries (e.g. policy questions, benefits enrolment), freeing HR Operations to focus on more complex challenges. Enterprise HR platforms are commonly used to streamline service delivery.
	HR teams increasingly use people analytics to inform decisions and demonstrate strategic value. Data is leveraged to predict workforce trends, measure employee engagement and optimize talent acquisition. CoEs now often include data scientists or analytics experts focused on workforce planning, attrition forecasting and diversity metrics. HR Business Partners (HRBPs) use these insights to advise leadership on evidence-based strategies.
Purpose and sustainability integration with diversity, equity and inclusion (DEI) specialization	HR has become a key driver of embedding purpose and sustainability into the organization's culture and strategy. CoEs collaborate with sustainability officers to integrate ESG goals into performance management systems and leadership development programmes.
	DEI functions have been elevated into their own CoE or embedded within HRBPs' strategic priorities. HR teams track DEI metrics (e.g. pay equity, representation), ensure inclusive hiring practices and implement programmes to foster belonging and reduce bias.

And yet, the prevailing (underpinning) model is still the classic *three-legged stool* and role titles seem much the same. Whilst these are laudable increments, they haven't really 'moved the needle' and certainly, the reputation of HR is still based in compliance and administration, not pioneering.

It's time for a new model. One that casts aside the previous orthodoxy and, whilst using many of the interactive adaptations mentioned here, reimagines, reinvents, resets and evolves for the huge paradigm shift that is upon us – from the Industrial Revolution and the Knowledge Economy through the AI era and into the Regenerative Age.

TABLE 3.4 The projected advancement of work paradigms 2025–2045

2025 Knowledge Economy	2035 Automation Era	2045 Regenerative Age
Profit	Philanthropy	Planet
Sectors	Intersections	Ecocentric
Place	Space	Anywhere
Company	Collective	Community
Contracts	Compendium	Choice
Compliance	Coalesce	Commitment
Hiring	Adding	Collaborating
Salary	Reward	Prosperity
Episodic	Adaptive	Evolutive
Jobs	Work	Craft

WHAT WE'VE COVERED IN THIS CHAPTER

1 **The evolution of the HR Operating Model.** Whilst we have perhaps fairly recently become more familiar with the term operating models, since the mid-1990s, we've owed a debt of gratitude to scholars, especially Dave Ulrich, who have given us an operating model that has seen us through the last three decades.

2 **Adaptations have been and are being made to the HR Operating Model.** But a symbolic, reimagined approach is yet to emerge, becoming a core catalyst for a shift to the new age of digital technology and business model reinvention.

3 **The adaptations and innovations in HR Operating Models**

   o The chapter detailed how HR has evolved through technology, people analytics and approaches like Agile HR, People Experience focus and tiered service models.

   o We explored modern adaptations, such as integrating DEI initiatives, leveraging self-service portals powered by AI and embedding sustainability and purpose into HR strategy.

4 **The connection between HR and organizational purpose**

   o We reaffirmed that the HR Operating Model is not standalone but deeply interconnected with the Organizational Operating Model, serving People, Culture, Learning, Performance and Purpose in alignment with broader business goals like Product, Service and Reputation.

- o The chapter emphasized the need for HR to move beyond compliance and administration to a more progressive, value-creating function.

5 **HR and leadership share in the criticism of the current work systems**

- o It appears that the 'easy target' of HR for being bureaucratic, policy-led, compliance-only and favouring 'the management' over people is still a prevailing view held by many. This leads us in the HR profession to improve this perception with an upgrade to the work 'operating system' and thereby the HR Operating Model which enables that 'upgrade'.

- o Criticism of HR often stems from broader systemic and leadership failings. The chapter explored how HR and leadership are jointly responsible for creating work systems that foster engagement, inclusivity and performance.

6 **The call for a new HR Operating Model**

- o While incremental improvements to the current model are notable, the chapter argues that a reimagined and revolutionary HR Operating Model is needed to meet the demands of advancing digitization, AI and more sustainable business practices and operations.

- o This model must integrate cutting-edge technology with timeless human principles to thrive in a rapidly evolving work environment.

7 **A vision for the future**

- o The chapter closed with a vision for HR to be a fusion core of energy and innovation, playing a pivotal role in organizational success and redefining the experience of work as move from the Knowledge Economy through the Automation Era and into the Regenerative Age.

References and Further Reading

Becker, G S (1964) *Human Capital: A theoretical and empirical analysis, with special reference to education*, Chicago: University of Chicago Press

Cappelli, P (2015) Why we love to hate HR... and what HR can do about it, *Harvard Business Review*, https://hbr.org/2015/07/why-we-love-to-hate-hr-and-what-hr-can-do-about-it (archived at https://perma.cc/J5AL-DLJW)

Deming, W E (1986) *Out of the Crisis*, Cambridge, MA: MIT Press

Drucker, P F (1973) *Management: Tasks, responsibilities, practices*, New York: Harper & Row

Edelman (2023) Edelman Trust Barometer 2023: Navigating a polarized world, www.edelman.com/trust/2023/trust-barometer (archived at https://perma.cc/L9P5-JGVH)

Effron, M and Ort, M (2018) *One Page Talent Management: Eliminating complexity, adding value*, Boston: Harvard Business Review Press

Frankl, V (1946) *Man's Search for Meaning*, Beacon Press

Gallup (2022) State of the Global Workplace

Kahneman, D (2013) *Thinking, Fast and Slow*, London: Penguin

Kellerman, B (2012) *The End of Leadership*, New York: Harper Business

Lewin, K (1951) *Field Theory in Social Science*, New York: Harper & Brothers

Mayo, E (1933) *The Human Problems of an Industrial Civilization*, New York: Macmillan

Maslow, A H (1943) A Theory of Human Motivation, *Psychological Review*, 50 (4), pp 370–96

McGregor, D (1960) *The Human Side of Enterprise*, New York: McGraw-Hill

Medina, J (2014) *Brain Rules: 12 principles for surviving and thriving at work, home, and school*, Pear Press

Pink, D H (2009) *Drive: The surprising truth about what motivates us*, New York: Riverhead Books

Porter, M E (1985) *Competitive Advantage: Creating and sustaining superior performance*, New York: Free Press

Putnam, R (2001) *Bowling Alone: The collapse and revival of American community*, Simon & Schuster

Royal, K (2019) Who's responsible for employee engagement, Gallup, https://www.gallup.com/workplace/266822/engaged-employees-differently.aspx (archived at https://perma.cc/6L7F-Q8HS)

Sinek, S (2014) *Leaders Eat Last: Why some teams pull together and others don't*, New York: Portfolio

Thaler, R and Sunstein, C (2008) *Nudge: Improving decisions about health, wealth, and happiness*, New Haven, CT: Yale University Press

Ulrich, D (1997) *Human Resource Champions: The next agenda for adding value and delivering results*, Boston: Harvard Business School Press

4

Additional perspectives on HR Operating Models

You never change things by fighting the existing reality. To change something, build a new model that makes the old model obsolete.

BUCKMINSTER FULLER, FUTURIST AND SYSTEMS THINKER

WHAT'S COVERED IN THIS CHAPTER

- **Demonstration of the range of thinking** others propose to give balance and different vantage points on future HR Operating Models and research into operating models.

- **Academic reviews and studies** of HR Operating Models put into consumable perspectives such as:

  o Gartner's perspective: Summary and critique of Gartner's frameworks for HR.

  o McKinsey's insights: McKinsey's research on HR and operating models.

  o Josh Bersin's innovations: Explore Bersin's views on HR trends and best practices.

  o Dave Ulrich's HR modelling and iterations: Analysing Ulrich's HR Operating Model and its impact on the industry.

Introduction

In Chapter 3, we covered what operating models for HR could and should be all about: evolution, adaptation, connectivity and shared accountability.

Over the last few years, it's become clear that the iterative evolution of the HR Operating Model has been called into being as many organizations have taken more sophisticated and technologically advanced approaches to delivering HR services and generating value and impact.

The need for a way to describe a more significant shift has been the subject of thought leadership, features, research and case studies, some of which we'll summarize in this chapter.

For busy (probably busier than ever) HR practitioners and leaders, the sheer volume of the written prose on the future options and potential models for HR is in itself somewhat overwhelming.

This book sets out to help equip, nudge and inspire HR to be a profession with the head, heart and guts to shift its operating system to have that impact.

I'll give each my own personal 'Move the needle' rating out of 10 but, of course, this is my own sense of how strongly the model will address the need to be at the forefront of future thinking and sustainable success for organizations and the people in them.

So, without further ado, let's get into HR operating models.

Gartner's view

Gartner's work on HR Operating Models presents a dynamic and forward-thinking approach to transforming HR into a more strategic and agile function. Their perspective focuses on four key imperatives for the future of HR:

1 **Building robust HR operations and service delivery:** This is about establishing a centralized team that services employees and managers, laying a solid foundation for strategic HR functions.

2 **Reinventing the HR Business Partner (HRBP):** Gartner sees HRBPs evolving into strategic talent leaders, aligned with business units to tackle specific challenges, rather than just performing administrative tasks.

3 **Creating a dynamic pool of HR problem solvers:** These HR professionals would be tasked with managing short-term projects, applying critical thinking and project management skills.

4 **Providing agile support with leaner CoEs:** Centres of Excellence should become smaller, more agile and focused on creating and updating policies that support HR and the workforce.

This model positions HR not only as a business enabler but as a change agent that can quickly adapt to the rapidly evolving needs of the business world. Gartner's approach integrates emerging technologies, promotes strategic alignment and prioritizes operational efficiency, allowing HR to scale while maintaining an employee-centric focus.

A key takeaway from Gartner's model is the emphasis on agility and data-driven decision making – but that has been talked about in HR circles for well over a decade now. It does provide a roadmap for HR teams to become more adaptable and strategic by evolving from transactional functions into those that shape and support broader organizational goals. Again, a common thread over the past decade.

However, while Gartner's framework has relevance and links to the operating model of now, it lacks an ambitious departure from now, and does not give enough specific, actionable details for implementation of a bigger departure from the orthodoxies of now. The framework sets a vision for HR transformation but does present a step-change. *More of the same, plus*. The model also assumes a level of technological sophistication that may not be present in all organizations.

Move the needle rating: 7/10. Gartner's vision for the HR Operating Model is compelling and highly relevant in the face of rapid change. It offers a future-forward approach that can significantly impact organizations, especially those that are ready to embrace the challenges of transformation. However, the practical application of these concepts within organizations of varying technological capabilities and maturity could present some challenges and HR needs something more significant to decouple itself from the prevailing models of now. This model stops short of that and is instead iterations of more of the same with additionality.

McKinsey's view

Global consulting and professional services firm McKinsey & Co cast their bid in December 2022 for HR Operating Model consideration and a vote for choice and more flexibility without being committed to a singular departure from the models of now (Durth et al, 2022).

FIVE EMERGING HR OPERATING-MODEL ARCHETYPES

- **Ulrich+:** An adaptation of the classic Ulrich model, where HR business partners develop specialized skills and assume execution responsibilities from centres of excellence (CoEs), which are scaled down to expert teams.

- **Agile:** Structuring HR functions along the employee lifecycle, aligning resources to the EX journey and integrating servicing and operations into workstreams with end-to-end service responsibility.
- **EX-driven:** Optimizing the employee experience (EX) by identifying and enhancing critical 'moments that matter' throughout the employee lifecycle, mirroring customer experience (CX) strategies.
- **Leader-led:** Empowering frontline leaders to manage HR responsibilities, fostering human-centric interactions and reducing organizational complexity.
- **Machine-powered:** Automating HR solutions to drive efficiency and capitalize on digitalization, utilizing AI and machine learning for data-driven decision making.

The report emphasizes that these models are not mutually exclusive; organizations often adopt a hybrid approach, selecting elements that best align with their unique needs and strategic objectives. The transition towards these new operating models is driven by the need for HR functions to become more adaptable, responsive and aligned with the overall business strategy in a rapidly changing environment.

More of the elements of their models are:

- **Adopting agile principles:** Implementing Agile methodologies to prioritize HR capacity and swiftly reallocate resources, facilitating rapid organizational change.
- **Excelling in EX:** Enhancing the employee journey to attract and retain talent amid widespread attrition.
- **Re-empowering frontline leaders:** Enabling leaders to foster human-centric interactions, reduce complexity and restore appropriate decision-making authority.
- **Offering individualized HR services:** Providing personalized HR services to meet diverse employee expectations.
- **'Productizing' HR services:** Developing tailored HR offerings with cross-functional teams assuming end-to-end responsibility.
- **Integrating design and delivery:** Combining design and delivery processes to address strategic HR priorities effectively and clarify ownership.

- **Transitioning to data excellence:** Leveraging data analytics, artificial intelligence and machine learning for informed decision making.
- **Automating HR solutions:** Utilizing digital tools to automate HR processes, enhancing efficiency and capitalizing on digitalization.

Critique of this model

McKinsey's HR Operating Model feels pretty bold and it is thought-provoking – a reasonable and practical compelling vision of what HR could be in a fast-changing world. But let's be brutally honest: it feels more like a manifesto than a blueprint or a playbook. It's fairly high on ambition but light on the gritty, practical realities of how to make it work in organizations with competing priorities, cultural inertia and resource constraints.

That said, for HR leaders willing to lean in, this (compendium) model can act as a catalyst and a reasonable *map of the territory*. It challenges the People profession to rethink our role, embrace agility and elevate employee experience, all while embedding technology and data into the core of our practice.

The opportunity here is to take these ideas and ground them in the specific context of our organizations – building something that works for our people, not just ticking theoretical boxes. It's not perfect, but it's provocative – and that's where transformation starts.

Move the needle rating: 7/10.

Deloitte's view

Deloitte's 2024 Global Human Capital Trends report introduces the concept of Boundaryless HR, advocating for a transformative shift in the HR function to meet the evolving demands of the modern workplace.

Key drivers of Boundaryless HR

- **Evolving work realities:** The traditional definitions of work, workplace and workforce are dissolving. Work is no longer confined to specific jobs, workplaces extend beyond physical locations and workers include a diverse array of employment arrangements.
- **Technological advancements:** Rapid developments in technologies, such as artificial intelligence and virtual collaboration tools, necessitate a more

integrated and flexible HR approach to effectively manage and support a dispersed and technologically adept workforce.

- **Human sustainability focus:** There's a growing emphasis on creating value for employees, enhancing their well-being, employability and equity, which calls for HR practices that transcend traditional boundaries.

Core elements of Boundaryless HR

- **Integration into business operations:** HR evolves from a siloed function to a discipline seamlessly woven into all aspects of the organization, collaborating across departments to address complex challenges.
- **Shared people responsibility:** The responsibility for people management extends beyond the HR department, becoming a collective accountability shared among all leaders and employees.
- **Multi-disciplinary solutions:** By combining HR expertise with other functional insights, organizations can develop holistic solutions that address multifaceted issues, enhancing adaptability and innovation.
- **Human-centric performance metrics:** Shifting focus from traditional productivity metrics to measures that reflect human performance and well-being, utilizing advanced data analytics and AI to capture a comprehensive view of employee contributions.

Implications of Boundaryless HR

- **Enhanced organizational agility:** A Boundaryless HR approach fosters a more responsive and adaptable organization, better equipped to navigate the complexities of the modern business environment.
- **Improved employee experience:** By integrating HR practices throughout the organization and sharing people management responsibilities, employees are more likely to feel supported and valued, leading to increased engagement and retention.
- **Strategic value creation:** HR's deeper integration into business operations enables a more strategic contribution to organizational goals, driving both human and business outcomes.

Critique of this model

Deloitte's Boundaryless HR model presents a progressive framework that redefines the HR function to be more integrated, collaborative and human-centric, aligning with the dynamic nature of today's work environment. It is more a string of concepts than an actual model, but the concept of Boundaryless HR chimes really well with the emerging sense that more responsive, adaptive and *unbundled* HR is needed in order to tackle the complexity and clustering of the business world's challenges.

It's a compelling case for a radical rethink of how to 'do' HR and what the value-creating and capability issues are.

Move the needle rating: 8.5/10.

The Talent Strategy Group

Rather than describe a new HR Operating Model, this is more a critique of the current reality and where things aren't working, as well as the existing ways HR 'sets out its stall' (Talent Strategy Group, 2024).

Titled 'It's (Still) the Mortar not the Bricks', this report from October 2024 starts by referencing that the 'world is changing fast' is rather hyped-up sales talk. Whilst accepting that much of work might look the same as it did in, say, the 1990s, underneath the surface there are a range of additional, different and evolving elements of work that are different enough to offset the view that it is largely hype.

I would counter that robustly thus:

- Work from anywhere (hybrid and remote) and increasingly alternative models of employment like contingent, gig working, side hustles and pools of freelancers with reductions in permanent, core teams are being planned by organizations I've come across.

- More widespread use of robotics, automation and AI is already present in workflows.

- Chatbots and machine-based interfaces for consumers and colleagues alike.

- Virtual and augmented reality in use for people who work on oil rigs for engine diagnostics.

- Genomics, forensic science and criminal prosecution – data modelling and digitized evidence have changed the face of those areas.

- Folding proteins and data-led drug discovery which accelerated the production of Covid-19 vaccines.

- The most high-value IPOs of recent years have come from very different entities like Air BnB, DoorDash and Shopify, with very different operating models.

There have been significant shifts in what work *is* and how it is *done*; there is also much more to come. Ray Kurzweil, a futurist and inventor, stated: 'The rate of change is accelerating, and the pace of change will continue to increase' (Kurzweil, 2005).

But for the sake of argument, much of the work might *look* like it did, with hierarchies, corporate functions and under-imaginative Organization Designs in most of the larger enterprises still calling the shots as high-performing giants of commerce.

So have operating models shifted that much in recent years? The answer is no and yes. Globalization and high-growth organizations have set the tempo for monetizing customer data, creating just-in-time supply chains and moving from brick-and-mortar to virtual and physical presence alongside the ubiquity of digital accessibility. We are seeing many long-standing organizations falter, fail and collapse.

Target operating models, though, appear to be driving much – if not all – of the transformational change activity in everything from those huge commercial and even non-profit organizations. So something is *in the air* around a different form of modernization of those operating models in an arguably disrupted and challenging world.

What this report does do very well is check the reality of what *current* HR Operating Models are all about.

That last point is telling. Operating models now coming into their own more and more as the dynamic of what work is and how it could get done is an underserved capability in HR.

Indeed, the report goes on to share that the effectiveness of HR functions hinges more on operational execution than on structural design.

While many organizations have adopted models like Dave Ulrich's three-pillar framework – comprising HR Business Partners (HRBPs), Centres of Excellence (CoEs) and Shared Services – the article argues that mere structural changes are insufficient. The real challenge lies in the 'wiring': clearly delineating roles, responsibilities and processes within the HR function.

The article strongly challenges consulting firms for promoting new HR Operating Models that are essentially variations of existing frameworks, often without addressing fundamental operational issues. It asserts that the core elements of work – such as organizational hierarchies, defined tasks and business strategies – remain largely unchanged, despite claims of a radically transformed work environment. Therefore, the focus should be on enhancing how HR operates within its existing structure.

TABLE 4.1 Current HR Operating Models

CHRO reporting lines	A significant 86 per cent of Chief Human Resources Officers (CHROs) report directly to the CEO, indicating HR's prominent position in organizational leadership. However, this structural alignment doesn't necessarily translate to impactful contributions, suggesting a need for CHROs to leverage their roles more effectively (or, indeed, be seen for the influence they can have in operational success).
Expansion of HR teams	There has been notable growth in HR personnel, particularly in Talent Acquisition and Diversity, Equity and Inclusion (DE&I) functions. This expansion reflects organizations' responses to evolving workforce demands and a heightened focus on inclusive practices.
Collaboration between HRBPs and CoEs	The traditional friction between HR Business Partners (HRBPs) and Centres of Excellence (CoEs) appears to be diminishing, with 56 per cent of respondents indicating these groups work well together. This improvement suggests progress toward more cohesive HR operations.
Dominance of specific CoEs	Total Rewards and Talent Management CoEs predominantly report directly to the CHRO, underscoring their critical roles within HR. Additionally, functions like Learning and Development, Assessment and Talent Acquisition often report into Talent Management, highlighting a hierarchical structure within CoEs.
Prevalence of service centres	A majority (68 per cent) of organizations have established formal HR service centres, typically centralized, to streamline HR service delivery and enhance efficiency.
Lack of training in new operating models	Notably, 60 per cent of companies that have updated their HR Operating Models did not provide formal training to facilitate the transition. This oversight may hinder the effective implementation of new HR structures and processes.

To improve HR effectiveness, the article recommends:

- **Clarifying accountabilities:** Ensuring that each HR role has well-defined responsibilities to prevent overlaps and gaps.
- **Enhancing collaboration:** Fostering better cooperation between HRBPs and CoEs to deliver cohesive HR services.
- **Investing in capabilities:** Developing the skills and competencies of HR professionals to execute processes efficiently.

In summary, the article underscores that the success of an HR Operating Model depends more on the quality of its implementation – the 'mortar' – than on its structural design – the 'bricks.' Organizations should prioritize operational excellence and capability building within their existing HR frameworks to achieve desired outcomes. So, it's a helpful critique that spotlights the status and challenges but offers no departing model to inspire and shape the shift this report states is needed.

Move the needle rating: 6/10.

Mercer's Target Integration Model

Mercer's HR Operating Model Design introduces the Target Interaction Model (TIM). This people-centric approach reimagines HR functions by prioritizing employee experiences and aligning HR services with organizational and employee needs (Mercer, 2024).

KEY COMPONENTS OF THE TARGET INTERACTION MODEL (TIM)

- **Employee-centric design:** TIM focuses on intentionally designing interactions between HR and employees, ensuring that HR services are tailored to meet the specific needs of the workforce.

- **Integration of digital tools:** The model emphasizes the use of purpose-built technology to enable seamless and effective interactions, balancing digital and human experiences to enhance efficiency and employee satisfaction.

- **Redefined HR roles:** By evaluating HR roles, processes and technology against workforce needs, TIM increases agility, reduces silos and pools resources across functions for various projects.

- **Strategic alignment:** TIM aligns HR services with business and people strategies, elevating HR to a strategic advisor role within the organization.

Perceived benefits of implementing a TIM

- **Enhanced EX:** By placing employees at the centre, TIM delivers relevant services and exceptional interactions, leading to measurable improvements in employee satisfaction, engagement and commitment.

- **Operational efficiency:** The model enables HR to streamline processes, often freeing up about 30 per cent of administrative load, allowing professionals to focus on strategic initiatives.

- **Agility and innovation:** TIM fosters an Agile HR environment capable of adapting to the future of work, introducing better ways of working and boosting talent attraction and retention.

In summary, Mercer's TIM approach transforms HR into a people-centred function that supports and actively drives organizational strategy and people priorities, contributing to true business value.

TIM strongly signals human-centricity in an overly mechanical world of work-related transformation. Its emphasis on designing around the employee experience feels *on-point*, especially in a world where engagement and retention are more costly and fragile than ever. By deliberately aligning HR services with business strategy and employee needs, Mercer positions HR as more than a support function – it becomes a key enabler of enterprise success.

The integration of digital tools, balanced with human connection, is particularly compelling. It's not about replacing HR with technology but enhancing it – freeing up time for strategic contributions while making employee interactions smoother and more meaningful. The focus on agility and resource pooling is another standout. TIM recognizes the reality of modern organizations: agility and adaptability aren't optional – they're survival tools.

There is a critical positive for this approach in its feasibility, which may actually make it too low on the sense of something different. Of course, not all transformation has to be about *from* and *to*, but in being different and making a difference, there may be too much subtlety and not enough audacity to capture attention, energy and galvanize effort.

While TIM's employee-centric focus is laudable, it risks oversimplifying the complexity of HR's role, particularly in larger, more hierarchical organizations. Designing bespoke employee interactions sounds fantastic in theory, but in practice, it requires a level of customization and resource investment that many HR teams simply don't have.

The reliance on digital tools, while forward-thinking, also assumes a baseline of technological maturity that isn't universal. Not every organization has the infrastructure – or the budget – to implement 'purpose-built' technology at the scale TIM envisions. Without this, the balance between digital and human interaction can quickly tip too far, leaving HR feeling impersonal.

Moreover, the model's promise to cut administrative load by 30 per cent sounds bold but needs more concrete proof. How does this scale across industries with wildly different needs and regulatory environments? Without detailed case studies or metrics, this risks sounding like a generic efficiency promise rather than a transformative outcome.

Lastly, TIM's strategic alignment narrative is strong but feels like it glosses over the heavy lifting required to shift HR into a true advisory – and critically, future-shaping – function. For organizations where HR is still fighting to prove its strategic worth, this could feel more like an aspirational target than an accessible roadmap.

Move the needle rating: 6/10.

EY's People Value Chain Model

EY's People Value Chain Model is a forward-thinking framework that reimagines HR as a digitally enabled, employee-centric and strategically aligned function. It integrates advanced technologies like AI, automation and machine learning to streamline operations while focusing on delivering seamless employee experiences. The model emphasizes agility, global scalability and strategic HR alignment with business objectives.

The framework comprises three core components:

- **Digital people team:** Automates up to 50 per cent of HR tasks to reduce administrative burdens and free HR professionals to focus on strategic contributions.
- **People consultants:** Agile HR advisors who closely align with business needs and act as strategic partners within their units.
- **Virtual global business services (VGBS):** Centralizes HR operations across geographies, ensuring standardized and efficient service delivery.

Digital innovation: This model's emphasis on automation and AI makes it highly relevant in an era where efficiency and data-driven decision making are crucial for HR's evolution. It allows HR to focus on high-impact areas rather than being bogged down by transactional tasks.

Employee-centric approach: EY views HR interactions as customer experiences, a refreshing approach to improving employee satisfaction and engagement. This approach is particularly valuable in retaining talent in a competitive job market.

Agility in HR: The introduction of People Consultants as Agile HR partners brings a much-needed dynamic element to HR, making it more responsive to shifting business needs and workforce expectations.

Scalability through VGBS: Centralizing HR operations through VGBS ensures consistency, cost efficiency and streamlined service delivery, which are critical benefits for multinational organizations.

Strategic alignment: The model underscores HR's role as a strategic partner, elevating its position within organizational decision making and aligning HR practices with broader business goals.

Whilst this may seem like Ulrich+ (like McKinsey), it does have more intricate roles/elements that make it stand out, such as service, cloud, automation, data and enablement layers linking to Workforce Vitality Engineers, Workforce Strategists, Performance Architects, Experience Amplifiers and People Enablement Technicians. These bold-sounding roles cater to the shifts in how work is reshaping.

Despite the boldness of some of the roles, this model is highly tech-dependent. It relies heavily on digital tools, which might not be feasible for organizations with limited budgets or technological maturity. Implementing AI and automation at scale can be cost-prohibitive and resource-intensive for many companies.

There are challenges with this model, though, as described in Table 4.2.

Overall, EY's People Value Chain Model is an ambitious and modern approach to HR transformation, offering exciting possibilities for organizations ready to embrace digitization, agility and strategic HR alignment. However, to be successful it requires careful consideration of resource availability, organizational culture and workforce needs. It's a model that inspires but also challenges organizations to balance efficiency with empathy and

TABLE 4.2 Challenges of EY's People Value Chain Model

Potential loss of human touch	While digitization enhances efficiency, it risks alienating employees by reducing personal interaction, especially in sensitive areas like performance management, grievances and career counselling.
Overemphasis on scalability	VGBS prioritizes standardization, which may not accommodate the nuanced needs of local teams or cultural differences across geographies. This could lead to friction or a perception of HR as disconnected from on-the-ground realities.
	The model assumes that all organizations are ready for such a high level of sophistication in HR. For smaller companies or those in traditional industries, the framework might feel overly complex and misaligned with their realities.
Implementation complexity	Transforming an existing HR function into the People Value Chain Model requires significant restructuring, change management and training. Without strong organizational commitment, the model risks becoming another ambitious, under-executed framework.

scalability with localized relevance. For those willing to make the investment, it has the potential to redefine HR as a driver of both business success and employee satisfaction.

Move the needle rating: 8/10.

The Chartered Institute of Personnel and Development (CIPD)

Valiantly bringing the spotlight to the HR Operating Model, the CIPD (both recently and in 2015) helped the profession look at the 'blueprint' and reflected on practice trends and general application of how to deliver value through the HR function.

We'll start with the (now) nostalgic look from 2015.

CIPD viewpoint on HR Operating Models – 2015

Ten years ago, but with (still) relevant and interesting reflections on the HR Business Partner/Ulrich model. It was probably never conceived to be transformational and so is perhaps more helpful in terms of where the thinking has evolved, been lacking and was a sign of the times (five years before the Covid-19 pandemic disrupted so much of how we approached our work in lockdown and isolation situations).

The CIPD report goes into depth about the challenges HR departments face as they transition from traditional to more modern operating models. It critiques the Ulrich model for focusing too much on structure over value creation and calls for more strategic and adaptable HR functions. A key focus is on integrating technology like cloud-based systems to streamline HR processes and improve decision making. The report advocates for greater specialization within HR roles, cross-functional collaboration and aligning HR strategies more closely with business objectives.

Key takeaways from the report:

1 **Critique of traditional models:**
   The Ulrich model – long the cornerstone of HR – emphasized efficiency through a division of labour into HR Business Partners (HRBPs), Centres of Excellence (CoEs) and Shared Services.

   However, the CIPD report argues that this model, while valuable in improving efficiency, has not fully enabled HR to deliver on its strategic potential. It has often resulted in siloed teams, with HRBPs focused on client servicing rather than strategic advisory, and CoEs detached from broader business needs.

2 **Demand for agility and flexibility:**
   The report emphasizes that businesses today require HR to operate with more agility. Organizations are facing fast-paced changes due to digital transformation, the rise of hybrid and flexible work and shifts in workforce expectations. Therefore, HR must be able to flex quickly to meet these changes. Rather than sticking to rigid structures, organizations should adopt flexible, Agile HR models that encourage innovation and adaptability.

3 **Importance of technology:**
   Technological advancements, especially cloud computing and data analytics, are transforming how HR operates. Cloud-based systems allow for real-time data access and automation of routine tasks, which enables HR professionals to focus more on strategic issues like workforce planning, talent management and employee experience. The report encourages HR leaders to invest in technologies that will streamline operations and allow for more data-driven decision making.

4 **Focusing on EX:**

There's a growing recognition that HR should be more employee-centric. This means that HR's focus should shift towards creating a seamless employee experience, from recruitment to retirement. The report argues that this will not only improve employee satisfaction and retention but will also create a competitive advantage for organizations in attracting top talent.

5 **Reskilling and specialization within HR:**

The report also touches on the need for HR teams to develop new skills, including data analytics, change management and digital literacy. Additionally, there is a call for increased specialization within HR roles, with experts in areas like talent management, employee experience and Organization Design working alongside generalists.

6 **Leadership and HR's strategic role:**

Finally, the document stresses the need for HR to take a seat at the executive table. The future of HR lies in its ability to act as a strategic partner, contributing to organizational strategy and long-term business planning. This involves not just being reactive to business needs but proactively shaping the workforce strategy to ensure business growth and success.

By integrating these shifts, HR can move from being a functional department to becoming a key driver of business value, adaptable to the changing landscape of work.

Move the needle rating: 5/10*

*But it was never really intended to show an alternative, merely a reflective piece.

CIPD HR Operating Models Review 2024

Timely for this book, Rebecca Peters at the CIPD has brought together a series of case studies, thought pieces and potential 'agitations' about the need for and shape of current adapted HR Operating Models and the future operating model for HR (CIPD, 2024a). Again, and understandably for a professional body, the work avoids recommending a specific model the entire profession should adopt, and is a spotlight on the work of organizations, scholars and practitioners.

Firstly, five organizations gave their take on HR Operating Model adaptations:

- **Peabody,** a prominent housing association, recognized the need to overhaul its HR function to support its business strategy effectively.

- **Homebase,** a major UK home improvement retailer, undertook a significant transformation of its HR Operating Model to become more agile and responsive.

- **Firstsource,** a global business process management company, recognized the need to revamp its HR function to better support its business objectives.

- **NatWest,** one of the UK's leading financial institutions, transformed its HR function to align with its broader strategy of fostering trust and customer focus.

- **Tesco,** one of the UK's largest retailers, transformed its HR Operating Model to stay competitive in a fast-changing retail market.

Table 4.3 shows the summary of all five as an amalgamation of their adapted HR Operating Model elements and results.

TABLE 4.3 HR Operating Model adaptations

Strategic alignment with business goals • HR evolved from a support function to a **strategic business partner**, embedding HR initiatives into broader organizational strategies.	• **Peabody** linked HR with workforce planning to meet housing sector needs. • **NatWest** aligned HR with its customer-centric strategy, embedding HR Business Partners into core business units.
Technology and digital transformation • All organizations leveraged technology to automate administrative tasks, enabling HR teams to focus on value-added activities like strategy and talent management.	• **Firstsource** used AI to streamline recruitment and predict workforce trends. • **Tesco** adopted digital tools for workforce planning and on-demand training.
Agility and responsiveness • Agile HR practices were embraced to increase responsiveness to market and organizational changes.	• **Homebase** applied agile workforce planning for seasonal staffing. • **NatWest** adopted cross-functional Agile HR squads to address key challenges like DEI and leadership development.
Employee-centric HR models • Organizations shifted to HR models that prioritize EX, engagement and well-being.	• **Tesco** enhanced engagement through real-time feedback mechanisms. • **NatWest** embedded mental health and well-being resources into its HR operations.

(continued)

TABLE 4.3 (Continued)

Integration of diversity, equity, and inclusion (DEI) • DEI became a core focus, with dedicated initiatives to improve representation, equity and inclusion across the workforce.	• **NatWest** established a DEI-focused CoE to promote inclusive leadership. • **Firstsource** prioritized cultural sensitivity in its global talent management.
Focus on talent mobility and development • Internal mobility and upskilling initiatives were key to preparing workforces for future needs.	• **Tesco** created career pathways and launched a digital learning platform for employees. • **Peabody** focused on leadership development to support organizational growth.
Simplification and process efficiency • HR processes were streamlined to improve efficiency and reduce complexity.	• **Homebase** decentralized HR roles, giving store managers direct access to strategic HR advice. • **Peabody** implemented people analytics dashboards to enhance workforce management.
Data-driven HR • Organizations increasingly used HR analytics to inform decisions, predict trends and measure success.	• **Firstsource** used AI to forecast attrition and workforce needs. • **NatWest** leveraged analytics to align HR initiatives with employee engagement metrics.
Embedded HR teams • HR teams were embedded into business units to provide tailored, localized support.	• **Homebase** placed HR Business Partners at the regional level for hands-on support. • **NatWest** aligned HR squads with key business areas.
Shift toward purpose and sustainability • HR played a role in embedding organizational purpose and sustainability into culture and practices.	• **Peabody** integrated purpose-driven leadership into its strategy. • **Tesco** focused on aligning its workforce strategies with its mission to serve communities.

Summary of common themes

These organizations demonstrate a shift towards:

- strategic, technology-enabled and Agile HR models;
- a strong focus on employee experience and development;
- data-driven decision making and embedding HR into core business functions.

I had the pleasure of being on a four-way podcast discussion, hosted by Nigel Cassidy, which features insights from Natalie Sheils, ex-Chief People Officer at Mosaic Group, Dave Ulrich, the pioneer of the HR Business Partner model, and me (CIPD, 2024b).

The discussion explored the evolution, current state and future of HR Operating Models.

Key themes and insights

1   **Evolution of HR Operating Models**
    Dave Ulrich reflected on his 1997 HR Business Partner model, emphasizing that while HR structures remain relevant, the focus must shift to delivering value beyond the organization – to customers, investors and communities. Ulrich critiques the tendency to focus on internal HR processes, urging a more outside-in approach where HR aligns practices with external stakeholder needs.

2   **Challenges with traditional models**
    Many HR structures, rooted in Ulrich's framework, have not adapted to modern demands like digital transformation and AI-driven change.
    Natalie Sheils noted that Covid-19 and technological disruptions have exposed limitations in traditional models, requiring HR to become more strategic and dynamic.

3   **Key adaptations for modern HR**
    Agility and experimentation: I highlighted the need for boundaryless HR that breaks down silos and promotes collaboration across disciplines.
    Technology and AI integration: Natalie emphasized leveraging technology to automate administrative tasks, freeing HR to focus on strategic goals like workforce planning and skill development.
    Customer-focused HR: Dave Ulrich advocated shifting the HR narrative from internal strategy to creating value for external stakeholders, such as improving customer experiences through effective employee engagement.

4   **Practical applications and case studies**
    Product-oriented HR: I described a banking case where induction processes were redesigned as an end-to-end product, leading to cost savings and improved employee retention.
    Talent strategy evolution: Natalie discussed embedding talent acquisition into talent management and intelligence to align workforce capabilities with business needs.

5 The future of HR Operating Models

HR must balance operational and strategic priorities, moving beyond 'either/or' thinking to embrace 'both/and' approaches, as Ulrich emphasizes.

Models must adapt to business context, focusing on skills, adaptability and collaboration rather than rigid structures.

HR's ultimate goal should be to combine systems and energy to address challenges such as climate change, technology and consumer demands.

Risks and rewards of remodelling

Risks: I warned that focusing too much on models can distract from outcomes, creating fear and resistance among HR professionals.

Rewards: A remodelled HR function can – and should – excite stakeholders, improve collaboration and align employee aspirations with organizational purpose.

The key themes from this discussion point to some common elements from the case studies and the absolute need to be deliberate, diversified and dynamic about shifting the HR Operating Model.

It is clear that the CIPD, Ulrich himself and many practitioners are looking ahead to an adaptation and iteration of the Business Partner model. Whilst some are only just moving to this model (based on organizational maturity more than 'living in a cave', I'm sure), there are clear benefits in being more sophisticated, adaptive and creative in how to interpret the model's aims and forms, rather than a simple 'lift and shift' in the hope HR can create more impact and value.

What is less clear is whether there should be a wholescale departure from the HR Business Partner/Ulrich model to something radically different.

The case studies in the CIPD research are adapting the model and iterating more than rebooting because of an upgraded operating system. But there are pragmatic and aspirational aspects to the way the CIPD has framed all of this work. And being a part of it is a real honour for me. There is a growing wealth of insight and an urge for HR leaders (in particular) to focus on their Operating Model more. I believe this 2024 focus from the CIPD is a real positive and gives the profession something to get behind and into. If I'm being picky, it's still a little gentle and could do with more urge and urgency. However, it's still a really positive step and a growing body of work. So bravo Rebecca and the CIPD.

Move the needle rating: 7/10.

The 'father' of modern HR and his take on an evolved model

Dave Ulrich's recent reflections on the evolution of the HR Business Partner model mark a significant contribution to the continuing transformation of HR Operating Models. In a LinkedIn article titled 'Update on the HR Business Partner model continuing evolution and relevance', Ulrich outlines how his influential framework has adapted to contemporary organizational needs and business landscapes. His insights not only reaffirm the model's relevance but also push HR professionals to reimagine their role as strategic enablers of value. Below is a deep dive into Ulrich's key updates and reflections on the model's evolution.

The foundation of the HR Business Partner model

First introduced in *Human Resource Champions* (1997), Ulrich's HR Business Partner model positioned HR as a strategic partner to the business. The model emphasized that HR's core responsibility is to create value – not just for employees and the organization but also for customers, investors and communities. This value-creation lens set the stage for HR's transformation from a back-office administrative function to a pivotal enabler of business outcomes.

The original model rested on four key roles:

1 **Strategic partner:** Align HR practices with business strategy.

2 **Change agent:** Lead and manage organizational transformation.

3 **Administrative expert:** Ensure operational excellence in HR processes.

4 **Employee champion:** Advocate for employee engagement and well-being.

This framework became foundational to HR's global practice, influencing operating models, talent strategies and Organization Design. However, as Ulrich reflects, the changing context of work has necessitated significant evolution in how HR operates.

Why an update was necessary

In his update, Ulrich acknowledges that the original HR Business Partner model was designed for an era defined by hierarchical organizations and predictable business cycles. Today, organizations face unprecedented complexity, driven by globalization, technological disruption and evolving stakeholder expectations. HR must adapt to these changes by focusing on the following shifts:

---

1 **From inside-out to outside-in:** HR must align its practices not just with internal organizational goals but also with external stakeholder expectations. Customers, investors, regulators and communities now demand that organizations demonstrate social responsibility, environmental sustainability and ethical governance. HR's value lies in enabling organizations to meet these external demands while supporting internal capabilities.

2 **From transactions to transformation:** The administrative aspects of HR, while still critical, are now largely automated or outsourced. This allows HR to focus on transformational work, such as shaping culture, driving innovation and building organizational resilience.

3 **From roles to results:** Ulrich emphasizes the importance of outcome-driven HR. Instead of focusing solely on fulfilling predefined roles (e.g. strategic partner or change agent), HR professionals should concentrate on delivering tangible results – be that improved employee engagement, enhanced customer satisfaction or increased investor confidence.

Key updates to the model

Ulrich's updated framework reimagines the HR Business Partner model with a sharper focus on impact and value creation. The updates in Table 4.4 capture the essence of his evolution.

10 CORE HR CAPABILITIES

Ulrich introduces 10 key capabilities HR must focus on to remain impactful and relevant in modern organizations:

1 **Establishing HR reputation:** Building trust and credibility within the organization.

2 **Serving HR customers:** Meeting the needs of employees, managers and external stakeholders.

3 **Determining HR purpose:** Clarifying HR's mission and aligning it with organizational goals.

TABLE 4.4 Updates to the Business Partner model

Value creation as the core metric	Ulrich reiterates that HR's ultimate accountability is to deliver value. He redefines this value not just in terms of efficiency or employee satisfaction but as measurable outcomes that matter to customers, investors and other stakeholders. For example: 1. **Customer Value:** How do HR practices improve customer experiences? 2. **Investor Value:** How does HR enhance organizational performance to attract investment? 3. **Community Value:** How does HR contribute to social and environmental goals?
Integration across stakeholders	The updated model integrates value creation across multiple stakeholders. HR must now operate at the nexus of EX, customer outcomes and investor returns, ensuring that actions in one area enhance the others.
Enhanced capability building	HR's role in capability building has expanded. This includes not only developing individual skills but also fostering collective organizational capabilities like • innovation • collaboration • agility Ulrich emphasizes that these capabilities drive competitive advantage in a rapidly changing world.
The 'three-legged stool' revisited	While the three-legged stool structure of HR (HR Business Partners, Centres of Excellence and Shared Services) remains relevant, Ulrich suggests a more integrated approach. Modern HR teams must operate seamlessly across these pillars, breaking down silos to ensure agility and responsiveness.
The role of technology	Digital tools and data analytics have become central to HR's effectiveness. Ulrich highlights the importance of using technology to generate insights, predict trends and personalize employee experiences. AI and predictive analytics, for instance, enable HR to anticipate workforce needs and proactively address challenges.

4 **Governing HR design:** Structuring HR processes and systems to drive efficiency and impact.

5 **Growing human capability:** Enhancing workforce skills and organizational capabilities.

6 **Using HR analytics:** Leveraging data to inform decisions and predict trends.

7 **Refining HR practices:** Continuously improving HR operations and services.

8 **Using digital/technology:** Harnessing technology to enhance employee experiences and HR efficiency.

9 **Advancing HR professionals:** Developing the skills and competencies of HR teams.

10 **Strengthening HR relationships:** Fostering collaboration and partnerships across the organization.

Practical implications for HR professionals

Ulrich's updates are not just theoretical; they have actionable implications for HR professionals. Key takeaways include:

1 **Embrace data-driven decision making:** HR must build competency in analytics to translate data into meaningful insights. This includes leveraging people analytics to forecast attrition, measure engagement and align workforce planning with business strategy.

2 **Cultivate external awareness:** HR professionals should stay attuned to external trends, such as changing customer expectations, ESG priorities and technological advancements. This external perspective ensures that HR initiatives remain relevant and impactful.

3 **Focus on agility and adaptability:** In a world of constant change, HR must operate with agility. This means adopting iterative approaches, fostering cross-functional collaboration and quickly responding to emerging challenges.

4 **Redefine success metrics:** Move beyond traditional HR KPIs (e.g. time-to-hire) to metrics that demonstrate broader business impact, such as customer retention, innovation rates and market share growth.

Critiques and challenges

While Ulrich's updated model is forward-thinking, its implementation may pose challenges for HR teams:

1 **Cultural resistance:** Organizations with entrenched hierarchies or legacy systems may resist the shift to a more integrated and outcome-driven HR approach.

2 **Skills gap:** HR professionals may need to upskill in areas like data analytics, design thinking and change management to meet the demands of the updated model.

3 **Balancing strategic and operational roles:** HR teams must balance their focus on strategic initiatives with the need to deliver efficient operational support, a challenge exacerbated by resource constraints.

Conclusion: the path forward for HR

Dave Ulrich's reflections remind us that the HR profession is continually evolving. The updated HR Business Partner model challenges HR professionals to think beyond traditional boundaries and embrace their role as drivers of organizational value. By focusing on value creation, leveraging technology and integrating across stakeholders, HR can cement its position as a strategic enabler of success in an increasingly complex world.

For HR leaders and practitioners, Ulrich's call to action is clear: **adapt, innovate and deliver results that matter** – not just within the organization, but in the wider ecosystem it serves.

It's time to be bold, and in much of Ulrich's thinking of late he himself is urging this. His phrase 'HR isn't about HR' is telling. He is challenging HR professionals to look beyond the internal mechanics of HR functions and focus on delivering value to external stakeholders.

In the context of evolving HR Operating Models, this perspective reframes HR as a conduit for broader organizational success.

HR is about enabling organizations to thrive by ensuring that employees are engaged, customers are satisfied, investors see returns and communities benefit from ethical and sustainable practices.

This external, outcome-driven mindset ensures that HR is not just a department and is at the strategic core of achieving the organization's purpose and impact.

People. Culture. Learning. Performance. Purpose

Dave Ulrich continues to be a prolific writer, thinker and narrator. We need him to provide that and a focal point for us all in the people profession.

Move the needle rating: 9/10.

Josh Bersin's vision for the future of HR

Josh Bersin, a globally recognized analyst in HR and workforce strategies, has been at the forefront of calling for an evolved HR Operating Model. His work highlights the inadequacy of traditional models in meeting the demands of a rapidly changing workforce and business environment. Through his research and frameworks, Bersin has outlined a vision for an HR function that is more integrated, technology-enabled and human-centric.

The need for a new paradigm

Bersin argues that legacy HR structures, often siloed and process-driven, fail to address the modern complexities of workforce dynamics. Organizations are facing unprecedented disruptions – from technological advancements to societal shifts – and HR must transform to navigate these challenges effectively. According to Bersin, the evolved HR Operating Model must prioritize:

- **Employee experience:** HR should act as the architect of meaningful and seamless employee experiences, addressing everything from recruitment to retirement. Bersin emphasizes the importance of listening to employees, leveraging feedback tools and designing HR services that meet their expectations.
- **Well-being and resilience:** In a post-pandemic world, HR must focus on holistic employee well-being, encompassing physical, mental and financial health. Bersin's research demonstrates that organizations investing in well-being see significant gains in engagement, productivity and retention.
- **Continuous learning and growth:** Bersin highlights that traditional learning management systems (LMS) are no longer sufficient. HR must create dynamic learning ecosystems that integrate into employees' day-to-day workflows, enabling them to acquire new skills rapidly and remain agile in their roles.

Technology and data as catalysts

A cornerstone of Bersin's evolved HR model is the integration of advanced technologies and data analytics. He advocates for HR to leverage AI and machine learning to automate repetitive tasks, personalize employee interactions and provide real-time insights into workforce trends. Key technology shifts include:

- **AI-driven decision making:** From predictive analytics for attrition risks to personalized career development recommendations, AI can transform how HR supports employees and the organization.
- **Digital HR ecosystems:** Bersin encourages HR leaders to move beyond standalone systems towards integrated platforms that connect talent management, payroll, employee engagement and workforce analytics seamlessly.

The 'Irresistible Organization' framework

One of Bersin's most impactful contributions is his concept of the 'Irresistible Organization', a framework for designing businesses that attract and retain top talent while driving sustainable outcomes. The core pillars of this framework include:

1 **Purpose and meaning:** Organizations must provide employees with a clear sense of purpose, aligning their work with broader societal and organizational goals.
2 **Trust and transparency:** Building a culture of trust through open communication and ethical practices is vital to creating a positive employee experience.
3 **Growth and development:** Bersin emphasizes the importance of fostering a culture of continuous growth, enabling employees to develop their careers while contributing to organizational success.
4 **Well-being and resilience:** Creating supportive environments where employees can thrive is a critical aspect of long-term organizational success.

Implications for HR Operating Models

To operationalize Bersin's vision, HR must embrace a flexible and integrated operating model. This includes breaking down silos, fostering cross-functional collaboration and aligning HR practices with business outcomes. Bersin's research highlights that organizations succeeding in these areas demonstrate:

- **Higher engagement levels:** By prioritizing employee experience and well-being, these organizations cultivate highly engaged and motivated workforces.
- **Improved business agility:** Integrated HR systems and data-driven decision making enable organizations to respond quickly to market and workforce changes.
- **Sustainable growth:** Organizations that adopt Bersin's principles not only attract top talent but also achieve long-term business success.

Bersin's Systemic HR: a holistic evolution

Building on his previous work, Bersin introduced the *Systemic HR* model in 2023, arguing that traditional HR structures – particularly those rooted in the siloed Ulrich model – fail to meet the complexities of modern business. Systemic HR is not just an operational shift, it's a fundamental redesign of HR as an interconnected, real-time and data-driven function.

Key principles of Systemic HR:

1 **HR as an ecosystem, not a function.** Rather than HR being a standalone department, Bersin advocates for HR operating as an integrated business capability that flows across functions, embedding workforce intelligence, employee experience and skills development into the entire organization.

2 **AI and skills intelligence as the core.** Systemic HR is heavily data-driven, leveraging AI-powered talent intelligence to personalize learning, predict workforce needs and dynamically allocate people to projects based on skill matching rather than static job roles.

3 **HR as a business enabler, not just a service provider.** Bersin shifts the focus from HR delivering predefined services to HR shaping how the business operates. This means aligning workforce design with organizational strategy, using talent data for proactive decision making and embedding agility at all levels.

4 **Employee experience as a continuous journey.** Traditional HR focuses on processes (hiring, onboarding, performance management), while Systemic HR looks at the employee lifecycle as a dynamic, constantly evolving

experience. It ensures work is structured around people rather than people fitting into rigid structures.

5 **End-to-end HR Operating Model.** Instead of fragmented teams (HRBPs, CoEs, Shared Services), Systemic HR calls for fully interconnected HR teams where expertise flows across functions, decisions are based on real-time insights and HR professionals operate as cross-functional consultants.

Implications for HR Operating Models

Systemic HR presents an opportunity to go beyond the 'lift-and-shift' approach of modifying existing models. It pushes HR towards a **networked, skills-based and AI-powered** approach that responds dynamically to business needs. Organizations that adopt this mindset see increased workforce agility, better decision making and a more engaged, adaptive workforce.

While some companies are beginning to implement elements of Systemic HR, it requires a fundamental cultural and technological shift. The challenge is not in adopting new technologies but in shifting HR's role from **process execution** to **business orchestration** – a step that many HR teams are not yet structured to take.

Systemic HR is one of the most ambitious shifts in HR thought leadership. It challenges HR to evolve beyond structures and into **dynamic, AI-powered, skills-based and employee-centric** practices. While not all organizations may be ready for this level of transformation, those that embrace it will likely be the ones leading the way in the future of work.

Bersin's insights provide a compelling roadmap for HR professionals looking to modernize their operating models and create meaningful impact within their organizations and beyond.

Move the needle rating: 9.5/10.

WHAT WE'VE COVERED IN THIS CHAPTER

1 **Exploration of leading frameworks:**

o A comprehensive review of McKinsey's HR Operating Model archetypes, emphasizing adaptability, employee experience and technological integration.

o Mercer's Target Interaction Model (TIM) highlights a people-centric approach that balances digital tools with human connection, enhancing employee experience and HR efficiency.

o EY's People Value Chain Model demonstrates how digitization, agility and global scalability can transform HR into a strategic enabler.

2 **Critical reflections on current HR models:**

o The Talent Strategy Group's critique underscores the importance of operational execution ('mortar') over structural design ('bricks') in HR functions.

o CIPD's reviews from 2015 and 2024 provided a reflective lens on the challenges and evolution of HR Operating Models, offering insight into how models need to adapt to a rapidly changing world.

3 **Case studies of organizational adaptations:**

o Key themes include strategic alignment, technology integration, agility, employee-centric practices and a focus on purpose and sustainability.

4 **Evolving the Ulrich model:**

o Dave Ulrich's updated HR Business Partner model was revisited, emphasizing the need for HR to create value beyond organizational boundaries for external stakeholders such as customers, investors and communities and his 10 core HR capabilities.

5 **Josh Bersin's call for an evolved HR Operating Model:**

o Josh Bersin's work emphasizes that traditional HR Operating Models are increasingly inadequate in addressing the complexities of the modern workforce, advocating for the use of AI and advanced analytics to drive decision making and personalize the employee journey.

6 **Challenges and future directions:**

o This chapter explored the barriers to implementing new HR Operating Models such as cultural resistance, skills gaps and balancing strategic with operational priorities.

o We discussed the need for HR to embrace agility, leverage technology and focus on external outcomes to remain relevant and impactful in a complex business environment.

With the world moving through 'versions' (we are in the midst of Web 3.0 and for some time Industry 4.0), it's a telling signal from the future that we need to build a significant upgrade to HR's operating system for the sake of the overall system work.

It is time to move HR from 2.0 to 3.0.

References and further reading

Bersin, J (2023) Systemic HR: The future of HR operating models, https://joshbersin.com/2023/12/introducing-the-systemic-hr-initiative/ (archived at https://perma.cc/DE4M-SN3F)

Buckminster Fuller, R (1973) *Operating Manual for Spaceship Earth*, New York: E.P. Dutton

CIPD (2015) *HR Operating Models: A review of trends and best practices*, London: Chartered Institute of Personnel and Development

CIPD (2024a) *HR Operating Models Review 2024*, London: Chartered Institute of Personnel and Development, www.cipd.org/uk/views-and-insights/thought-leadership/insight/hr-models/ (archived at https://perma.cc/CQ34-NCQF)

CIPD (2024b) HR's next top operating model [podcast], www.cipd.org/uk/knowledge/podcasts/hr-top-model/ (archived at https://perma.cc/Z9BA-JSZW)

Deloitte (2024) 2024 Global Human Capital Trends: Boundaryless HR, www2.deloitte.com/content/dam/insights/articles/glob176836_global-human-capital-trends-2024/DI_Global-Human-Capital-Trends-2024.pdf (archived at https://perma.cc/KG42-UJ5S)

Durth, S, Gandhi, N, Komm, A and Pollner, F (2022) A new approach to human resources, McKinsey, www.mckinsey.com/capabilities/people-and-organizational-performance/our-insights/hrs-new-operating-model (archived at https://perma.cc/U69K-FQRZ)

EY (2024) The People Value Chain Model: HR in the digital era, www.ey.com (archived at https://perma.cc/RXU4-PJTC)

Gartner (2023) *HR Transformation and Operating Models: Future-proofing the function*, Stamford, CT: Gartner

Kurzweil, R (2005) *The Singularity is Near: When humans transcend biology*, New York: Viking

McKinsey & Company (2022) HR's new operating model, www.mckinsey.com/capabilities/people-and-organizational-performance/our-insights/hrs-new-operating-model (archived at https://perma.cc/6VBU-YB3A)

Mercer (2024) Target Interaction Model: Unlocking the employee experience, www.mercer.com/en-jo/insights/people-strategy/hr-transformation/why-the-target-interaction-model-is-the-key-to-unlocking-the-employee-experience/ (archived at https://perma.cc/4Y9N-PLTV)

Talent Strategy Group (2024) It's (still) the mortar, not the bricks: HR effectiveness in a changing world, https://talentstrategygroup.com/its-still-the-mortar-not-the-bricks/ (archived at https://perma.cc/PL4T-6NMW)

Ulrich, D (1997) *Human Resource Champions: The next agenda for adding value and delivering results*, Boston: Harvard Business School Press

Ulrich, D (2024) Update on HR Business Partner model continuing evolution and Relevance, www.linkedin.com/pulse/update-hr-business-partner-model-continuing-evolution-dave-ulrich-vqwoc/ (archived at https://perma.cc/2RQV-JFVB)

5

HR 3.0: The genesis, Systems and People Operations

Web 3.0 is about empowering users and decentralizing control. In the same way, HR 3.0 must empower employees, decentralize decision making and create intelligent, skills-driven talent ecosystems.

INSPIRED BY GAVIN WOOD, CO-FOUNDER OF ETHEREUM

WHAT'S COVERED IN THIS CHAPTER

- **Concept overview:** Define HR 3.0 and its core components. Built on four domains: Science, Systems, Products and Process

- **Differentiators:** Highlight what makes HR 3.0 distinct from previous models. Especially the shift from more intersectional approaches to how HR work is done across those domains (so examples of deliverables and their flow through this model) and the different capabilities and roles needed in this more progressive model.

- **Philosophy and principles:** Discuss the guiding principles of HR 3.0, focusing on meaning, relationships, versatility, agility, people science, systems, product management, People Operations and data-driven decision making.

Introduction

In the previous four chapters, we covered operating models, how HR has shaped its professional field, some iterations on that and a look ahead to the future and how all forms of models – Business Operating and HR Operating Models – are changing and will change further.

Without any form of hyperbole, things will shift significantly in the coming years as we move from the *Knowledge Economy* into the *Automation Era* (how rapidly we are yet to truly know) and then into the *Regenerative Age* (more action to restore a balance to the planet and the diminishing of destructive extraction and overuse of planetary resources). Whether we are man-made climate change deniers or not, shrinking ice caps and the planet's temperature pose some serious challenges that will continue to feature in how we live our lives and run our businesses.

So how does a new HR Operating Model help with any of that?

The short answer is that any systemic change and adaptation has to start *somewhere*.

An HR Operating Model shift will position the professionals within any HR team to better serve *People, Culture, Learning, Performance and Purpose*, and link those tangible and intangible elements to *Product, Service, Financialization, Reputation and Diligence*.

Aligning people, their skills and talents, creating a vibrant and positive culture, helping people learn, develop and add capabilities to their ways of working, and measuring and rewarding performance are the lifeblood of any organization that aspires to continuously improve and sustainably succeed in such challenging times.

The current operating models – and many of those proposed by scholars, researchers, providers and analysts – see the need to adapt but perhaps fall short of an entirely new model.

This book aims to showcase a potentially new model significantly different from the previous incarnations of HR Operating Models.

The genesis of a new operating model for HR

On an autumn afternoon in September 2022, having seen the world react to and recover from the pandemic's effects, I started to think about the HR Operating Model and why it hasn't significantly evolved. I looked around and, for two solid days, researched who was saying what about HR Operating Models.

I found the interesting things I've featured in this book and have since been active in keeping abreast of anything significant in this area.

I sensed a lack of something genuinely new, inventive and provocative, so I put pen to paper (admittedly, a digital pen and writing tablet) and started sketching.

In my consulting business, I had already created a model for People Experience at work (Figure 5.1).

FIGURE 5.1 Our unique 42@work model for a flourishing experience of work

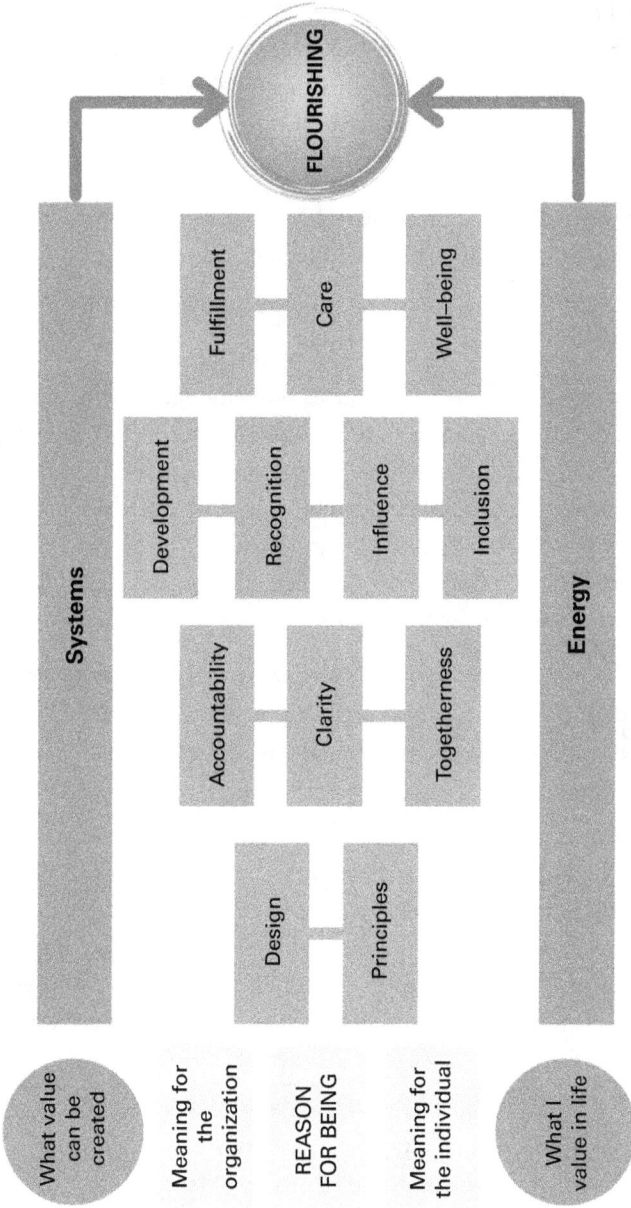

Ultimately, this model aims to create a state of flourishing for people and the organizations they work for.

Flourishing comes from the 5th century BCE term (apparently used by philosopher Aristotle) *Eudaimonia* – the highest form of human good. It's beyond happiness or hedonistic pleasure and is about a sense of fulfilment, joy and making an impactful difference in your life that is sustainable and helps you realize who you are, what you're 'about' and what you're 'here' for.

The model starts with two forms of value:

1 what we as individuals **value in life** – our morals, ethics, sense of mission and how we wish to see and experience the world;

2 what **value is created** by an organization, enterprise or collection of people.

From these, we also have two senses of meaning: individual meaning (what life is all about) and meaning for the organization (why it exists, what it is there to serve). These combined create a merged sense of the *reason for being* in a working role, performing tasks and activities and linked to that higher sense of meaning, purpose and value.

Two 'forces' framing those value elements and the reason for being/meaning elements are *systems* and *energy*.

• We use systems of work, behaviours, rituals, routines, processes, tasks, interconnected engineered activities and tools, technologies and frameworks to direct our working efforts towards positive and productive outcomes.

• We have and use energy – our physical, mental and emotional energy as individuals, as well as the energy that comes from completing things, creating things and doing things that manifest the value aspects and mission/purpose rationale. The organization creates energy – sometimes great, sometimes good and sometimes not so good – and we might label that culture. An organizational energy that might be shaped by, or itself shape, its processes, systems, business and operating model and product and service line.

In between those two framing elements are things we have to do to connect the systems and energy.

We have *design* and *principles*:

• The design of systems and approaches that utilize, generate and enhance our energies (intellect, skill, labour, commitment, etc.).

- The principles are the codes, the attitudinal and behavioural needs that combine with technical capabilities, skills and proficiencies. Trust, appreciation, patience, morals and guidance are also principles.

Then, we move from these two pillars to three core features that help us perform well, learn and adapt, and have a sense of fortitude and collegiality:

- **Accountability** – what I am accountable for doing in my work; what others are accountable for that I link with and rely on, and how they depend on me. And also how the organization is accountable to me (contracts, compliance, reward, recognition, safety, etc).

- **Clarity** – am I clear on what, how, why, when and with whom I'm doing things, and are others – leaders, colleagues, partners, etc. – clear with me on their expectations and needs? That information is shared with me and helps me do what I do to the best of my ability. Do people communicate, engage and involve me, and do I do the same when things are challenging, go wrong, are going brilliantly well, and where help is needed and can be offered?

- **Togetherness** – are we aligned and connected? Do we believe in and trust each other, becoming 'greater than the sum of our parts'? Without this, we're isolated, individualistic contributors, but how much more can we do when camaraderie, belief, sharing and a spirit of collective endeavour create gain and impact?

Then there are four areas we will more readily recognize as part of the HR service proposition:

- **Development** – how we learn, build, grow and discover more of what we could be and do in our work. How does the organization afford/allow me to develop?

- **Recognition** – how we are rewarded, appreciated and receive benefits from what we do for the impact we have and the results we achieve.

- **Influence** – how we can shape our working environment and future options. How can we make changes that help us know and be better at what we do?

- **Inclusion** – do we belong as our true selves, with all the differences that add up to who we are and what we can bring to our work? I may have a different ethnicity, social class, language, accent, disability or caring responsibility to others, but am I a strong and true part of something bigger than myself?

In these 'spaces', we might feel that everything is good or something is not quite right. These are pivotal areas for us in describing our sense of an experience of work that is good, indifferent or not so good.

Yet more likely, the final three areas either contribute to or make us feel something is missing in achieving a flourishing state:

- **Fulfilment** – does my work fulfil me? Do I get a kick from it? Do I feel a positive impact and am I accomplished in what I do? Do I fulfil my obligations to the organization and does it provide fulfilment for me?

- **Care** – do I care about my work, colleagues and what I do? Do I feel the organization (its leaders, my manager, team and colleagues) cares about me and what I do? Do I feel looked after and do I look after the interests of the team, function and organization?

- **Well-being** – is my work making me healthier or am I ailing? Does it give me an adrenaline rush or am I filled with stress and cortisol? Do I work long hours and feel exhausted, or does my work buoy me so that I'm in flow and feel it adds to my mental and physical wellness?

Because if there's a negative in any of these three areas, *flourishing* will not be the word you'd use to describe your working experience.

Using this model (influenced by the 42@Work model)

This model is then meant as a design tool (left through right, Figure 5.1) and a diagnostic/correcting tool (right through left) to find ways to boost and build things towards a state of flourishing.

Because a flourishing enterprise is made up of flourishing people – else it might be financially successful but is it truly flourishing? Not likely.

After this appraisal of the ultimate deliverable for HR, I started plotting the current model, roles, tools and services, and that's when it hit me: **what we currently have is no longer fit for purpose.**

It will get us by, but it won't help HR teams flourish, which in turn impairs the likelihood of the entire organization and its people flourishing.

None of the model's components were well served by the existing HR Operating Model, with some gaps, crossovers and overemphasis, so something more progressive was needed:

- Where could HR practitioners amplify the sense of meaning?

- How could a culture of trust truly be delivered when HR itself has to navigate silos of its own doing and a lack of accountability, clarity and togetherness?

- Can a more holistic approach (and as Deloitte coined as a phrase in its 2024 Human Capital Trends report, 'Boundaryless HR') be enacted upon and deliver value?

It made me realize that we've been toiling in HR for some time with a model that does not service our needs in the best way possible.

We cannot keep tinkering with an infrastructure and blueprint that requires constant maintenance and annexing.

We need a new model to declare a new way to handle more complex work, workflows and solution provision. That is so pioneering that it could bring about something different in how organizations set out their operating models. There would be fewer divisions and more intersectional spaces and roles that traverse them along value chains without resource hoarding and gaps being created in ownership and accountability, impact and value creation.

I saw six elements coming into play – not business partners, recruiters or L&D facilitators. That's the current paradigm.

I saw **Systems Designers** as super-practitioners for everything that requires a system: hiring, selection, reward, talent planning, careers, workflows, and Organization Design and structures into organizational and individual performance and effectiveness.

I saw **evidence-based HR** not just from the realms of a raft of spreadsheets but from the compelling utilization of other forms of evidence – **people and behavioural science, organizational and occupational psychology** and all forms of performance psychology, learning psychology, design psychology and social sciences.

I saw essential and underpinning **operational management** (deployed recruitment campaigns, unionized relations and negotiations, workforce planning, onboarding and legislative compliant strength) as the domain of **People Operations and practice leads**.

I saw the absolutely vital need for the **data side of performance** relating to people, given its *special-ops* feel with analysts dedicated to working out the tricky calculations of how well people are performing and how we can improve things where that performance is sub-par.

I have been advocating for the HR profession to view the things it does for people and the organization as products, thereby adopting a **product manager** mindset with all the positive additionality that design thinking and human-centric design can bring. And this stood out for me as a shift we need to make to be taken more seriously by business colleagues who see us as 'tea and tissues' for dispute resolution rather than the builders of business value,

FIGURE 5.2 The HR 3.0 Operating Model

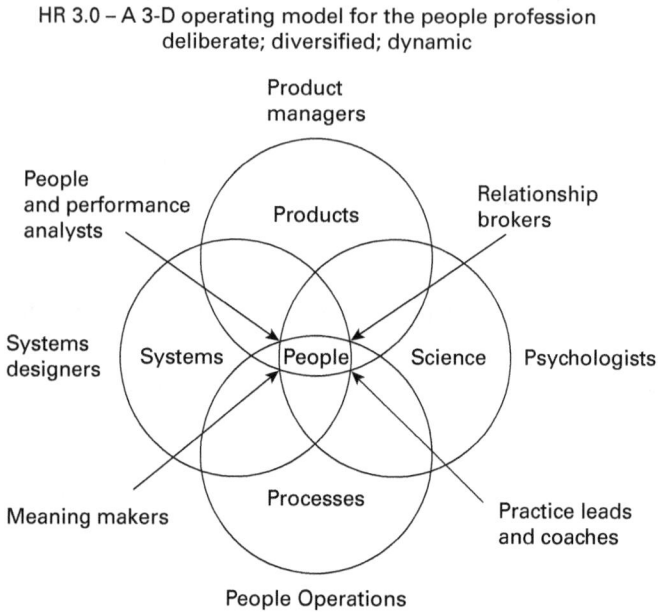

HR 3.0 – A 3-D operating model for the people profession
deliberate; diversified; dynamic

Product
managers

People
and performance   Products   Relationship
analysts   brokers

Systems
designers   Systems   People   Science   Psychologists

Meaning makers   Processes   Practice leads
and coaches

People Operations

creating humanistic and positive things that help people do their best work in fair exchange for a vibrant culture and recognition.

I also saw the need for the **Chief People Officer** not to be a senior administrator and VP of 'keeping tribunals at bay' but as the manifestation of the organization's soul, amplifying the **meaning and purpose** of why this organization exists and is exceptional, and what to do about that if it is not a meaningful enterprise.

In thinking about Web 3.0 as the movement to where digital technology is headed, I coined the name **HR 3.0,** and I then designed Figure 5.2.

Before we go into the terminology used in this graphic, I must share some of the principles behind this model:

1 **Symbolic:** It represents a shift from anything else an HR team, department or function is currently using. That is symbolic and can be both exciting and, of course, a little disconcerting or even scary. It is meant to be a bold step away from the existing model and paradigm. A new blueprint, to use our earlier metaphor.

2 **Adaptable:** It is deliberately open to as much interpretation and adaptation as it is definitive. It's definitive in suggesting that things like **systems, science, products and processes** are vital. Yet it doesn't mean every team

has to have psychologists working in their midst. Access to psychology will be helpful to even the smallest HR team or even sole practitioner. Knowing the sciences of motivation and how to create valuable policies needs more than knowledge of employment law, critical though that is.

3 **Intersectional:** The criticism of most operating models is that they can make things more compartmentalized, and in defining entities and elements within them, they can create a degree of separation between those parts in the attempts to develop their distinction. The more intersectional a model, the more likely the parts will come together outside of linear flows. So, this was very deliberate. And of course, you could create Olympic rings, but the use of four circles (rather than the classic Venn of three) was already present in the thinking around **Systems, Science, Products and Processes.**

4 **People:** At the heart of it – although in early iterations of this, I had People where the Science circle is. I had one of those *what was I thinking?* moments and shifted that into this iteration. Science is crucial to link with Systems (and then intersects with Products and Processes) **because of** and **for** people. People should be at the epicentre of what HR is there to do, not a specific domain – the core of it all.

5 **Roles:** No vast list of roles. Operating models don't need that. Your organization's design work creates that. However, as this HR Operating Model starts to 'come to life', people will inevitably want to know and see the roles that are needed within it. Of course, this will depend on the nature, size/scale and type of organization, so I've purposefully under-prescribed that with this sketch.

6 **Impact:** Every operating model exists to create impact and value. Again, this model will need to be clear for those who want to shift to this evolved version, which is contextual to the organization. What is implied in this model is that impact is a shared endeavour across intersectional areas and is all about people at the heart of this evolved version. It's not that assets, materials, intellectual property, capitalization and market uniqueness aren't important, because they are. The **overall** organizational operating model deals with that. This is about People – the entire reason HR exists.

7 **Framed:** There is a very intentional thing in having a subtitle to this model (HR 3.0) as having a foundation in three dimensions:

a. **Deliberate** – specific, purposeful, profound and planned in making shifts that matter to the outcomes that create value for the organization's people.

b. **Diversified** – this model needs to usher in a more diversified HR approach to its portfolio now and in the near future. HR is beyond the simplified realms of personnel and even a business partnering model.

c. **Dynamic** – this model is adaptable, adjustable and agile. Its users can shift from the previous incarnation to be more responsive, emergent and experimental.

3-D also describes less of a flat two-dimensional model that is linear and predictable and more something akin to CAD drawings of real objects in three dimensions, not just something like a 2-D process chain.

How I see the HR 3.0 model working

In later chapters, we'll talk to practitioners who have started incorporating this model into their approaches and are transitioning to their version of it. It is vitally important that the model is scoped and shaped in your organizational context – you may not have the size, scale, complexity or need for all of this model in a simple 'drop' into your existing HR team or department.

So it's important to note that this is a *blueprint* you should adapt to your situation. Suppose you don't need full-time psychology-qualified practitioners to deploy the *Science* aspect or have a small team of analysts to look at people and performance data. In that case, you'll have an adapted version of this with relevant levels of capability and application in your team, or will engage external expertise to be a part of your resource model as a more *on-demand* contingency.

First, let's take the underpinning element of this model, People Operations.

People Operations

CONTEXT AND HERITAGE

You may already have a *shared service* approach from the HR Business Partner/Ulrich model, with centralized administrative support, which is both colleague/customer facing/interacting and supports the Centres of Excellence (Recruitment, Employee Relations and Learning and Development administration) and Business Partners (Project Management and Data Queries).

You may be a smaller or even standalone/solo HR 'function' – you will likely be engaged in a fair degree of HR transactional work in those circumstances, and of course, the whole spectrum of what HR is there to do. In the main, though, there is always an underpinning operational aspect to HR through a range of services, support, interventions and processes.

Having a new operating model for HR is not to overlook what is essential, and in many cases, highly functioning from previous models. It is to position any areas of optimal value even more strongly for an evolved approach, recognizing both the opportunities to leverage such strengths and the impacts any significant shifts in the operating model might have on an already functioning area.

Having a Shared Service Centre may have been a key area of focus, and therefore the last thing you want is to jeopardize the ongoing success of this function by shifting the Operating Model. Equally, the opportunities to improve this high-performing function are there alongside additional and evolved services in other areas of HR.

Increasingly, People Operations will rely more on technological access and actions by our service users. This isn't just a relabelling of *HR Administration* to *People Operations*. It is recognizing that regularly occurring, foundational elements of providing service to people are crucial to creating a stable and confident set of solutions to the problems people face and the things they need.

Digitization and accessibility

The People Operations area will increasingly be where the most significant utilization of digital technologies and automation will take place, and will also consider the most accessible and convenient way to deliver something of value for our people.

There is also a strong demand that more efficient People Operations be a way to create resource capacity and capability for the multitude of complex challenges HR now faces, whilst also for itself modernizing, evolving and improving speed, accuracy and the impact of administrative and functional services.

I often hear it said that in order to transform HR we must do so by 'getting the basics right'. And it is true that a baseline of strong and valuable services helps us 'level up' to those more complex areas and push on way beyond current boundaries and expectations.

It would be foolish to say that all People Operations work will be automated, therefore we should merely focus on that, even if the HR technology vendor community is clearly moving that way – from chatbots now supported by large language models that can handle more nuanced and natural language queries online, to AI-enabled screening and sifting of job applications and beyond.

It's more than 'outsourcing digitally'. It's designing and deploying superior digitized solutions for **information**, allowing for increased personalization of value through **interaction**.

It does feel vital that HR administration is not overlooked or overplayed, as we clearly see a shift in the expectations, services needed and complexity of what people need in working in a more turbulent and fast-changing world.

So it is with this model that People Operations is in no need of any further abstract or trendy title or total reimagining – it needs to be contextually evolved and to give us a way of building a stronger Operating Model for HR with that as our underpinning strength.

People Operations will be (at least) three-fold in this model:

1 Effective and efficient **transactional delivery**. Enabling everyday queries on people matters to be smartly and supportively serviced and answered.

2 Ongoing assimilation of **upgraded digitized solutions** to give people access to what they need in the flow of their working lives.

3 Additional, exceptional and personalized services that are where **dialogue and empathy are vital** because they go beyond the utilization of information and need sensitive, ethical and appropriate levels of human interaction

Far from being administrative hubs, these are human-centred design experts in service provision and synergies with the best digitized solutions, helping them focus on people's complex and nuanced needs.

Transition to People Operations

We do have a challenge on our hands, though – perception and HR's own capability to digitize its services create a mixed bag of success and some clear room for improvement in our reputation as process reengineers for the better.

We sadly hear that whilst looking for efficiencies, systems 'upgrades' don't feel like that, especially to people across the organization and perhaps line managers.

People can be more trusting of other people they've come to know, who can solve their problems – they become familiar, comfortable or dependent on others to help them. And indeed, they may feel there's something impersonal and a little lacking in not getting help from another person. So there's a common feeling that more automation is more impersonal and invites the enquiry, 'Just what are you here for, HR?'

Of course, there are some real success stories, where people who just want a quick answer are given a fully digitized solution. For them, it's a clearer, more accessible, swifter and seamless process.

I think it's important to distinguish between our approach to setting out People Operations and how it might differ from a *service centre* offering.

In looking at servicing needs, we move from HR areas (recruitment, payroll, learning, etc.) and place more emphasis on the *experience our colleagues have*. They require information at crucial points for them, when and in a way that reflects what matters to them most.

To some people, the default response is 'I need to speak to someone', when the reality is 'I need more information and a way to find a solution for my need'.

However, we (HR) have a handling and positioning issue. The historical default is that *you (HR) solve my problem, for me*.

In that case, this kind of dependency may feel like a superior level of service is being offered when, in reality, people may be unwittingly reducing or even eliminating the sense of agency people feel over solving their problems, finding what they need and constructing their own solutions.

Parent-child dependency is perhaps in play (or, in HR's case, *nanny-child*, perhaps).

When we position a shift to more automation, self-service and information-providing interventions, we need to show this is a continuously better way for people to get what they need, when and how they need it, to prove it is the most efficient, effective and helpful way to provide a service.

It requires us to ensure we are fully aware of what people might need and that our information sources, compliant processes and guidance are optimal.

In essence, we adopt human-centred design principles. This does not mean it is a *white-glove concierge service* at all times; it means HR becomes fixated on what makes a positive and impactful experience for people who need help, input, guidance or a resolution to an issue.

In attempts to show value and service, HR has somewhat inculcated this dependency, when the reality is that maturing and adaptability direct us to evolve and build capabilities so that we move away from this form of dependency and create new forms of more sophisticated and powerful interaction and co-creation.

One such evolution is the move from basic contracting and management of work – role, execution, value – and into deeper understanding beyond that surface layer of performance. We have moved through stages of what we've called 'employee engagement' and into the realms of understanding the experience of work that appears to enable a greater sense of balanced and adaptable performance, responding and navigating an ever more complex world of work and business operations. With this in mind, this model needs to absolutely deliver a stronger form of People Experience.

People Experience

The business world has for some time focused on what they worked out about customers and their loyalty, continued buying of our services and products, and advocating our products and services, endorsing and encouraging others to do the same.

We called this **customer experience**.

And this thinking is now coming into the internal workings of an organization, because we are designing services, support, interventions and guidance (our products) for our own people based on the employee lifecycle, which we often call the journey of people at work.

In this lifecycle, there are identified archetypal stages: pre- and onboarding; initial learning, performance and integration into their role; skills and capability development; performance feedback; careers; life events (parental/caring leave, study, illness, secondments) and of course, in some cases, off-boarding/exit. And whilst we can map out as many permutations as possible for what people will need from the organization as a guiding and caring employer, the uniqueness of life means there will always be adapted exceptions to what standard offers we can create.

There is always much more going on in the 'middle' of the lifecycle than we can provide specific solutions for in a nice, tidy journey map. It would become incredibly cluttered as people's circumstances (life events/episodes) change. And yet, this is perhaps when our colleagues might need us the most, where a non-prescriptive instance requires a uniquely personal solution. In such circumstances, People Operations needs to go beyond standardized information supply and services and become much more interaction-based. However, this will only happen if they are liberated through digitized information provision and query handling for the predictable, repeat instances.

HR 3.0 – elevating People Operations

HR 3.0 aims to show how to present an elevated perspective, from purely information and processes in People Operations to consultative, helpful, solutions-focused operational activities that require a distinct human interaction. *Exceptional exception handling*, I suppose.

In the more challenging forms of interaction – people struggling mentally because of a bereavement, stress from financial fragility, inappropriate behaviour from a colleague causing them anxiety – we need more than a policy and information to handle these situations. Business partners often pick this up, and advisers and, and in some cases, employee relations specialists get involved.

This is where the intersectional aspect of HR 3.0 provides that space more coherently than at present. In the present model, there is perhaps too much distinction and separation. Such things 'fall between stools' and get picked up, but in reality, who owns the initial contact through to a solution? In a more evolved People Operations sense, beyond the initial information submission and signposting, human interaction is managed and given ownership for the challenge people are facing.

Intersecting with practice leads

HR's current system allows for the adoption of a formal 'case work' approach, where it becomes formalized and involves employment law. There are also 'tickets' that are raised for helpdesk-like queries (leave allowance, maternity leave paperwork, etc.).

Somewhere in this is a way to log, administer and progress queries to resolution where it is not as formal as a potential conduct or conflict issue and not as simple as information and administration.

People Operations seems to be the prominent owner of this, with input from specialists on a 'commissioned' basis so that this work is logged, tracked and allocated. It is managed sensitively and efficiently. Where People Operations work intersects with specialist advice, it is more proficiently handled and resolved so that people feel they are cared for and handled well, and can see how they will obtain a solution to their issue.

It is underestimated that someone handling this kind of query from a colleague goes beyond process or legislation and is someone who understands science and psychology, giving us evidence and expertise in handling stressful situations our colleagues might be experiencing.

This work often involves supporting line managers who are unsure how to handle their team members. It may require escalation to medical professionals and referral to counselling services. Much of this happens now, with very willing HR practitioners doing their utmost, but a more robust system could help, with the right skill level, tracking progress and capturing anonymized data on the nature of the work, outcomes and value created in such areas.

Increasingly, work of this nature is more in demand than exceptional. Levels of stress, anxiety and mental health challenges are higher than ever. A more strategic and impact-assessed approach would help those linking with business leaders to show how work in this area reflects the current state of morale, performance and collective strength, and whether bigger, more systemic actions are required to counter pressures, demands and uncertainty.

In this instance we go beyond processing tickets to use our deeper and more interpersonal problem resolution to aggregate into signals of a system, energy, behavioural or operational issue that needs the attention of systems designers, science-based practitioners and product managers.

Of course, People Operations requires a range of products, and we will cover this in more detail in Chapter 6. Our next logical link, though, is People Operations' dependency on and impact on our Systems.

HR 3.0 – focusing on Systems

Our horizontal factor in the model starts with Systems. This could have been a 'wrap around' to the entire HR 3.0 model, as the model is in itself an operating model that depicts the system we operate in, use and create. However, it still intersects with all other elements and isn't the only driver to successful delivery of HR value. It needs the sciences, products and processes to learn from, design with and through, and bring the whole thing to life.

With so many areas, services, interaction points, deliverables and 'moving parts', the systems used for HR teams are complex, diverse and not as clear-cut and linear as those used in the supply chain, production and reporting.

Systems Thinking is where we'll start, and a recognition of how powerful this field has become over the last few decades, growing into a more formally recognized discipline in society and, acutely, in the world of work.

Systems Thinking: a critical lever in HR 3.0

With arguably a more complex operating 'backdrop' than in living memory, HR leaders are increasingly called upon to navigate and anticipate such challenges and design people strategies that adapt to evolving organizational needs.

HR 3.0 is a model that places people at its heart and is supported by innovative systems, products, processes and science. A key enabler of this vision is Systems Thinking, a mindset and approach that helps HR professionals see the bigger picture, connect the dots and drive impact across the entire organizational ecosystem.

What is Systems Thinking?

Some may know this, but not all: Systems Thinking is an approach to problem solving that considers the interrelationships, patterns and dynamics of *the parts within a larger whole*. In organizations, it means moving beyond siloed thinking to understand how people, processes, policies and technologies interact as part of a complex, adaptive system. Rather than isolating issues like retention or productivity, Systems Thinking invites us to explore why these challenges arise by examining the systemic forces at play.

This shift in perspective is powerful for HR. It helps us identify root causes, foresee unintended consequences of changes and create strategies that align with the organization's overall goals and values. Systems Thinking is not just about fixing problems – it is about deliberately and dynamically designing resilient, sustainable systems that support growth, innovation and people's well-being.

Systems Thinking in action: from fragmentation to integration

Consider a common HR challenge: addressing low engagement scores in an employee survey. A traditional response might involve quick fixes like recognition activities or wellness initiatives. While valuable, these solutions often focus on symptoms, not causes.

A Systems Thinking approach, however, takes a deeper dive. It asks questions like:

- How are leadership behaviours impacting engagement?
- What role do organizational structures or workloads play in shaping employee experiences?

- Are our systems (like performance management or rewards) aligned with the culture we want to foster?
- How do external factors (industry trends or economic conditions) influence the system?

By zooming out and identifying the interconnected factors at play, HR can co-create systemic solutions that address the root causes – whether it's a misalignment of values, outdated processes or unclear communication channels.

The role of Systems Thinking in HR 3.0

In HR 3.0, the Systems area operates as a dynamic source of connecting and enabling energies for the entire model. It ensures that HR strategies, tools and initiatives are designed with a systems-aware mindset. Here's how it comes into play:

Holistic workforce strategies: HR 3.0 requires us to think beyond roles and job descriptions and embrace more progressive and dynamic approaches, such as skills-based workforce design. Systems Thinking helps map the interdependencies between talent supply, skills development and business demand, enabling more intelligent workforce planning.

Agile and adaptive HR processes: In our volatile environment, static processes no longer suffice. Systems Thinking supports the creation of feedback loops that allow HR processes – like learning, recruitment or DE&I – to evolve based on real-time insights, shifting needs and broader forms of value being created across disciplines, service areas and meeting the company's customer demand.

Cross-functional collaboration: Systems Thinking emphasizes breaking boundaries from silo working. It ensures and enables collaboration across departments and enables HR strategies to integrate seamlessly with business goals, technology investments and operational realities, irrespective of structural parameters people have created.

Data-informed decision making: HR has more access to data than ever before. Systems Thinking ensures that we don't just collect and analyse data in isolation but use it to uncover patterns, test hypotheses and drive strategic action that benefits the whole system.

Resilience and well-being: Organizations are ecosystems and people are at the heart of it all. Systems Thinking helps HR underscore the importance of designing systems that not just promote mechanical efficiency and productivity but also consider culture, mental models, psychological safety, inclusion and long-term resilience.

Building Systems Thinking capability in HR

To embed Systems Thinking in HR practices, fostering this capability across teams is important. This could start with:

- Training and tools: introduce HR teams to Systems Thinking frameworks like causal loop diagrams or systems mapping. These tools help visualize relationships and anticipate ripple effects.

- Unleashing curiosity and dialogue – such as asking 'Why?' more often.

- Encourage deeper questioning when analysing problems.

- Looking for patterns, dependencies and underlying structures that influence outcomes.

- Experimenting and learning: adopt an iterative approach to HR initiatives. Pilot programmes, gather feedback and refine strategies based on what the system reveals.

- Engage multiple perspectives: Systems Thinking thrives on diversity. When designing HR strategies, include voices from different teams, levels and backgrounds.

A new mindset for HR

Systems Thinking helps us expand our thinking, horizons and considerations. As we embrace a model like HR 3.0, Systems Thinking offers a lens through which we can make more thoughtful, impactful decisions. This will enable us to create HR practices that aren't just efficient, adaptive, inclusive and aligned with the organization's broader purpose.

In today's interconnected world, nothing exists in isolation and it probably never has. In the current turbulence, it's more complex, challenging, chaotic even. Therefore, Systems Thinking has perhaps never been more crucial than it is now.

By mastering Systems Thinking, HR becomes a true architect of change – designing systems that unlock the potential of individuals, teams and organizations alike against that backdrop of uncertainty, turbulence and unpredictability.

This is why we need more space and work dedicated to Systems and the concept/roles of Systems Designers.

Everything is a system and therefore, in the world of work, Systems Designers are critical in constructing the methods for how all the moving parts – human, mechanical, intellectual, digital and emotional – connect in an optimized, adaptable and efficient manner to create something HR needs to be known much more – engineering Organizational Effectiveness (OE).

OE is the third underutilized aspect of Organizational Development (OD), along with Organizational Design. OE needs much more prominence as the point of great design and continuous development. It's aligned to purpose, mission, vision and values and delivered through the Business and Operating Model and aligned, committed and capable people.

Throughout this book we will look more into OE and HR's role not as the sole determinant of OE, but the custodian of OE as a regular and focused element of OD/D in service of the organization's reason for being.

WHAT WE'VE COVERED IN THIS CHAPTER

In this chapter, we introduced HR 3.0 as a new and progressive operating model for HR – one that shifts from conventional structures to a more adaptive, science-informed and intersectional approach.

We outlined the **four core domains** that define HR 3.0:

- **Science** – leveraging people science, behavioural psychology and data-driven insights.

- **Systems** – applying Systems Thinking to create holistic, integrated HR practices.

- **Products** – designing HR interventions with a product management mindset.

- **Processes** – ensuring seamless execution through people-centred operational excellence.

We focused specifically on **Processes** (and the role of People Operation) and **Systems**.

We explored why existing HR models are no longer fit for purpose in today's evolving landscape, moving from the knowledge economy into the automation and regenerative eras. This shift demands HR professionals move beyond siloed functions and actively shape the culture, learning, performance and purpose of their organizations.

Key takeaways include:

- **Flourishing as the ultimate goal** – drawing on Aristotle's concept of *eudaimonia*, HR should create workplaces where people and businesses thrive together.
- **A fresh HR paradigm** – the model moves away from traditional HR Business Partnering towards intersectional roles such as Systems Designers, People Scientists and HR Product Managers.
- **HR as a systemic enabler** – rather than functioning as a service provider, HR should be a strategic architect of work, culture and capability.
- **The importance of Systems Thinking** – viewing HR work through a systems lens ensures solutions are holistic, interconnected and designed for adaptability.
- **People Operations as the core 'platform'** – moving beyond administrative HR to a modern, digitized, empathetic and experience-driven function.

This chapter set the foundation for understanding how HR 3.0 is both a mindset and a practical model that can be shaped and owned by HR teams to fit their organizational context.

Next, we will dive deeper into how HR products and sciences work within this model, ensuring HR moves from reactive service delivery to proactive value creation.

References and further reading

Aristotle (350 BCE) *Nicomachean Ethics*, translated by W.D. Ross, Oxford: Oxford University Press.

Bersin, J (2023) Systemic HR: The future of HR operating models, https://joshbersin.com/2023/12/introducing-the-systemic-hr-initiative/ (archived at https://perma.cc/FV3X-V6X8)

Deloitte (2024) 2024 Global Human Capital Trends: Boundaryless HR, www2.deloitte.com/content/dam/insights/articles/glob176836_global-human-capital-trends-2024/DI_Global-Human-Capital-Trends-2024.pdf (archived at https://perma.cc/T3KE-SYRM)

Laloux, F (2014) *Reinventing Organizations: A guide to creating organizations inspired by the next stage of human consciousness*, Brussels: Nelson Parker

McKinsey & Company (2022) Five Emerging HR Operating-Model Archetypes, www.mckinsey.com (archived at https://perma.cc/WL8K-CNKK)

Meadows, D H (2008) *Thinking in Systems: A primer*, White River Junction, VT: Chelsea Green Publishing

Senge, P M (1990) *The Fifth Discipline: The art and practice of the learning organization*, New York: Doubleday

Wood, G (2014) Ethereum: A secure decentralized generalized transaction ledger, https://bravenewcoin.com/assets/Whitepapers/Ethereum-A-Secure-Decentralised-Generalised-Transaction-Ledger-Yellow-Paper.pdf (archived at https://perma.cc/ET43-7ZWL)

6

Core principles of HR 3.0: Products and Science

Great products don't happen by accident. They come from deeply understanding people's needs and iterating towards value.

MELISSA PERRI, **AUTHOR OF** *ESCAPING THE BUILD TRAP*

WHAT'S COVERED IN THIS CHAPTER

- **Agility and product management:** Examine the importance of agility in HR operations and the nature of a wholescale shift to product management that creates value.

- **Data and analytics:** Showcase the role of analytics in shaping HR strategies, particularly the emerging real-time data using generative AI.

- **Science:** Using People and Behavioural Science, Occupational and Organizational Psychology, and Social and Performance Science as key additional aspects to the emerging field of evidence-based HR and a key domain in HR 3.0

- **Technology integration:** Detail the use of digital tools and platforms in HR 3.0.

In Chapter 5, we looked at the genesis of the HR 3.0 Operating Model and two of the key domains within it – **Process** (and People Operations) and **Systems** (and the role of Systems Designers).

We will explore these domains and capabilities/roles within them in more detail later but for this chapter we will look at the other two: **Products** and **Science**.

Products: a shift from compliance to value

HR has long been viewed as the custodian of policies, the enforcers of compliance and the gatekeepers of workplace rules. But this framing has done us few favours. While well-intentioned, it often positions HR as a bureaucratic function rather than a value-creating one. If we want to elevate HR's role, we must move beyond seeing ourselves as service providers and start thinking like product managers.

From policy enforcers to product designers

In the tech world, Product Management has transformed how digital applications and platforms are designed – creating tools that are intuitive, useful and seamlessly embedded into the flow of work. No one reads a manual before using an app; it's designed to be self-explanatory.

HR's 'products' – whether policies, processes or people programmes – should follow the same principle. Instead of being seen as rigid compliance mechanisms, they should be framed as tools that help people navigate work effectively, fairly and with clarity.

Historically, HR's primary 'product' has been the **policy**. But policies, as we know them, are often:

- **Reactive** – invoked only when something has gone wrong.
- **Legalistic** – written in jargon that feels distant and cold.
- **Negative** – framing rules as barriers rather than enablers.

This traditional approach creates a disconnect between HR and the people we serve. Many employees don't even realize a policy exists until they unintentionally breach it – booking the wrong type of train ticket, showing up late based on perceived flexibility or misunderstanding a performance expectation.

Using more imagination – what if policies were designed differently?

We could reimagine the starting point for policies framed not as rules to be obeyed but as practical guides that help people make better decisions.

Shaping policies as usable products

A Product Management approach to HR would shift our focus to user experience, ensuring policies and people processes are:

- clear and intuitive – written in everyday language, designed for real-life scenarios;

- psychologically engaging – using positive framing that appeals to people's intrinsic motivations;

- flexible within boundaries – offering clear guidance while allowing for situational discretion;

- designed for adoption – tested with real users to ensure usability rather than just existing as legal documents.

For example, instead of a policy that dictates, 'Employees must always book fixed-time train tickets to reduce travel costs', we might say, 'We ask you to treat the company's resources as carefully as your own. Flexible tickets are available where unpredictability requires them, but where possible, fixed-time tickets ensure we can use any savings you make into other important areas of our work.'

This subtle shift in language transforms the policy from a rigid rule into a shared responsibility, encouraging compliance not through enforcement but through understanding.

From 'doing just enough' to willing compliance

When policies are seen as barriers, people may look for ways around them. When they are positioned as enablers, people choose to follow them. The challenge for HR is not just to create policies, but to design them as products that people trust, understand and willingly engage with. A Product Management mindset challenges HR to rethink everything we build – from performance management to learning, inclusion and employee well-being. By designing for real people, real work and real needs, HR can transition from a function that is seen as an enforcer of rules to one that delivers products that help people and organizations thrive.

Of course, policies are not the only products HR creates (Table 6.1).

We may see many of these as standardized offerings and perhaps have come to expect certain levels of support, enabling and guidance. During exceptional times like the pandemic and wars affecting us all, we suddenly become more focused on what we can use to create value and make sense in our work, and what helps us navigate crises and handle chaos.

Using Product Management techniques in all of HR's 'offers' has seen a more human-centred, adaptive and value-creating approach to what those offers are, not just in how we construct them, and certainly not just by peppering people with more policies, but by being deliberate and diversified

TABLE 6.1 HR products

Employer brand	An appealing narrative setting out the company purpose, mission, values, culture and all it means to work somewhere IS a product. It's not just PR – and if it is over-glamourized PR, then your overall product (the organization's entire reason for being) needs a lot more work to be true, virtuous and appealing to people.
Recruiting/talent acquisition framework	Everything from the interest brought on by the employer brand, to the offer letter for a role and everything in between (including any 'sorry, not this time/it's us/you' etc.). A series of products (application, initial assessment, responses, selection processes including any tests, interviews and trials, exchanging essential information and documentation, and working out the contract and offer to start date, time, place, etc.) of which all need both a sincere, personal touch, and an efficient process and systems utilization.
Onboarding	The exciting, eager and energizing start to a role that creates that vital first impression and likely lasting connection to the things beyond the appeal and selection processes. Products here need to create clarity, comfort, confidence and assurance and tap into that exciting (and somewhat nervous) energy. Again, a list of products and features that help people step into their new working life with you are provided through HR's design and for utilization by people, their teams, managers and the company overall.
People experience	Ongoing performance, development, relational, knowledge and know-how needed to become an effective colleague and part of the team. It is where you get into why you wanted the role, and the role was seen as right for you. ALL manner of products occur here. Setting clear expectations, imbuing the culture and values and building relations with your colleagues, partners, customers and community. Looking to the future, building a career, strengthening your place in the world and living your life with this work as a key enabler for all you want to be. And how to handle things that aren't as desired, difficult, awkward and different from expectations.
Change and continuous improvement	Transitioning work that handles shifts and changes. Organizational, market/sector and customer changes; internal shapes, systems, structures and assembly of your work in how, where, what on and with whom you do your best. And of course, deliberate, designed and opportunistic transitions, be they a new role you identify as desirable, a promotion, project work and more. Products are many in many scenarios and circumstances that require change, adaptation and evolution.

(continued)

TABLE 6.1 (Continued)

Justice and resolution	Conflict is not how we might choose to be but arises nonetheless. Either collective conflict or at an individual level, any differences escalating into conflict require more formal utilization of legal, ethical, moral and procedural products that come into play where we cannot resolve our differences without further intervention.
Wellness, inclusion and belonging	A level of congruence and inclusivity is where HR's products are pertaining to a sense of satisfaction, fulfilment, appreciation, recognition and reward that gives us the comfort that we're doing a good job and benefits beyond that sense of pride. It's also supportive, adaptive and enabling products where we hit difficulties in our health, relationships, home life challenges, traumas, emotional and other forms of challenges. HR's product line here is often where companies provide resources that go beyond the standard work tools and frames and are much more about us as fallible and fragile human beings in need of something assuring.
Ending and exit	At times, it comes to an end and people (have to) move on. Either because the role isn't what is really needed or wanted, or there may have been performance, development or relational factors within or beyond your control that have determined it has to come to a close. Sometimes the company will end it – redundancies and market squeezes impact on your role – or you see something better elsewhere and choose to take your next step under someone else's banner. We tend to think of the ending only when it's near or clearly emerged as our preferred option. And in this are more products from HR's line in handling the governance, fairness and a dignified way to say 'goodbye' to each other.

in how we construct our products, how we offer them and let our colleagues know what they're for, and how we measure the effectiveness and dynamic needs of a changing world and people's changing needs.

What does an HR Product Manager do?

A Product Manager is a problem solver, architect and translator – working at the intersection of user needs, business goals and operational feasibility.

In the tech world, Product Managers don't just build software; they design experiences that people actually want to use. They gather insights, test assumptions, refine iterations and ensure products evolve with changing needs.

APPLYING THAT TO HR

An HR Product Manager takes the same product-thinking approach but applies it to people-focused solutions, ensuring HR's offerings are valuable, intuitive and designed with the user in mind.

They don't just roll out another initiative; they build products that integrate seamlessly into the way people work.

HR Product Management in action: three scenarios

Let's imagine an HR Product Manager stepping into three big-ticket challenges.

---

1. STRATEGIC WORKFORCE PLANNING AS A PRODUCT

The challenge: The organization is struggling to predict talent needs, leading to reactive hiring, skill shortages and workforce inefficiencies.

The HR Product Manager's approach:

- User research: Interviews with leaders, employees and external analysts to map fundamental skills needs (not just assumptions).
- Prototyping: Piloting AI-driven skills forecasting dashboards, helping teams see what skills are depleting, emerging and at risk.
- Iterate and adapt: Testing on-demand talent marketplaces, enabling internal mobility before external hiring is needed.
- Success looks like: Workforce planning isn't a PowerPoint deck, but an interactive, predictive and self-adjusting system that leaders actively use.

Key mindset shift: Workforce planning isn't an HR report – it's a decision-making product leaders rely on.

---

2. GENERATIVE AI IN HR SERVICE DELIVERY

The challenge: HR service teams are overwhelmed with repetitive queries, slowing down response times and frustrating employees.

The HR Product Manager's approach:

- User journey mapping: Understanding the most common friction points where employees struggle to find answers.

- AI as a product: Deploying a generative AI assistant that can answer 90 per cent of policy and process queries while seamlessly escalating complex cases to HR experts.

- Testing and refinement: Running controlled A/B tests on chatbot responses to optimize for accuracy, tone and clarity.

- Success looks like: HR teams spend more time on solving higher-stakes problems, while employees get instant, human-like responses to standard queries.

Key mindset shift: AI isn't replacing HR – it's a product that frees HR to focus on high-value, human-centric work.

---

3. CULTURE OF PERFORMANCE AS A PRODUCT

The challenge: Traditional performance management is a painful, bureaucratic process – managers dread it, employees fear it and HR struggles to make it meaningful.

The HR Product Manager's approach:

- Reframing performance: Treating performance feedback as an everyday habit, not an annual event.

- Product thinking: Designing real-time performance check-ins via collaboration tools (Slack, MS Teams) with nudges for managers to give timely feedback.

- Pilot and scale: Starting with a test group of teams, measuring engagement and scaling based on feedback.

- Success looks like: Employees feel supported, managers find it effortless and HR stops chasing overdue appraisals.

Key mindset shift: Performance isn't an HR admin task, it's a cultural product designed for continuous improvement.

What makes an HR Product Manager different?

Unlike traditional HR, which often launches initiatives based on best practices, an HR Product Manager:

- starts with the user and the system they are in, focusing on real problems, not assumed ones;

- designs for adoption and creating value, ensuring HR solutions are fully utilized and deliver value for people and the organization;
- iterates constantly, adapting based on feedback and data, external drivers, science and technological advancement;
- measures success, using data, engagement and behavioural shifts, not just compliance.

A more flourishing future of work needs HR to be more product-led

HR is at a key inflexion point. It needs to continue delivering processes, and yet, it can instead build better products that solve critical problems in ways that people want to engage with and see the value in them.

If we want HR to matter more in the next stage of evolution in work, we do need to think and act like product designers, not just policy writers.

HR 3.0 isn't just about changing what we do – it's about how we think and the additional value we can create.

Agility and Product Management in HR 3.0

The traditional model of HR – structured around rigid policies, annual cycles and hierarchical decision making – has long struggled to keep pace with the rapid changes in work, technology and employee expectations. HR 3.0 represents a shift from static, compliance-driven operations to a more dynamic, responsive and value-creating function. At the heart of this transformation lies **Agile HR** – an approach that embraces adaptability, iterative development and customer-centric thinking.

This is where **Product Management** emerges as a vital paradigm for HR. Rather than viewing HR as a service function delivering predefined programmes and policies, HR 3.0 treats HR initiatives as **products** – designed, tested, iterated and improved based on data, user feedback and changing business needs.

The shift from process-driven to product-driven HR

In traditional HR models, processes dictate how HR operates. Whether it's performance management, recruitment, learning or rewards, these areas are typically managed through fixed cycles and sequential workflows, often detached from evolving business priorities. In contrast, a Product Management mindset reshapes HR's role by focusing on:

1 Defining value: HR teams must identify what value they are creating – whether for employees, managers or the business – and articulate it in terms of outcomes rather than processes.

2 User-centric design: Just as Product Managers develop solutions based on customer needs, HR should design policies, programmes and digital experiences based on employee and stakeholder feedback.

3 Continuous iteration: Instead of launching massive, one-size-fits-all initiatives, HR 3.0 prioritizes incremental improvements, testing new ideas in pilot groups before scaling.

4 Data-driven decision making: Product Management in HR involves measuring success through real-time analytics and using insights to refine and optimize HR solutions.

Agile HR: principles and practices

Agile HR applies Agile methodologies – originally designed for software development – to HR operations. At its core, Agile HR is about breaking work into small, manageable increments, ensuring rapid feedback loops and fostering cross-functional collaboration. Table 6.2 shows key Agile HR practices.

TABLE 6.2 Key HR Agile practices

Cross-functional HR teams	Moving away from siloed HR departments (e.g. L&D, Talent Acquisition, Rewards), Agile HR structures teams around multi-disciplinary squads that work on solving specific people challenges.
Scrum and Kanban	HR teams adopt Scrum (sprints, stand-ups, retrospectives) or Kanban (visual workflows, continuous improvement) to manage HR projects efficiently.
Minimum Viable Products (MVPs)	Instead of rolling out fully developed HR programmes, Agile HR tests small-scale pilots, gathers feedback and refines before full implementation.
Employee personas and journey mapping	Borrowing from design thinking, Agile HR builds employee personas and maps their experiences to create personalized HR solutions.

The role of Product Owners in HR

In Agile environments, Product Owners define and prioritize work that delivers value. In HR, this role might be taken on by HR Business Partners (HRBPs) or new roles specifically designed to oversee people products.

A people Product Owner is responsible for:

- identifying HR priorities based on business strategy and employee needs;
- managing HR product roadmaps, ensuring iterative development and alignment with organizational goals;
- working with data and feedback loops to refine and enhance HR offerings.

For example, instead of viewing learning and development as a static catalogue of courses, an Agile HR function might create an adaptive, AI-driven learning ecosystem, where learning paths evolve dynamically based on employee skill progression and business demand.

REAL-WORLD EXAMPLE
Performance management as a product

Traditional performance management relies on annual appraisals, static competency frameworks and manager-led evaluations. An Agile, product-driven approach would:

- treat performance management as a product – continuously refined based on data and feedback;
- use real-time performance analytics instead of yearly ratings;
- implement frequent, lightweight check-ins rather than rigid appraisal cycles;
- provide AI-driven nudges and feedback loops tailored to individual employees.

Companies such as Google, Atlassian and ING have successfully transitioned to continuous performance models, eliminating outdated processes in favour of real-time feedback and coaching.

Conclusion

The integration of Agile and Product Management into HR 3.0 marks a significant departure from traditional, process-heavy HR models. By embracing value-driven, iterative and employee-centric approaches, HR can become a true driver of business agility. Product thinking allows HR to remain proactive rather than reactive, ensuring that every initiative aligns with business strategy and employee needs.

HR teams that adopt Agile and Product Management principles will find themselves not just supporting transformation, but leading it.

Progressive approaches to data and analytics in HR

HR 3.0 represents a major shift from traditional, process-driven HR functions to a more data-informed, agile and strategic operating model. In this new paradigm, data and analytics are no longer auxiliary functions that provide periodic reporting but core enablers of evidence-based decision making, workforce optimization and strategic foresight.

To do more with data and analytics in HR, organizations must:

- move beyond descriptive metrics (what happened) to predictive and prescriptive analytics (what will happen and how to respond);
- leverage real-time and dynamic insights rather than relying on static, historical data;
- integrate AI, machine learning and automation to enhance workforce intelligence;
- expand the role of People and Performance Analysts, who bridge HR strategy with data science.

This section explores progressive ways HR can maximize the value of data and analytics, along with the critical role of People and Performance Analysts in shaping the future of work.

The evolution of data-driven HR

Traditionally, HR has relied on simple, backward-looking metrics such as turnover rates, headcount reports or employee satisfaction scores. While these provide useful snapshots, they do little to drive proactive decision making. HR 3.0 will bring in a more sophisticated, forward-thinking approach, leveraging real-time data, AI-driven analytics and business intelligence tools. This evolution is evident in how organizations are shifting from traditional to progressive HR analytics (Table 6.3).

This transformation is not just about technology – it's about building a data culture within HR. This means training HR teams in data literacy, statistical thinking and analytical problem solving to ensure that insights drive business impact.

TABLE 6.3 HR metrics into progressive analytics

Traditional HR Metrics	Progressive HR Analytics
Absenteeism reports	Predictive models for absenteeism risk
Engagement survey results	Sentiment analysis from internal platforms
Employee turnover rates	AI-driven retention risk scoring
Learning & Development spend	Skills-based workforce analytics and capability gaps

Real-time HR analytics: moving beyond annual reporting

One of the most significant shifts needed in moving to an HR 3.0 Operating Model is the transition from static reporting cycles to real-time workforce intelligence. This means HR teams can:

- detect trends as they emerge rather than waiting for quarterly or annual reviews;

- act immediately on workforce issues, such as productivity declines, well-being concerns or early attrition risks;

- enable Agile workforce planning, ensuring HR strategies adapt dynamically to business needs.

REAL-WORLD EXAMPLE
AI-driven employee listening

Companies like Microsoft and Salesforce now use AI-powered sentiment analysis to gauge employee engagement in real time. Instead of relying on annual engagement surveys, they analyse:

- collaboration data (e.g. Teams, Slack, email patterns);

- feedback from performance check-ins and pulse surveys;

- employee behaviour signals, such as workload spikes or reduced participation in meetings.

This allows HR leaders to take proactive actions, such as adjusting workloads, offering mental health support or improving team collaboration.

Predictive and prescriptive analytics: from insight to action

A key advantage of modern HR analytics is predictive and prescriptive capabilities. Instead of merely tracking what has happened, organizations can anticipate what will happen and take preventive measures.

Predictive analytics in HR

Predictive models use historical data, AI and machine learning to forecast trends such as:

- turnover risk – identifying employees at high risk of leaving based on engagement, compensation trends and external job market signals;
- flight risk drivers – analysing reasons behind attrition (e.g. lack of career growth, pay disparity, leadership issues);
- performance forecasting – predicting which employees are likely to become high performers or need additional development;
- diversity and inclusion success rates – modelling how hiring patterns impact long-term workforce diversity.

Prescriptive analytics in HR

Prescriptive analytics goes one step further – it not only predicts outcomes but recommends specific actions to optimize results. Examples include:

- AI-powered learning recommendations – adaptive learning platforms suggest personalized courses based on employees' career paths and performance;
- optimized workforce scheduling – AI recommends staffing adjustments based on real-time business needs and employee availability;
- dynamic compensation strategies – predictive pay analytics help HR optimize salary adjustments to reduce attrition while maintaining cost efficiency.

People and performance analysts: the new data translators in HR

The rise of HR analytics has created a demand for specialists – People and Performance Analysts – who combine HR expertise with advanced analytical skills to deliver:

1   The translation of people data into business insights:

    o connecting workforce data with business outcomes, ensuring HR strategies align with financial and operational goals;

    o creating HR dashboards that visualize key trends in real time.

2 Predictive models for workforce strategy:

    o developing attrition risk models to help retain top talent;

    o designing career path simulations to identify future leaders.

3 Data-driven decision making in HR practices:

    o guiding HR teams in using data-backed evidence for policy decisions;

    o running A/B testing on HR interventions (e.g. testing different benefits packages for impact on retention).

The rise of the HR data science function

Forward-thinking companies are creating dedicated HR data science teams that work alongside People and Performance Analysts to:

- develop machine learning models for workforce planning;
- use network analysis to map internal collaboration patterns;
- integrate HR, finance and operational data for full workforce intelligence.

REAL-WORLD EXAMPLE
Data-driven HR in action

Company: A global tech firm with 30,000 employees.

    Problem: High attrition rates among mid-career professionals, leading to increased hiring costs.

HR analytics approach

1 Data integration: the HR team merged data from performance reviews, compensation, exit interviews and employee engagement platforms.

2 AI-driven insights: predictive models identified key attrition drivers (e.g. career stagnation, lack of leadership opportunities).

3 Targeted interventions:

    o a personalized learning and mentorship programme was introduced for employees at risk of leaving;

o   leadership development fast-tracks were created based on AI recommendations.

4   Outcome: attrition among mid-career professionals dropped by 27 per cent within 12 months.

Ethical considerations in HR data and analytics

With the increasing power of workforce analytics, HR must also navigate ethical risks, including:

- bias in AI models – ensuring predictive models do not reinforce discrimination (e.g. biased hiring or promotion algorithms);
- data privacy and consent – being transparent with employees on how their data is used;
- responsible monitoring – avoiding surveillance-style analytics that harm workplace trust.

Organizations should adopt ethical AI frameworks and HR data governance policies to ensure fairness, transparency and accountability.

HR 3.0 will strengthen the data-driven, agile and deeply integrated delivery of the business strategy. By leveraging real-time analytics, predictive intelligence and the expertise of People and Performance Analysts, HR can optimize workforce decisions, enhance employee experience and drive measurable business impact. The challenge is not just adopting new tools, but embedding a data-first mindset across HR teams. Organizations that successfully do this will transform HR from a support function into a strategic powerhouse, shaping the future of work with evidence-based, high-impact people decisions.

The role of Science in HR 3.0

HR 3.0 represents a shift from traditional HR practices to a more scientific, evidence-based and human-centred approach to workforce strategy. Central to this evolution is integrating People and Behavioural Science, Occupational and Organizational Psychology, and Social and Performance Science – disciplines that provide a deeper understanding of human behaviour, motivation, performance and workplace dynamics.

As HR moves beyond process-driven models to a more adaptive, data-informed and human-centric function, the use of scientific research and methodologies becomes crucial. Evidence-based HR is no longer just about policies and compliance – it is about leveraging scientific insights to create better work environments, improve decision making and drive high performance.

This section explores how scientific disciplines contribute to HR 3.0, shaping workforce strategies in talent management, leadership development, employee engagement and Organization Design.

Evidence-based HR: the scientific foundation

Historically, HR decisions have often been based on intuition, best practices and past experiences. However, as workplaces become more complex and fast-changing, organizations must rely on empirical research and data to drive decisions. This is where evidence-based HR (EBHR) emerges as a crucial framework.

EBHR is built on:

- Academic research: findings from psychology, neuroscience, sociology and management science.
- Organizational data: workforce analytics, employee feedback and performance metrics.
- Professional expertise: the practical experience of HR leaders and practitioners.
- Stakeholder perspectives: insights from employees, leaders and external market trends.

By combining scientific principles with real-world data, HR professionals can develop more effective policies, interventions and strategies that are tailored to human behaviour and workplace realities.

People and Behavioural Science: understanding workplace psychology

Behavioural Science helps HR teams understand, predict and influence employee behaviour through the study of motivation, decision making, biases and habits. Insights from this field are transforming HR functions.

TABLE 6.4 Key HR domains and links to sciences

Recruitment and hiring: reducing bias in decision making **Problem:** Traditional hiring processes are often subject to unconscious biases, affecting diversity and inclusion	Science-driven solution: • Using blind recruitment techniques (e.g. removing names and personal details from CVs). • Applying structured interviews and AI-driven assessments to improve hiring accuracy. • Designing behavioural nudges that prompt hiring managers to overcome biases in selection.
Performance and motivation: applying neuroscience to employee engagement **Problem:** Many traditional performance management systems rely on annual reviews, which fail to capture real-time engagement and productivity	Science-driven solution: • Using self-determination theory (SDT) to design autonomy-supportive workplaces that enhance motivation. • Applying gamification principles (e.g. reward systems, progress tracking) to encourage continuous learning and high performance. • Implementing real-time feedback loops based on dopamine-driven reinforcement strategies to sustain engagement.
Organizational change: behavioural interventions for adoption **Problem:** Resistance to change is one of the biggest barriers to organizational transformation	Science-driven solution: • Using nudge theory to encourage small, incremental changes in behaviour. • Designing habit-forming interventions to help employees adapt to new processes. • Leveraging social proof and peer influence to drive cultural shifts.

Occupational and Organizational Psychology: designing high-performing workplaces

Occupational and Organizational Psychology (OOP) is one of the most established scientific fields in HR. It provides insights into how workplace environments, leadership styles and team dynamics impact performance and well-being.

Some areas where we already apply this are shown in Table 6.5.

TABLE 6.5 Additional HR domains and links to sciences

Job design and well-being: the science of work	• Job crafting: Encouraging employees to shape their roles in ways that align with their strengths and interests. • Psychological safety: Creating environments where employees feel safe to voice opinions, take risks and innovate. • Workload balance: Using cognitive load theory to design workflows that prevent burnout and optimize cognitive performance.
Leadership development: neuroscience of decision making	• Emotional intelligence training: Leaders who understand how emotions shape decisions make better, more empathetic choices. • Adaptive leadership: Using cognitive flexibility training to help leaders manage VUCA (volatility, uncertainty, complexity, ambiguity) environments. • Resilience building: Applying positive psychology principles to develop mental toughness and stress management techniques for leaders.
Hybrid work and collaboration:	• Optimizing remote team performance. • Cognitive flow in remote work: Designing schedules that enhance focus and minimize digital fatigue. • Virtual trust-building strategies: Using psychological frameworks to strengthen remote team cohesion and collaboration. • AI-powered team dynamics: Leveraging organizational network analysis (ONA) to map informal communication flows and improve collaboration.

Social science and performance science: enhancing human capital

HR 3.0 also integrates insights from social science and performance science, which explore human interaction, group dynamics and high-performance behaviours.

SOCIAL SCIENCE IN HR: CULTURAL AND WORKPLACE SOCIOLOGY

• Social identity theory: understanding how group affiliations (e.g. gender, ethnicity, organizational role) shape workplace interactions and inclusion efforts.

- Network science in collaboration: using data to map social connections and identify key influencers within organizations.
- Cultural intelligence (CQ): applying sociological insights to navigate global and diverse workplaces.

PERFORMANCE SCIENCE: THE BIOLOGY OF PRODUCTIVITY

- Chronobiology in work scheduling: designing work rhythms based on circadian science to maximize energy levels.
- Neurofeedback for learning and development: using EEG and cognitive assessments to optimize learning experiences.
- Movement and productivity: applying ergonomic research to improve workplace environments and prevent physical strain.

HIGH-PERFORMANCE WORK CULTURES: LESSONS FROM ELITE ATHLETES

HR teams are increasingly borrowing strategies from sports science and elite performance coaching to build resilient, high-performing teams. Key applications include:

- mental rehearsal and visualization techniques – used in leadership training and high-stakes decision making;
- biofeedback for stress management – helping employees regulate heart rate variability (HRV) to reduce stress and improve focus;
- team cohesion strategies from sports psychology – enhancing collective performance through goal-setting and accountability structures.

REAL-WORLD EXAMPLE
Scientific HR in action

Company: A multinational financial services firm with 50,000 employees.

Challenge: Employee engagement scores were low and productivity was declining due to hybrid work challenges.

Science-based HR solution:

1 Behavioural Science applied to hybrid work:
   - used psychological nudges to encourage deep work and reduce *video call fatigue*;
   - designed an 'intentional collaboration model' to balance remote vs in-office interactions.

2 Performance science for energy management:

- o reorganized meeting schedules based on chronobiology insights, aligning critical thinking tasks with peak cognitive hours;
- o implemented recovery breaks based on sports psychology techniques to sustain performance.

3 Occupational psychology for leadership development:

- o trained managers in neuroscience-based coaching techniques to improve engagement;
- o used AI-powered feedback tools to enhance self-awareness in leadership behaviours.

Result: Employee engagement scores improved by 35 per cent, with a 20 per cent increase in productivity and lower burnout rates.

In conclusion

HR 3.0 is calling for a strong sense and utilization of science.

It blends psychology, neuroscience, social science and performance science to create more intelligent, human-centred work environments.

Organizations that embrace these disciplines will enhance employee experience and drive measurable business impact, positioning HR as a true strategic partner in the modern enterprise.

Technology integration in HR 3.0: digital tools and platforms for a smarter workforce

HR 3.0 significantly shifts from process-driven HR to a tech-enabled, data-driven and human-centred function. Technology integration is at the heart of this transformation, allowing HR to move beyond administrative tasks and focus on strategic workforce optimization, employee experience and organizational agility.

In this new model, digital tools and platforms are not just support systems – they are core enablers of HR strategy, allowing organizations to:

- automate repetitive tasks, freeing HR professionals to focus on high-value work;
- leverage AI and analytics to improve decision making;

- personalize employee experiences through digital solutions;
- enhance collaboration, engagement and learning with integrated digital ecosystems.

This section explores key technologies shaping HR 3.0, their impact and how organizations can maximize their potential.

The evolution of HR technology: from systems of record to intelligent platforms

Historically, HR technology focused on record-keeping and compliance through HRIS (Human Resource Information Systems) and ERP (Enterprise Resource Planning) systems. While these systems improved efficiency, they were not designed for agility, real-time decision making or employee-centric experiences.

HR 3.0 shifts HR technology from static systems of record to dynamic systems of intelligence, including:

- cloud-based platforms that integrate multiple HR functions;
- AI-driven solutions for recruitment, engagement and learning;
- employee self-service (ESS) tools for greater autonomy;
- real-time workforce analytics for predictive insights.

Modern HR technology ecosystems blend HRIS, AI, machine learning (ML), automation, and employee experience tools to create intelligent and adaptive HR functions.

AI and automation: transforming HR decision making

AI and automation fundamentally reshape HR operations, enabling faster, smarter and more personalized HR services.

AI IN TALENT ACQUISITION
Recruitment is one of the most AI-transformed HR areas. AI-powered tools:

- automate resume screening, ranking candidates based on job fit;
- use natural language processing (NLP) to analyse job descriptions and remove biased language;

- implement chatbots for candidate engagement, answering FAQs and scheduling interviews;
- use predictive analytics to assess cultural and skills fit, reducing turnover risk.

Example: Unilever uses AI-driven hiring tools, including video interview analysis and behavioural assessments, to improve hiring accuracy and reduce bias.

AI IN EMPLOYEE EXPERIENCE AND WELL-BEING

- AI-powered digital assistants provide employees with on-demand HR support (e.g. benefits queries, leave applications).
- Sentiment analysis tools gauge employee morale in real time, allowing HR to respond proactively.
- AI-driven well-being platforms offer personalized recommendations for mental health and stress management.

Real-world example: Microsoft's *Viva Insights* integrates with Teams to analyse work habits, detect burnout risks and suggest productivity improvements.

AUTOMATION IN HR OPERATIONS

- RPA (robotic process automation) eliminates repetitive HR tasks (e.g. payroll processing, compliance reporting).
- Self-service HR portals allow employees to manage HR transactions independently.
- AI-powered workforce planning optimizes headcount based on business demand.

Learning and development (L&D): the rise of AI-powered adaptive learning

HR 3.0 and a Product Management approach will shift L&D from one-size-fits-all training programmes to personalized, AI-fuelled and human relational learning experiences.

KEY INNOVATIONS IN DIGITAL LEARNING

- AI-driven skills mapping to align learning with career goals.
- Adaptive learning platforms that tailor content based on employee performance and preferences.
- Microlearning and gamification to increase engagement and retention.
- VR- and AR-based simulations for hands-on training experiences.

Real-world example: Walmart uses VR training for employees, reducing onboarding time and improving skills retention.

LEARNING EXPERIENCE PLATFORMS (LXPS)

Unlike traditional learning management systems (LMS), LXPs curate personalized learning paths by:

- using AI recommendations to suggest relevant courses;
- integrating social learning, allowing employees to learn from peers;
- leveraging content from multiple sources, including Massive Online Open Courses (MOOCs) and company knowledge bases.

Real-world example: Degreed and EdCast use AI to recommend training based on job roles, interests and skills gaps.

Employee engagement and collaboration: the digital workplace

HR 3.0 places employee experience at the centre by integrating collaboration tools, recognition platforms and engagement analytics into a seamless digital ecosystem.

HR TECH FOR EMPLOYEE ENGAGEMENT

- Real-time pulse surveys (e.g. Peakon, Culture Amp) to gauge sentiment and engagement.
- AI-driven recognition platforms (e.g. Bonusly) that reward performance with peer-to-peer feedback.
- Digital EX (employee experience) platforms integrating well-being, career development and internal communication.

COLLABORATION TOOLS FOR THE HYBRID WORKFORCE

- Cloud-based collaboration (e.g. Slack, Microsoft Teams) for remote and hybrid teams.
- AI-driven workflow automation to streamline approvals and HR tasks.
- Digital workspace analytics to track productivity trends and collaboration patterns.

Real-world example: Atlassian uses AI-driven collaboration analytics to improve hybrid team performance and optimize workflows.

People analytics and workforce intelligence

One of the biggest advantages of HR 3.0 technology integration is real-time workforce analytics, allowing HR teams to make evidence-based decisions.

PREDICTIVE ANALYTICS IN HR

- Turnover prediction models to identify employees at risk of leaving.
- Diversity and inclusion analytics to measure representation and hiring trends.
- Performance forecasting to assess high-potential talent.

PRESCRIPTIVE ANALYTICS: TURNING INSIGHTS INTO ACTION

- AI-powered analytics provide recommendations for workforce planning.
- HR data visualization tools (e.g. Tableau, Power BI) enable data-driven decisions.
- Organizational Network Analysis (ONA) maps internal collaboration and influence structures.

Real-world example: IBM uses AI-driven 'proactive retention programmes' based on predictive analytics, reducing turnover rates by 30 per cent.

Blockchain in HR: the future of secure HR transactions

Blockchain technology is emerging as a game-changer in HR, particularly in credentials verification, payroll security and smart contracts.

APPLICATIONS OF BLOCKCHAIN IN HR

- Tamper-proof digital resumes for verifying candidate credentials.
- Smart contracts for automated payroll and compliance processes.
- Decentralized identity management, improving data security and privacy.

Real-world example: SAP and Velocity Network are piloting blockchain-based HR credential verification to streamline hiring.

REAL-WORLD EXAMPLE
Technology-driven HR transformation

A global e-commerce company with 100,000+ employees who were challenged by:

- HR processes that were manual and inefficient, slowing down hiring and engagement;
- employee engagement that was declining due to poor digital experience;
- the lack of real-time analytics that prevented HR from making strategic decisions.

Tech-enabled HR 3.0 solution:

1 AI-powered recruitment tools reduced hiring time by 40 per cent.
2 Automated onboarding via chatbots improved new hire experience.
3 Personalized learning platforms increased engagement in training by 50 per cent.
4 Predictive analytics on retention risk enabled proactive retention strategies.

Outcome:

- Workforce productivity improved by 30 per cent.
- Employee engagement scores went up by 25 per cent.
- The HR team tackled more strategic initiatives rather than administrative work.

Technology integration is the cornerstone of HR 3.0, enabling HR teams to be more strategic, data-driven and employee-centric. The future of HR is AI-powered, analytics-driven and deeply embedded in digital ecosystems, ensuring that HR not only keeps pace with business transformation but leads it.

HR leaders who embrace digital tools will create more adaptive, intelligent and high-impact people strategies, making HR a true driver of business success in the digital era.

WHAT WE'VE COVERED IN THIS CHAPTER

In this chapter, we explored the core principles that define HR 3.0, emphasizing a shift from traditional, compliance-driven HR to an agile, product-led and technology-enabled function. The key takeaways include:

1   **The shift to Product Management in HR:**

   o   HR should adopt a Product Management mindset, designing HR initiatives as products that are user-centred, continuously iterated and data-driven.

   o   HR 'products' include policies, talent acquisition frameworks, onboarding experiences, learning and development programmes, and performance management systems..

2   **Agility and product thinking in HR 3.0:**

   o   HR must embrace Agile methodologies – prioritizing iteration, user feedback and rapid adaptability over static, one-size-fits-all solutions.

   o   The HR Product Owner role is emerging – responsible for workforce experience, talent products and data-driven HR solutions.

3   **Progressive approaches to data and analytics in HR:**

   o   AI-driven workforce intelligence helps anticipate attrition risks, optimize workforce planning and personalize employee experiences.

   o   HR data science functions are growing, with specialized roles such as People and Performance Analysts to bridge HR strategy with advanced analytics.

   o   Ethical considerations, such as AI bias, data privacy and responsible monitoring are critical in HR's data evolution.

4   **The role of science in HR 3.0:**

   o   People and Behavioural Science helps HR understand and influence employee motivation, decision making and engagement.

   o   Occupational and Organizational Psychology provides insights into workplace design, leadership effectiveness and psychological safety.

   o   Performance science and social science contribute to high-performance cultures, adaptive work models and employee well-being strategies.

5   **Technology integration in HR 3.0:**

   o   HR is evolving from process-driven to tech-enabled and digital-first, leveraging AI-powered talent acquisition, employee experience tools and adaptive learning platforms for personalized skill development.

References and further reading

Ariely, D (2008) *Predictably Irrational: The hidden forces that shape our decisions*, New York: HarperCollins

Bersin, J (2023) The role of generative AI In HR is now becoming clear, https://joshbersin.com/2023/09/the-role-of-generative-ai-in-hr-is-now-becoming-clear/ (archived at https://perma.cc/PXN3-AJWM)

Christensen, C M (1997) *The Innovator's Dilemma: When new technologies cause great firms to fail*, Boston: Harvard Business Review Press

Deloitte (2024) 2024 Global Human Capital Trends: AI in HR and workforce intelligence, www2.deloitte.com/content/dam/insights/articles/glob176836_global-human-capital-trends-2024/DI_Global-Human-Capital-Trends-2024.pdf (archived at https://perma.cc/X73H-J6LT)

Kahneman, D (2011) *Thinking, Fast and Slow*, London: Penguin

Lewin, K (1951) *Field Theory in Social Science: Selected theoretical papers*, New York: Harper & Row

Laloux, F (2014) *Reinventing Organizations: A guide to creating organizations inspired by the next stage of human consciousness*, Brussels: Nelson Parker

McKinsey & Company (2022) Generative AI and the future of HR, www.mckinsey.com/capabilities/people-and-organizational-performance/our-insights/generative-ai-and-the-future-of-hr (archived at https://perma.cc/UK7J-KACF)

Perri, M (2018) *Escaping the Build Trap: How effective product management creates real value*, Boston: O'Reilly Media

Pink, D H (2009) *Drive: The surprising truth about what motivates us*, New York: Riverhead Books

Senge, P M (1990) *The Fifth Discipline: The art and practice of the learning organization*, New York: Doubleday

Thaler, R and Sunstein, C (2008) *Nudge: Improving decisions about health, wealth, and happiness*, New Haven, CT: Yale University Press

Ulrich, D (1997) *Human Resource Champions: The next agenda for adding value and delivering results*, Boston: Harvard Business School Press

7

Implementing and transitioning to HR 3.0

Structure is not strategy. The real challenge is designing an operating model that turns intent into everyday action.

ROGER L MARTIN, PROFESSOR EMERITUS AND FORMER DEAN OF THE ROTMAN SCHOOL OF MANAGEMENT AT THE UNIVERSITY OF TORONTO AND AUTHOR OF *PLAYING TO WIN*

WHAT'S COVERED IN THIS CHAPTER

- **Strategy development:** A narrative and compelling case, a roadmap and an actionable plan for organizations to transition to using the HR 3.0 Operating Model.

- **Key tools and frameworks:** Introduce tools and frameworks for successful implementation that are both existing, emerging and adjacent practices for HR and People professionals.

- **Change management:** Strategies for managing organizational change and gaining buy-in.

- **People, planet and prosperity-centric design:** Explore how HR 3.0 prioritizes the need for a more balanced and progressive people experience in work, and planet-pro ways to deliver value in business through HR.

Getting started

HR 3.0 is still a conceptual HR Operating Model – and this book introduces it to the world, alongside other progressive designs reflecting the need for a reimagined way to create value from the work of People professionals and HR functions/teams in a very changeable world.

It is much like the HR Business Partner model concept in 1997, built from the perspectives of other parts of the business operating world and responding to a very different working world. Just prior to the dot com boom (and bust), this model ushered in a new approach for HR to become a more strategic player in the game of work. Now, 30 years later, we are increasingly impacted by:

- advancing technologies and sciences;

- challenging social, political, environmental and economic conditions;

- aspirations, needs and desires of people facing all of those factors and increasing life expectancy;

- the velocity, intensity, complexity and ferocity of change, transformation and adaptation.

So the conditions of both the introduction of the prevailing model for HR – the Business Partner model and HR 3.0 – are creating a 'perfect storm' of challenge, opportunity and desired outcomes.

In 1997, the HR profession faced the opportunity and the challenge to remodel its former personnel and industrial relations heritage into a more business-aligned, specialized and broadened approach to create impact.

And we are now faced with the realization that perhaps a 30-year-old model – with adaptations of course – has reached its 'due by' date and it's time for something new. Certainly our other suggested models in Chapter 4 are demonstrating and urging the need for an 'upgrade' or wholescale new version. Enter HR 3.0 as that version-controlled shift, perhaps?

So, what do you do first if you are intrigued enough by the HR 3.0 Operating Model?

Introducing the HR 3.0 Operating Model into your organization is not just a structural change – it's a cultural and philosophical shift. To succeed, HR leaders should approach this with clarity, intentionality and a focus on impact. Here are some suggestions for how to begin.

We will use an adapted approach for value creation pioneered by a partner organization of mine, The Bridge Partnership, using an adapted approach from Professor David Wessels, who co-authored the book *Valuation: Measuring and managing the value of companies.*

It begins with the establishment of a strategy and the choices we make

In a business sense this would be through questions like *Where do we play?* and *How do we win?* Establishing markets, sectors, geographies and scale will all inform and be contained in the Business and Operating Model (as we've already highlighted).

We then look deeper into the Operating Model for more of the systems we bring in through our Organization Design and goal-setting into financial measures and actual accounting measures.

Professor Wessels' work on *driving value creation* emphasizes financial capital returns through key metrics such as:

a Return on Total Assets (ROTA);

b Return on Capital Employed (ROCE);

c Return on Capital Invested (ROCI), linking these to an organization's earning potential and strategic growth.

In an HR context, these financial measures underscore the importance of aligning people strategies with value creation – ensuring that workforce investments, capability building and leadership development directly contribute to financial returns:

- HR can drive higher ROTA and ROCE by optimizing talent allocation, improving workforce productivity and implementing strategic workforce planning that maximizes human capital efficiency.
- By leveraging HR analytics and performance metrics, HR leaders can demonstrate the tangible impact of people investments on financial outcomes, reinforcing the function's role as a value creator rather than a cost centre.

Before we get too deep into accounting methodologies, Wessels' work led to ways to set the enterprise up to deliver increased ROTA and ROCE through a looping method of adaptive business practices, many of which we all recognize, just not in the order and flow adapted by the Bridge Partnership.

Establish how we drive sustainable performance

- Purposeful advantage – *why we exist*
- Culture advantage – *how we run our business*
- Change leadership [Agile] advantage – *how our people lead change*

Whilst not necessarily revelatory, those three core parameters form into the flow of critical thinking in establishing the actions, structures, flows of work, alignment, adaptable practices and organization of resources into a coherent, high-functioning business or business unit.

The starting point in establishing all of this is with leaders (in particular) facing into two distinct forces – the **Current Reality** and the **Awakening of Possibilities.** Without immediately crafting these into a vision, strategy or tagging them to company values, a more exploratory, interrogative and imaginative method reveals how much of our intellectual and actual capability resides in our thoughts about how to make something run efficiently and effectively with renewable, adaptive and responsive ways to operate in complex operating environments.

From this, we can take the thinking into more recognizable realms taught on our MBA programmes: our **Purpose, Vision, Values and Emergent Strategy** (not the actual document per se but more the narrative and aspired direction of travel, plan of action and performance measures). This is often referred to as 'The Leadership Agenda' and moves us from the quality of our *awareness* to the quality of our *thinking.*

We can then use our thinking and capture of these elements to take us into our quality of *action* and the capitalization of our transformational capabilities and resources, established through our **Vibrant Culture,** in our **Liberated Teams** and through our **Leadership Partnerships.**

It also takes us into the quality of our organizing (many would say our Organization Design and Development) – our:

- enabling structures and systems;
- congruent processes;
- fluent communication;
- excelling capabilities and practices;
- having the right people;
- in a facilitative environment, and (crucially for HR and People Managers);
- aligned people systems – this is where our operation becomes the engine room and beating heart of performance, learning, culture and sustainable delivery of our mission.

We will now use this model and flow to explore how to get going and implement your version of HR 3.0 as your operating model for HR, People and Culture.

Stage 1: Quality of awareness and ambition levers

We explore this through two lenses:

1 confronting reality

2 awakening possibilities

In this stage, we're finding out what we are **most and least** comfortable with about our current operation, future potential and our sense of efficiency and effectiveness.

Making a list of those most and least comfortable factors is a solid place to start in testing the current performance and desired aspirations. Whilst this may seem subjective and without evidence, the 'lived experience' and imagination of possibilities has validity to then define and test throughout the rest of this model's flow.

Here are some plausible deductions from an archetypal HR Leadership Team conducting this exercise.

TABLE 7.1 Confronting the reality of HR deliverables and impact

Workforce planning and skills gaps: We recognize that while we have strong recruitment processes, we struggle with workforce planning for future skills needs.
Employee engagement and retention: We feel confident in our employee benefits but realize through exit interviews that career progression opportunities are unclear.
Diversity, equity and inclusion (DEI): Leadership acknowledges that they are committed to DEI but struggle to translate policy into meaningful impact.
Performance management: We are comfortable with technical skill evaluations but struggle with embedding behavioural competencies into performance reviews.

TABLE 7.2 Awakening possibilities for HR deliverables and impact

Agile workforce planning: We recognize that moving away from rigid job descriptions to skills-based hiring could create more adaptability.
AI & HR tech: While automation in HR may seem daunting, leveraging AI-driven tools for talent analytics or personalized L&D pathways could redefine efficiency.
Experimenting with new work models: If flexible working has been adopted in pockets, we should explore how to scale hybrid, asynchronous or outcome-based work models for greater impact.
From performance reviews to continuous feedback: If annual reviews feel ineffective, we envision a transition to real-time performance coaching with data-backed insights.
Evolving HR's role: Instead of being a compliance-driven function, we aspired to reposition HR as a *Product and Value Creator* – shaping experiences, culture and business outcomes rather than just managing transactions.

From this stage of the flow we have identified some 'where to play' and 'how to win' factors that we want to get behind and do something about.

It's a start but it needs to be sense-checked and embedded into something more coherent, visionary, practical and aligned to business goals and successes. So we then head to our next stage.

Stage 2: Quality of thinking and directional levers

Here, we are ready to stress-test our thinking on ambitions and realities through four key lenses:

1 **Our purpose.** Why we exist and what we serve in the world.
2 **Our vision.** As an enterprise, we should have one – what we aspire to be, deliver, create value and have impact on.
3 **Our values.** How we have agreed, as a business, we will be. Our code of conduct, our espoused sense of behavioural norms and attitudinal convergence. Are we fast, deliberate, visionary, reliable, pioneering, credible, etc.
4 **Our emergent strategy.** We may have a drafted business strategy and/or a people strategy – what we would be looking for is a congruence in that our strategies are explicit, enabling and reflective of the aspirations and reality. If there is a link, we are clearly aligned. If there is not, we may need to do either some research or diagnosis and then with that evidence, seek to have our aspirations and reality included.

Working through these critical factors and turning those strategic objectives into packages of work, projects, products and service line enhancements and additions gives us our leadership agenda. It's then that we can turn our attention to the crucial elements that will help us deliver – which is our next phase.

Stage 3: Quality of action and transformational levers

As with any shift and significant change, we need three really key aspects as we go from concepts and plans into activities:

- leadership coherence, cohesion and collaboration
- liberated, enabled and supported teams
- a vibrant and powerful culture

I'm going to start with culture as this is a REALLY important part of this next phase of shifting from HR 2.0 to HR 3.0 and is something we are stewarding across the organization anyway.

In defining culture, many people say this term represents 'the way things are done around here'. It is that but I believe it is more explicit in the sense of 'how does being part of an organization/team/community make me feel?'

Sure things get done in a particular way, but that's still processes and decisions and rituals (which make up some of the elements of culture). Culture, though, is woven in the sense of belonging, trust, participation, challenge, support, excitement, possibility, drive, determination, stamina, care, attention, reciprocity, recognition, appreciation, valour, voracity and virtue.

So culture is more likely about feelings than how to process things. *If the organisation/team/function had a soul, it's that.*

How we behave, the rules we are bound by, the intellect we deploy and acquire, the comradeship, the inclusion and support, the care, the diligence and the integrity of what is promised in the work we do all impact our feelings.

So, if human capital is the differentiator that truly sets apart the most admired, balanced and successful enterprises on the planet, is culture the determinant of whether that human capital is invested, spent and used well? It quite likely is.

But without a strong, stabilizing and inspiring culture, there's a price to pay for that success. It isn't always 'bankable' and some companies may have huge cash balances in the black, but if culture is in the red, beware.

Do you, therefore, over-index culture over everything? No. But under-indexing culture is a drain you may not notice and could catch you out when you least expect it. I often say that when your processes, technology and even leadership fail, your culture will see you through.

Which is why, in shifting from one operating model to another, culture is really important to not only 'get off on the right foot' but to create a strengthening layer as you emerge into new processes, roles, accountabilities, systems, decision making, spans of control and interoperation across people, teams and the new spaces being created by the operating model.

Vibrant culture in this instance doesn't mean hedonistic party culture; it means that culture is an energy force, a palpable sense of something that binds you all and holds you together even when there are fragile systems and processes emerging or not tested yet, and that the exploration and discovery of the new operating model's cadence, flow and impact are still not yet fully evident.

In looking more closely at a vibrant culture in readying to move to HR 3.0, there are some exercises and approaches that could really help define and activate things.

Exploring and capturing the essence of vibrant culture

Before designing interventions, the team must define what a vibrant culture *looks, feels and acts like* in their part of the organization (or as a whole). For this work on looking to shift to the HR 3.0 Operating Model, we'll keep it 'close to home' and focus on the specifics of the vibrant culture within the HR team.

Culture spectrum mapping would help you surface the current state and aspirations for culture (see Table 7.3) and create a coherent, managed and long-standing programme of activities that will build culture, create change and channel behaviours.

Review these at team gatherings, embed them into performance and team agreements and have them build meaning and create value as much as your operational processes.

Culture in action storyboarding can identify how people actually experience culture and where gaps exist:

- Ask the team to pair up and create short 'storyboards' or narratives about 'culture moments' – both good and less so.
- Review and analyse common themes to bridge the gap between stated culture and lived reality.
- Set up actions from the gap analysis and how to check progress and track culture shifts.

TABLE 7.3 Culture spectrum mapping examples

1	Create a visual spectrum with opposing cultural attributes, such as: • *Risk-averse* ↔ *Experimentation-led* • *Hierarchical* ↔ *Empowered teams* • *Process-heavy* ↔ *Agile and fluid*
2	Work with the team to place where the HR team is on a spectrum or a range of different parameters on their own spectrum.
3	Then, plot where the team wants to be through three horizons – this year, next and beyond.
4	Discuss the cultural shifts needed and how we can enable them.
5	Plot the actions in a backlog of tasks that are prioritized and linked/connected.
6	Allocate leads for the tasks and create a Scrum Board (to-do; doing and done columns) to review progress on your culture-building work.

Actioning a vibrant culture through HR 3.0

The HR 3.0 model requires HR to move from being passive culture custodians to culture designers.

'HR AS PRODUCT DESIGNERS' – CULTURE MVPS (MINIMUM VIABLE PRACTICES)
Treat culture like a product – design, test and iterate:

- Break the HR team into **cross-functional squads** with employees from different areas.

- Assign each squad a challenge (e.g. 'How can we embed psychological safety?' or 'How can we reward innovation beyond monetary incentives?').

- Have teams **prototype** small interventions (e.g. peer recognition rituals, a network of culture mentors, micro-learning nudges).

- Pilot these MVPs in **low-risk environments** and measure impact before scaling.

THE VIBRANT CULTURE OPERATING SYSTEM (OS) CANVAS
Ensure that culture is embedded in daily operations.

- Adapt the business model canvas into a culture OS canvas, with sections for:

  o key cultural drivers (e.g. autonomy, collaboration, diversity);

  o mechanisms and rituals (e.g. decision-making forums, leadership storytelling);

  o HR 3.0 levers (e.g. skills-based talent models, networked leadership);

  o metrics (e.g. engagement, attrition, cross-functional collaboration rates).

- The HR team can then co-design this with their wider colleagues from different functions and departments.

Utilizing vibrant culture for business impact

CULTURE X BUSINESS PERFORMANCE LINKAGE WORKSHOP
Align culture interventions with business KPIs. A vibrant culture isn't just about experience – it must drive organizational outcomes:

- The HR team maps how culture factors (e.g. trust, agility, psychological safety) correlate with key business outcomes (e.g. innovation speed, customer satisfaction, revenue growth).

- Test a hypothesis – such as 'If we strengthen our learning culture, how does that impact talent retention and innovation?'

- Co-design culture interventions with direct business ROI to create a culture strategy that is business-relevant, not just a 'feel-good' initiative.

CULTURE INTELLIGENCE DASHBOARD
Create a real-time, data-driven culture pulse check:

- Define three to five core culture indicators (e.g. cross-team collaboration, leadership trust, employee voice).

- Use a mix of pulse surveys, network analysis and sentiment tracking.

- Set up monthly culture check-ins where leaders respond to real-time insights rather than waiting for an annual engagement survey.

- Culture shifts from a soft concept to a measurable business asset.

A closing thought: a vibrant culture is a system, not an initiative

For HR 3.0 to embed a vibrant culture:

- it must be systemic – linked to leadership, incentives and operations
- it must be iterative – tested and evolved like a product
- it must be measurable – connected to business outcomes

By applying these exercises, HR moves from being the 'owner of culture' to enabling a self-sustaining, high-impact culture system.

Into operational mode – our delivery agenda

We've now got to the point where we've dealt with much of the intellectual, social and conceptual elements of how we would plot much of what we need to move forward with introducing our new HR 3.0 Operating Model. But – and there is a but – it won't be 'real' until we look at how we **organize**.

In Chapter 1, we explored the linkages and differences between an operating model and Organization Design. They are connected but distinct. Operating models are the conceptualization of how we operate, and the Organization Design is exactly that – how we get the moving parts into a flow so that people and our processes are systematically aligned for optimal efficiency, effectiveness and overall performance.

In using this value creation model, we're now at the point where a lot of operational, tactical and procedural things come together.

The list of elements then is:

1 **enabling structures and systems**

2 **congruent processes**

3 **fluent communication**

4 **excelling capabilities and practices**

5 having the **right people**

6 in a **facilitative environment,** and

7 (crucially for HR and People Managers) **aligned people systems**

It is at this stage that our practitioner colleagues will be most acutely attuned to see what their role and experience of this new model will be like.

In traditional Organization Design, we use much of what Professor Henry Mintzberg calls his 'Nine Parameters'.

Aligning HR 3.0 with Mintzberg's Nine Design Parameters

As HR teams transition to HR 3.0, it is essential to rethink how we design roles, processes and structures. Henry Mintzberg's *Nine Design Parameters* offers a valuable framework to ensure that the fluid and intersectional nature of HR 3.0 is aligned with organizational effectiveness. By leveraging these parameters, we can redefine HR roles from rigid, task-based positions to more open and adaptive functions that enable agility, collaboration and value creation.

TABLE 7.4 Using Professor Henry Mintzberg's Nine Parameters

Job specialization → adaptive roles and skills-based HR	Traditional HR models emphasize job specialization, with fixed roles such as HR Administrators, LandD Officers, and ER Specialists. HR 3.0 moves toward skills-based work, where HR professionals develop broad competencies across multiple domains (e.g., data analytics, behavioural science, digital HR tools). This shift encourages fluidity and cross-functional contributions rather than siloed expertise.
Behaviour formalization → Agile HR practices	Mintzberg's model recognizes that rigid rule enforcement limits adaptability. HR 3.0 embraces principles over policies, emphasizing human-centred decision making and real-time problem-solving instead of bureaucratic compliance-heavy processes.

(continued)

TABLE 7.4 (Continued)

Training and indoctrination → continuous learning and growth mindset	While traditional HR roles focus on predefined training, HR 3.0 fosters continuous skill development, leveraging digital learning platforms, coaching and micro-learning. HR teams must develop adaptability as a core competency, ensuring professionals can shift roles and respond to new challenges.
Unit grouping → cross-functional HR teams	Instead of siloed HR functions, HR 3.0 clusters roles around strategic outcomes, such as employee experience, workforce planning and organizational agility. This approach mirrors agile, product-based teams that continuously iterate and adapt to organizational needs.
Unit size → flexible HR capacity and fluid resourcing	Traditional HR structures assign work based on headcount, while HR 3.0 optimizes talent flow based on demand, leveraging gig-based HR professionals, cross-functional project teams and AI augmentation to manage workloads dynamically.
Planning and control systems → data-driven HR decision making	HR 3.0 integrates predictive analytics, AI-driven insights, and real-time feedback loops to drive decision making rather than relying on static annual reports or workforce audits.
Liaison devices → networks and HR ecosystems	Mintzberg emphasizes coordination mechanisms such as task forces and project groups. HR 3.0 takes this further by leveraging networks over hierarchy, enabling HR professionals to collaborate across business units, external partners and digital platforms in real-time.
Decentralization → distributed decision making in HR	HR 3.0 decentralizes authority, giving people and teams agency to make decisions at the closest point of impact. Instead of HR acting as a central enforcer, it enables employees and managers to access self-service, AI-driven HR solutions and peer-to-peer decision-making frameworks.
Horizontal and vertical specialization → T-shaped HR professionals	HR 3.0 encourages professionals to develop both deep expertise (vertical) and broad, intersectional skills (horizontal). HR teams transition from rigid role descriptions to T-shaped roles, blending technical, strategic and interpersonal capabilities

Mintzberg's Nine Parameters framework offers so much that even more unorthodox or experimental versions of operations can apply. It shows how even the most traditional HR functions can recalibrate themselves towards a more fluid and adaptive model, which HR 3.0 has at its very core. However, there is still a lot to do in shifting mental models and the ways people have become accustomed to operating in their roles, functions, specializations and 'lanes'.

Preparing HR teams for open and adaptive roles

To transition from static, narrowly defined HR roles to open and adaptive HR functions, organizations should implement:

- **Skills-based work allocation:** Move away from rigid job descriptions by mapping skills to projects, rather than roles to departments.

- **HR capability academies:** Introduce continuous learning initiatives focusing on digital literacy, business acumen, Systems Thinking and behavioural science.

- **Agile work practices:** Shift HR teams to work in cross-functional sprints, using iterative problem solving and rapid experimentation.

- **Mentorship and job rotation:** Encourage rotational assignments across different HR domains to develop multi-disciplinary thinking.

- **Empowerment through technology:** Equip HR teams with AI-powered decision-making tools, real-time dashboards and self-service solutions to drive decentralized autonomy.

- **Psychological safety and experimentation:** Foster a culture where HR professionals are encouraged to experiment (safely), fail fast and iterate without fear of rigid performance consequences.

Conclusion

By aligning HR 3.0 with Mintzberg's Nine Design Parameters, HR teams can ensure their function evolves into a dynamic, skills-driven and intersectional function. This transition moves HR from a support function to a strategic enabler of business success, where fluid, adaptable roles replace static, traditional job titles.

HR professionals of the future will not be confined to the role of an 'HR Administrator' or 'L&D Officer' but will instead become **HR Strategists, Culture Architects, Workforce Scientists** and **Employee Experience Designers** – driving real business impact through adaptive, integrated and human-centred design.

Creating a transition plan

Transitioning to HR 3.0 requires shifts in mindsets, processes and collaboration. The traditional approach to this would be to:

- communicate the benefits of HR 3.0 clearly to all levels of the organization;
- appoint change champions across departments to advocate for and support the transition;
- provide training and resources to help HR professionals adapt to new ways of working.

With HR 3.0 this is a much bigger shift and HR is likely to be pioneering a more fluid and adaptable way of structuring and working that goes beyond this linear approach.

In HR 3.0 we are operating less in silos, with vertical and tightly bound discipline-based roles, and instead we are moving to **spaces** and intersections in those spaces. More specifically:

- **Product** space
- **Process** space
- **Systems** space
- **Science** space

with people at the centre intersection of all four spaces, and the sense of meaning and purpose connected to the four spaces/zones with people at the heart of it.

In helping the HR team shift to spaces from their previously tightly defined realms, we would be wise to invite the team to map the work the HR team does into those spaces. This can be done by constructing a **Systems Map** to show how things flow and interconnect, through things like analysis, decisions, actions, evaluation, adaptation, delivery and measurement of effectiveness.

This team approach to all the work we have to do in an HR function of whatever size will provide a really powerful reflective exercise that proves:

1 How complex and intertwined a lot of our work is.

2 How there are flows that are standardized and many that are more variable, handling complex people, culture, learning and performance elements.

3 How we allocate responsibilities and use our capabilities in those workflows. There are many administrative processing inputs and outputs, alongside specialized, expertise-based interventions in design, deployment and evaluative work unique to HR.

4 The volumes of repeat, regularized work and the lower-volume but high-intensity work, which we might call exceptions.

5 How all of this aligns to business goals and strategy, people's needs and aspirations, and how it fits into compliance, value-add, pioneering and advanced approaches to people, culture, learning and performance.

This work will involve classic Organization Design principles of looking at the capabilities needed to do work of a standardized and variable/complex nature, and map that to the capabilities we have to form into newly cast roles.

As a reminder, HR 3.0 does not provide a 'laundry list' of roles, which we're perhaps used to in the existing operating model approaches. Instead we have a few 'starting point' roles, like:

- **Practice leads** – this is a role where a specialist expert role might currently exist in the form of a Centre of Excellence (CoE) – an ER specialist, a learning and development practitioner, a reward analyst. We are suggesting HR 3.0 does not need such roles to form into a CoE but to create capability pools of people who can deliver on such expert areas but also leverage other expertise they have, such as project management, drafting skills or creative design.

- **Systems designers** – creating (again) a pool of people who have skills in designing systems of work; implementation, integration and ongoing operation of digital systems; or learning and performance systems that support real-time, self-directed learning and not just courses and events.

- **Data analysts** – specialists in complex data sets around people and performance who can elevate our information systems to go beyond demographic and absence reporting into more dynamic and deductive data trails that help the business with its sustainable performance and reporting.

- **People scientists and psychologists** – ok, not every one- or two-person HR team can afford the 'luxury' of qualified people science or psychology degrees and experiences. However, the point of this is to show how much we can and should use more people science as part of our evidence-based HR approaches. For too long, the profession has been somewhat mired by accusations of not truly being a profession of the likes of financial accountants, research and development and supply chain expertise. And in pursuing a more robust and appropriate level of evidence to back up our practice, we've *doubled down* on the pursuit of spreadsheet-friendly data, when in reality, it's that AND strongly evidenced people science, psychology and behavioural economics. So if you are a one- or two-person HR team, what are the relevant and appropriate sciences that bolster the work you do? Because adding that capability will help you leverage and strengthen your position, arguments and decisions. There isn't enough science in the boardrooms of any company (bar perhaps consumer behaviours). This role/space will strengthen not only HR's value creation, but the entire enterprise.

- **Product Management** – where we craft the 'consumables' that create value for our colleagues. Policies, programmes, compliance and experiences of work which are valuable and deliver the more standardized elements of our people proposition

- **Relationship brokers** – where we handle our internal clients in a trusted, strategic and interpersonal sense to help them deliver the best outcomes in their part of the operation. Client account management is used in the commercial world but is a single point of contact offering solutions and enabling the drive to excel in all aspects of people, culture, learning and performance. Not a quasi-HR advisor/business partner – a collaborative force going beyond functional leadership and traditional management.

- **Meaning makers** – the force for good and encapsulation of the sense that people belong to something worthwhile that includes and inspires them to achieve and do their best in the balanced, dedicated application of their skills and creativity. Perhaps the most radical (but also in conversations with HR professionals the most applauded) addition to our roles in HR. Purpose and meaning are seen in study after study of the psychology of work to be crucial and yet they are absent in all bar some leaders' strong assimilation of purpose and meaning in how things run. A meaning maker in HR is not unique to the Chief People Officer or HR Director but sits very firmly in their *centrifugal force* element of representing the entire function at a senior level.

More on the Meaning Maker role

I prompted one of our AI chat tools to explain this role and here's the output from that prompt – which is (perhaps) surprisingly on point for an application that has no experience of being a people professional in the real world.

The Meaning Maker role in HR 3.0 is about translating work into purpose, culture into lived experience and strategy into human connection. In a world where employees seek more than just being paid, HR must go beyond transactional tasks to curate narratives, rituals and environments that make work meaningful. The Meaning Maker fosters psychological ownership, ensuring that employees see their contributions as valuable and impactful. They design experiences, embed purpose into everyday work and amplify shared stories that align people with the organization's mission. Whether through culture storytelling, designing purpose-driven career pathways or human-centred leadership practices, the Meaning Maker ensures that HR is not just a function, but the custodian of meaning, belonging and purpose in the workplace.

Meaning making doesn't just sit in one role. It's in all HR roles in this model, although a senior figure in the team who can 'steward' this concept into actuality would be helpful. So for ease of implementation, perhaps the HR Director or Chief People Officer can initially assume this stewarding role.

Here are some examples of how this might play through some 'use cases'.

The Product Management function has recut all our policies to aspire to more noble, elevated senses of guiding behaviours and complying with employment legislation.

As a final review, a Meaning Maker applies the ultimate tests:

- Does this policy (product) strengthen the connection to the meaning and purpose of working here and delivering on our ambitions and mission?
- How does it make people feel about belonging here?
- How inclusive and inspiring is it?
- Does it make people feel proud to work here and likely engender a stronger psychological and emotional contract to their commitment to us as their employer?
- Does it give team leaders confidence and assurance that they can gracefully and powerfully handle any potential breaches of our code of conduct, negating the need for early HR intervention?
- Would this product be the envy of our competitors, and would they instantly want to replicate it and use what we've carefully crafted?

These might seem like unnecessary and overly comforting elements for functional processing. Still, the acid test goes beyond compliance and into the emotional psyche of people who have chosen to join us through their employment.

Meaning Maker, then, is more an overarching role to all who work in HR. As the guardians of the people proposition and employee experience, if we cannot find how our work is strengthened, supported and enabled by the meaning and purpose of working here, we're still transacting and not transforming how our people feel and can apply themselves to working with us.

In a world that is increasingly harder to make sense of, meaning and purpose at work is a powerful sanctuary for people and our approach to embedding meaning and purpose allows us to be inclusive, participative and more noble in how we can show our duty of care and still be a high-performing, commercially astute and results-driven organization.

Real-world example: In responding to a restructuring request from a senior leader to their relationship broker who is experiencing higher volumes of work and increased turnover due to stress being placed on the under-resourced nature of their team, Systems Designers and people and performance analysts have worked with our People Operations team to assess the volumes and turnover rates, exit interviews and sample surveys from the team.

The pressures aren't necessarily just under-resourcing, they are about inefficient systems and management approaches.

So the Systems Designers get to work with the Product Management team and relationship brokers and a proposed Organization Design and Management Capability Programme is crafted.

Before submission of the strategy and plan, a Meaning Maker again casts a *critical friend* review and asks similar questions:

- Does this Organization Design and Capability Programme (product) strengthen the connection to the meaning and purpose of working here – and particularly in this division – and will it deliver on our ambitions and mission whilst solving this systemic problem?

- How does it make people feel about belonging in that team?

- How inclusive and inspiring is it?

- Does it make people feel proud to work there and will it likely engender a stronger psychological and emotional contract to their commitment to us as their employer?

- Does it give team leaders confidence and assurance that they can gracefully and powerfully handle the new systems and approaches to manage their workloads differently?

- Would this design and product be the envy of our competitors, and would they instantly want to replicate and use what we've carefully crafted?

A luxury additional stage we cannot afford? Or an opportunity we cannot miss to strengthen the value HR creates and the impact of the solution on our people, performance, learning and culture? I think the answer to that is clear and it is the latter.

People, planet and prosperity-centric design: HR 3.0's role in shaping additional forms of value

Introduction

The evolution of HR has reached a critical juncture where business value must be redefined to encompass not just economic returns but also human and environmental well-being. HR 3.0 is a transformative approach that seeks to integrate people, planet and prosperity-centric design into the core of organizational strategy, ensuring that work is meaningful, sustainable and beneficial to society. Drawing on Colin Mayer's work on *Prosperity* and his six forms of value, this book explores how HR 3.0 prioritizes a balanced and progressive employee experience while aligning with business sustainability and ethical imperatives.

HR 3.0 and the new value proposition

Traditionally, HR has been viewed as a functional discipline focused on hiring, managing performance and ensuring compliance. HR 3.0 shifts this paradigm by embedding value creation across multiple dimensions – people experience, environmental impact and business sustainability. Mayer's six forms of value – material (physical), financial, intellectual, social, human and natural – provide a robust framework for HR 3.0's expansive role in shaping the future of work.

People: elevating the employee experience

HR 3.0 acknowledges that employees are not just resources but active participants in creating business success. A people-centric approach ensures that individuals have meaningful work, opportunities for development and a sense of purpose within their organizations. This is closely tied to Mayer's human and intellectual values, which emphasize the need for organizations to invest in employee growth, well-being and creative potential:

1 **Human-centred design for work:** HR 3.0 applies human-centred design to workplace experiences, ensuring work is engaging, inclusive and aligned with employee aspirations.

2 **Skills-based organizations:** Moving beyond rigid job roles, HR 3.0 promotes skills-based structures, allowing employees to apply their talents dynamically across projects and teams.

3 **Employee well-being:** Well-being is not an HR initiative but a strategic priority. Organizations integrate mental health, work-life balance and personal growth into their operating models.

Planet: the role of HR in sustainability

Business success cannot be achieved at the expense of the environment. HR 3.0 integrates planet-pro approaches that embed environmental consciousness into HR policies, leadership development and organizational culture. Mayer's natural value reinforces the idea that businesses have a responsibility to sustain and regenerate natural resources rather than deplete them:

1 **Sustainable work practices:** Hybrid work models, digital transformation and conscious consumption of resources (such as energy and materials) reduce corporate carbon footprints.

2 **Green HR policies:** HR 3.0 champions eco-conscious policies, from sustainable travel policies to responsible supply chain engagement.

3 **Culture of environmental stewardship:** HR plays a role in embedding sustainability into corporate values, ensuring employees understand their role in promoting environmental responsibility.

Prosperity: redefining business success

Mayer's financial, social and physical values provide a broader lens through which organizations should define prosperity. Financial success alone is insufficient; organizations must create holistic prosperity that benefits employees, customers, communities and the planet:

1 **Beyond profit-first metrics:** HR 3.0 supports alternative success measures, such as social impact scores, employee engagement indexes and community investment returns.

2 **Purpose-driven leadership:** Organizations thrive when leaders embrace stakeholder capitalism – considering the interests of employees, society and the environment alongside shareholders.

3 **Regenerative business models:** HR fosters models that contribute positively to society, such as circular economy initiatives and community-oriented business practices.

The interconnection of people, planet and prosperity in HR 3.0

HR 3.0 does not treat people, planet and prosperity as separate domains but as an interconnected ecosystem. Businesses that optimize for one dimension at the expense of others ultimately undermine their long-term viability. Sustainable organizations design HR models that:

- enable employees while minimizing environmental impact (e.g. remote work strategies that reduce emissions while enhancing flexibility and engagement);
- create regenerative prosperity through equitable wages, upskilling and sustainable supply chains (e.g. companies investing in fair trade and ethical labour practices);
- align business objectives with societal needs (e.g. incorporating corporate social responsibility into HR strategies to foster community development).

Implementing HR 3.0: practical strategies

To operationalize the prosperity elements of HR 3.0, organizations can adopt the following approaches:

1 **Redesign the employee value proposition (EVP):** Move beyond compensation and benefits to offer a work experience that aligns with sustainability and purpose-driven work.

2 **Embed sustainability in talent development:** Train employees on environmental responsibility, ethical decision making and social impact within their roles.

3 **Adopt a skills-based approach to work:** Transition from traditional job roles to skill ecosystems where talent is deployed based on competencies and interests.

4 **Develop metrics for holistic prosperity:** Implement measures that assess the impact of HR strategies on people, planet and profit.

5 **Strengthen ethical leadership:** Encourage leaders to make decisions that balance financial performance with social and environmental responsibility.

Conclusion

HR 3.0 represents a paradigm shift towards a people, planet and prosperity-centric design that redefines the role of HR in business success. Inspired by Colin Mayer's six forms of value, this approach moves beyond transactional HR functions to create a holistic and sustainable business ecosystem. By embedding human, intellectual, natural, financial, physical and social value into HR strategy, organizations can achieve a new model of prosperity – one that uplifts employees, sustains the planet and delivers meaningful economic and social benefits for all stakeholders.

The road ahead

Getting started with HR 3.0 is not a one-size-fits-all approach. It's a journey that requires customization, experimentation and collaboration. As you adopt this model, remember that its ultimate goal is to create a flourishing organization where people thrive, systems align and products and processes drive meaningful outcomes. With HR 3.0, the possibilities for impact are vast.

WHAT WE'VE COVERED IN THIS CHAPTER

This chapter explored the practicalities of implementing HR 3.0, emphasizing that its transition requires more than structural change – it demands a cultural, strategic and operational shift.

We framed HR 3.0 as an evolution beyond legacy models like the HR Business Partner approach, embracing a fluid, skills-based and value-driven way of working. This shift responds to technological advancements, economic shifts and changing workforce expectations.

To establish a strategic foundation, we introduced value creation principles from Professor David Wessels and The Bridge Partnership, covering:

- **Purposeful advantage** – why we exist

- **Culture advantage** – how we run our business

- **Change leadership advantage** – how we lead change

We outlined a three-stage implementation approach:

1 **Quality of awareness and ambition levers** – confronting reality (workforce planning, DEI, talent retention) and envisioning new models (skills-based hiring, AI-driven talent intelligence).

2 **Quality of thinking and directional levers** – aligning HR 3.0 with organizational purpose, vision and strategy to position HR as a business enabler.

3 **Quality of action and transformational levers** – operationalizing vibrant culture through Culture Mapping, Culture MVPs and the Culture Intelligence Dashboard.

We also explored Mintzberg's Nine Design Parameters and the shift from traditional HR roles to adaptive, open roles (e.g. Practice Leads, Systems Designers and Meaning Makers).

Finally, we emphasized HR 3.0 as a holistic transformation embedding people, planet and prosperity-centric design, moving beyond economic value to drive intellectual, social and environmental impact.

References and further reading

Bersin, J (2023) Systemic HR: The future of HR operating models, https://joshbersin.com/2023/12/introducing-the-systemic-hr-initiative/ (archived at https://perma.cc/YA9B-D4KK)

Deloitte (2024) 2024 Global Human Capital Trends: HR 3.0 and the future of work, www2.deloitte.com/content/dam/insights/articles/glob176836_global-human-capital-trends-2024/DI_Global-Human-Capital-Trends-2024.pdf (archived at https://perma.cc/KQ8X-XHJW)

Martin, R L (2013) *Playing to Win: How strategy really works*, Boston: Harvard Business Review Press

Mayer, C (2018) *Prosperity: Better business makes the greater good*, Oxford: Oxford University Press

McKinsey & Company (2022) HR's new operating model, www .mckinsey.com/capabilities/people-and-organizational-performance/our-insights/hrs-new-operating-model (archived at https://perma.cc/5DAX-FV7J)

Mintzberg, H (1979) *The Structuring of Organizations: A synthesis of the research*, Englewood Cliffs, NJ: Prentice-Hall

Ulrich, D (1997) *Human Resource Champions: The next agenda for adding value and delivering results*, Boston: Harvard Business School Press

Wessels, D and Koller, T (2020) *Valuation: Measuring and managing the value of companies*, 7th edn, Hoboken, NJ: Wiley

8

Real-world applications influencing HR 3.0

The problem is never how to get new, innovative thoughts into your mind, but how to get the old ones out. Every mind is a building filled with archaic furniture. Clean out a corner of your mind, and creativity will instantly fill it.

DEE HOCK, FOUNDER OF VISA

WHAT'S COVERED IN THIS CHAPTER

This chapter looks at **innovative practices** that have shaped what HR 3.0 has become and showcases a **progressive** and more **dynamic** version of HR strategy in practice and impact.

Introduction

HR 3.0 represents a fundamental shift in how organizations design and execute their people strategies. But it only really 'exists' (at the moment) in this book.

How can we represent examples of people doing what this HR Operating Model is enabling when it's completely new?

While conceptual frameworks and best practices provide valuable guidance, the most compelling evidence of HR 3.0's potential effectiveness comes from real-world applications that are doing progressive, adaptive and pioneering work, unknowingly informing and helping shape what HR 3.0 has become.

This chapter explores how various organizations – across both the private and nonprofit sectors – have successfully implemented HR 3.0 principles.

These real-world examples (which are widely available) illustrate the diverse ways that HR functions in well-known organizations leverage agility, data and analytics, science, technology and people-centric design to create more adaptive, high-impact people teams and functions.

None of these examples are down to the creation of a new operating model for HR, and are more adaptations, iterations and additions into the existing operating models – which in itself proves that you do not have to transform completely into something new. There is an opportunity within radical adaptations to the operating model that become so profoundly different from the original version, that it could be more helpful to map, plot and describe that evolved state.

In these real-world illustrations we can see how challenges, opportunities and circumstances combine to create new versions of the HR Operating Model and in their own ways have influenced my thinking behind the potential shift to HR 3.0. Featured organizations are Santander Talent Development, Novartis Capability Pools, Barnardo's, Collinson, Reward Gateway Edenred, Jaguar Land Rover (JLR), NatWest Bank PLC and The Children's Society (TCS).

Diverse industry examples: HR teams who have influenced HR 3.0

Barnardo's: transforming HR in a non-profit context

Barnardo's, the UK's largest children's charity, recognized the need to modernize its HR functions to support its mission of aiding vulnerable children and families. Facing challenges such as outdated systems, inefficient processes and a lack of real-time data, Barnardo's embarked on a comprehensive HR transformation.

Documented/case study challenges faced over the last few years have been around:

- Outdated systems: Barnardo's had been using the same enterprise resource planning system since 1999, with limited updates, leading to a cumbersome user experience and inefficient processes.
- Data management issues: The organization grappled with maintaining accurate and accessible HR data, hindering effective decision making and reporting.

- Volunteer management: With approximately 22,000 volunteers, Barnardo's faced difficulties in tracking volunteer contributions and managing related data efficiently.

Lately, Chief People Officer Sarah Eglin has introduced some of the emerging concepts in HR 3.0 by realigning her team's structure, flow, efforts and operations.

HR 3.0 INFLUENCING APPROACHES

- **Agile HR practices:** Introduced cross-functional HR squads to improve responsiveness.
- **Data-driven decision making:** Leveraged analytics to enhance workforce planning and service delivery.

Collinson: commercial operations with purpose-led high performance

A global leader in travel experiences and loyalty solutions, Collinson recognized the need to enhance its employee experience and align HR more closely with business outcomes. Under the leadership of (then) Chief People Officer Bertie Tonks, the organization embarked on a transformative journey, integrating data analytics and AI into their HR practices.

HR 3.0 INFLUENCING APPROACHES

1 **Agile and product-centric HR:** Leading all HR deliverables and services through Sprint-based approaches to design, development and delivery. The Collinson HR team became fully skilled in using Minimum Viable Products (MVPs) through experimentation and operating with a Scrum-based method on projects.

2 **People analytics:** AI-driven insights. Collinson utilized AI to analyse workforce data, enabling the prediction of employee engagement trends and the identification of factors influencing retention and satisfaction. This proactive approach allowed HR to implement targeted interventions, fostering a more engaged workforce.

3 **Flexible work models:** Hybrid working environment. In response to evolving workplace dynamics, Collinson adopted hybrid work models supported by digital collaboration platforms. This shift not only provided employees with flexibility but also maintained productivity and team cohesion.

4 **Digitally powered learning:** Personalized development programmes. Leveraging AI, Collinson offered tailored learning experiences aligned with individual career trajectories. This personalization empowered employees to take ownership of their development, enhancing both skill acquisition and career progression.

Reward Gateway Edenred

Reward Gateway Edenred – a prominent provider of employee engagement solutions – recognized the importance of embodying its product line to other HR teams by fostering a high-performance and engaged workforce within its own organization (during and after a merger between Reward Gateway and Edenred). To achieve this, the company implemented a comprehensive people strategy, focusing on people-centric digital-first approaches to enhance employee experience and drive organizational success congruent with their services to the world of work.

HR 3.0 INFLUENCING APPROACHES

1 **Agile and product-based working:** Particularly in People Experience and Performance Support, the teams operated in Scrums, using iterative, Sprint-based approaches to designing, developing and delivering learning and personal development and an enhanced People Experience.

2 **Real-time recognition and reward systems:** Digital engagement tools, leveraging its own platform to implement real-time recognition and reward systems, enabling employees to acknowledge and celebrate each other's achievements promptly. This approach fostered a culture of continuous appreciation and motivation.

3 **A culture of appreciation and recognition:** Reward Gateway's own research highlighted the powerful performance stimulation that came from a culture where people felt recognized and appreciated in their work, modelling this themselves into their own People Experience and advising HR clients on the approaches to take using their platform and advisory support.

4 **Employee-centric HR design:** Prioritizing well-being and personalization. By utilizing data analytics, Reward Gateway designed a People Experience that prioritized employee well-being and offered personalized development support.

Jaguar Land Rover (JLR): investing in culture and skills

JLR is transforming significantly to align its workforce with the company's strategic shift towards electric vehicles (EVs) and digital innovation. This initiative is part of JLR's broader 'Reimagine' strategy, aiming to position the company as an electric-first, modern luxury automaker.

HR 3.0 INFLUENCING APPROACHES

1 **Capability-based workforce planning:** Skills-focused talent development. JLR has transitioned from traditional job roles to a skills-based approach, emphasizing the development of competencies essential for EV production and digital technologies. This strategy ensures that employees are equipped with the necessary skills to thrive in an evolving automotive landscape.

2 **Future-ready upskilling:** Advanced training programmes. The company has implemented AI-driven tools to identify skill gaps and predict future talent needs. Through its Future Skills Programme, JLR has trained over 20,000 employees and partners in electrification and digital skills, including more than 2,400 manufacturing employees in EV competencies and nearly 3,000 engineers in electrification technologies.

3 **Workforce agility:** Cross-functional project teams. JLR has established agile, cross-functional teams to foster innovation and accelerate project delivery. This collaborative approach enables diverse skill sets to converge, driving creative solutions and enhancing operational efficiency. The JLR People Team use Design Thinking, Persona Mapping and Agile Sprints to deliver on their culture, learning and People Experience enhancements.

4 **People services excellence:** JLR's HR contact centre handled over 2,000 weekly queries ranging from routine questions to time-critical well-being situations, reducing response times and improving service levels. By integrating AI, JLR created a Virtual Assistant capable of promptly addressing 51 topics and facilitating swift human escalation when necessary. The result was a 26 per cent reduction in queries requiring human intervention and a 15 per cent rise in service satisfaction.

The Children's Society (TCS): talent, diversity and mission-led performance = People Experience

A UK-based charity dedicated to supporting vulnerable children and young people has recently undertaken significant HR transformations to enhance employee well-being and organizational responsiveness. These initiatives are part of the charity's commitment to creating a supportive work environment that aligns with its mission-driven objectives. Whilst much of what TCS does in HR might not look that radical, at the heart of it is a hugely people-centric, dynamic and future-focused agenda for inclusive, participatory and ambitious mission.

HR 3.0 INFLUENCING APPROACHES

1 **People Experience-framed work proposition:** TCS has emphasized a human-centred approach to its people agenda, focusing on both employees and volunteers. This strategy aims to foster a unified 'TeamTCS', promoting inclusivity and a sense of belonging. Their commitment is evident in their dedication to creating an environment where all individuals feel valued and empowered to contribute effectively.

2 **Purpose-led people agenda:** Central to TCS's organizational strategy is a deep commitment to its mission and the well-being of its people. The People Experience strategy is designed to build unity and ensure that both employees and volunteers are engaged and aligned with the charity's objectives. This participative approach underscores the role of HR in fostering meaning and purpose within the organization.

3 **Using design and Systems Thinking for people, culture and digital transformation:** Taking persona mapping and intersectionality as a starting point, the People Agenda at TCS is as strong on inclusivity as any you're likely to see and is a highly participative culture of activism, innovation and dedication to the much-needed work of improving the lives of children and young people. Taking an approach to shaping leadership roles in two areas – technical/specialists and people/projects – is a departure from most orthodox management constructs.

Santander Talent Development

A global financial institution, Santander UK has implemented structured talent development programmes to nurture internal capabilities and foster leadership growth.

HR 3.0 INFLUENCING APPROACHES

Adoption of Agile and product management principles: Santander has embraced Agile as a core component of its operational strategy, aiming to improve adaptability and dynamic operations and change. The bank's Agile transformation began 10 years ago with the establishment of a Centre of Global Excellence, which has since influenced various units, particularly the Talent team. A Product Management approach was in play throughout the team, using the full range of Agile and Scrum in design, development and delivery approaches for all stages of Talent, from acquisition to development/management

Novartis

Novartis, a global healthcare leader, has reimagined its workforce planning by transitioning from traditional role-based hiring to a skills-based development approach. This strategic shift aims to enhance organizational agility and foster innovation in a rapidly evolving industry.

HR 3.0 INFLUENCING APPROACHES

1 **Digitally-enabled talent matching:** Novartis has developed its Skills Operating System for an agile workforce that integrates both internal and external skills data. This system utilizes machine learning to align employee capabilities with current and future business needs, ensuring a dynamic match between talent and organizational objectives.

2 **Internal gig marketplace – 'Propel':** To promote cross-functional collaboration and continuous learning, Novartis launched an internal talent marketplace named Propel. This platform allows employees to engage in short-term projects, gigs and mentorship opportunities beyond their usual roles, thereby broadening their skill sets and career horizons.

3 **Learning and development personalization:** Continuous upskilling programmes. Emphasizing a culture of lifelong learning, Novartis offers AI-driven social learning platforms that provide personalized learning experiences. These platforms curate content and connect employees with experts to support their development, ensuring the workforce remains adept at navigating new business challenges.

NatWest Bank PLC

NatWest – a prominent UK banking institution – has strategically implemented automation and AI-driven solutions to enhance its HR functions, streamline governance processes and improve overall employee experiences.

HR 3.0 INFLUENCING APPROACHES

1 **Automated HR processes:** AI-driven governance and compliance: NatWest has integrated the Appian low-code platform to automate its governance workflows, significantly reducing manual, time-intensive processes. This automation has led to improved employee experiences, reduced frustration and enhanced record retention.

2 **Employee self-service platforms:** AI-powered virtual assistant 'Ask Archie'. To provide real-time HR support, NatWest introduced Ask Archie, a 24/7 AI chatbot designed to answer frequently asked employee questions on various topics. By incorporating generative AI capabilities, Ask Archie delivers more targeted and conversational responses, streamlining access to information and allowing HR teams to focus on complex issues.

3 **Predictive workforce analytics:** AI-enhanced workforce planning. While specific details on predictive workforce analytics at NatWest are limited, the bank's broader AI initiatives suggest a commitment to leveraging AI for improved decision making. By integrating AI into various processes, NatWest aims to enhance operational efficiency and strategic planning.

Reflections on pioneering HR team and HR Operating Model shifts

All of these examples are not enabled because the HR teams/functions are operating in the HR 3.0 model – it's still a concept that isn't as prevalent as the dominant Ulrich/Business Partner model or variations thereof.

They do speak to the essence of a more intersectional, agile, purposeful approach to developing and delivering HR products and services that enable businesses to perform. All have a strong transformational and digital element that cuts across our verticals and divisional approaches.

These examples not only reflect elements of HR 3.0 (unbeknownst to them), they also demonstrate how some organizations are already operating in ways that align with its principles and are more deliberately progressive, diversified and dynamic.

By using publicly available stories and research – rather than direct interviews – there is no 'leading the witness' or any sense of bias or coercion. Stories are linked to HR 3.0 as an organic and credible evolution rather than a prescriptive framework.

In designing this new HR Operating Model, I have drawn inspiration from next-stage, adaptive and pioneering practices that challenge traditional structures and offer fresh ways to map HR's role in value creation, workforce agility and business impact. These case studies serve as tangible proof that HR 3.0 is not just theoretical – it is already taking shape in organizations rethinking how they work, develop talent and drive impact.

Again, many of these examples may not consider their deliverables as products and manage them within a product management framework; however, iterative, user-centric production combined with a clear, Design Thinking-derived problem-solving focus and a consumable quality to those deliverables suggests that these organizations are adopting a product management approach, perhaps just implicitly subconsciously.

With that in mind, it's heartening to sense that HR 3.0 has come into my thinking and now into a plausible shift for the HR Operating Model not from my own constructs but from those of HR practitioners and progressive practices adjacent to HR, so I'm seeing myself as a 'conduit' for that.

It also leads us to another conclusion: HR 3.0 is not a *freeze-unfreeze-refreeze* Kurt Lewin-type change model. It is an evolutionary iteration and a chance to look at the flow of work, the deployment of creativity and capabilities and some approaches to take in HR that should be iterative, evolutionary and adapted to context.

I see – with the greatest respect in the world to the prevailing model – some HR teams dogmatically forcing themselves into Shared Services, Business Partnering and Centres of Excellence when maybe that's not how they should deploy themselves and their functions.

HR 3.0 is a way of departing from an existing orthodox operating model for HR and shaping it for your context, with your existing and future capabilities, alive and responsive enough to be shaped how you need it to be.

How would I want HR leaders to respond to this new operating model and a shift in practice and strategy?

The ideal response I'd look for from any HR leader and people professional is this:

- **Curiosity:** What are these new spaces, elements, practices, methods and roles?
- **Analysis:** What is most compelling in this new operating model's framework for solving problems, creating value and helping the HR/People and Culture function to be ahead of the curve?
- **Scale:** Whilst the HR 3.0 Operating Model has four domains, and several espoused roles, how these are used to shape roles, accountabilities and thereby tackle workflow and tasks depends on the need and the resource required.

In some larger organizations, we might see the full range:

1 People and Performance Analysts

2 Systems Designers

3 Product Managers

4 Relationship Brokers, and perhaps even

5 Psychologists can be deployed alongside

6 Practice Leads for

   a. Employment Law and Employee Relations

   b. Reward and Recognition

   c. Internal Communication and Engagement

   d. Well-being

In smaller HR teams, the work will be contextualized to the scale and maturity of the organization and amalgamated into one or more roles. An HR Manager in a small manufacturing enterprise might be a People Analyst and a Systems Designer and deploy science and products depending on the needs of that business.

An operating model built for change *and* stability

One thing the HR 3.0 model does do is cover *business as usual* and any form of change. So it is both an operational model and a project/transformational model. This is very deliberate in the sense that organizations no longer have long periods of stability and then the occasional change programme. Twenty-first-century work is a constant shift between regularized change and adaptive operations.

The domains of **Product, Systems, Science** and **Process** are not differentiating between operational and transformative activities and are more indicative of the spaces where HR gets done.

Processes will include much of what we call *People Operations* now – so that function and its roles, accountabilities, technological solutions, data, information and intelligence obviously still exists. And if it's helpful, it can be shown through roles assembled in an organization chart.

Similarly, training programmes, online learning content and access to coaching exist in the Learning and Development professional area. And in HR 3.0, we will see a lot of the work sits in Products (as they are often created/built by Learning Designers) and any administration is a service that resides in the Process domain with People Operations. Statistical and evaluative work to gauge the impact of training programmes sits with People and Performance Analysts.

Working in a more dynamic, project-oriented manner requires effective workflow management systems to support the tasks and activities and a real sense of ownership.

An operating model built to flex

Unlike the blueprint metaphor we introduced in Chapter 1, the HR 3.0 Operating Model is not intended to be a fixed design. Instead it is more a starting point for it to be adapted in context.

What *is* encouraged is to depart from – or perhaps redraw the lines of – the three pillars of the Business Partner Model. It is not a map across Centres of Excellence into Systems Designers or Recruitment Administrators into People Operations.

It is designed to give HR teams a chance to realign what they do and how they do it away from fixed verticals/spaces.

What these real-world examples have done is a mixture of applied HR 3.0 'thinking', some of the philosophy of it and some of the practices recommended by it.

Departing from a range of intricately defined roles is another deliberate aspect of this as an operating model. In the main, we've already established that Organization Design will do that.

However, there are some roles that are indicative of the areas and domains that will add value through this operating model. For example People and Performance Analytics is described as a practice field and role that does not sit neatly in Science, Products, Systems or Processes/Operations.

Performance Analysts will operate in ALL of those spaces, depending on the nature of the work that needs data and analytical inputs. People and Performance Analysts will either be part of a pool of analysts, a single role deployable across a range of areas needing analyst input, or part of someone's role alongside other skills/areas covered. In the model, there are deliberate intersections and People and Performance Analysts will operate in the heart of the model.

HR Advisor work (conduct, grievances), Employee Relations and Employment Law are still specialist areas of work that won't go away just because we want to create a more agile and dynamic HR Operating Model. This is where the role of **Practice Leads** comes in – leading in an area of practice.

Again, no need to distinguish Practice Leads as being 'based' purely in People Operations. There is a similar intersectional feel to Practice Leads who will use Science, Products and work with and shape Systems and Processes.

Conclusion

Curiosity, analysis, scale and context are four key determinants of whether the shift to a new operating model for HR using HR 3.0 is viable, useful and desired – desired being an optimal aspect of this trio of decision-making parameters.

Do you – as an HR team/function – want and need to create more agility, responsiveness, fluidity of resources, focus on value-creating products, use of sciences and evidence, data and analytics utilization, Systems Thinking and a designed approach to diversifying your service offer?

If some or all of those parameters apply, I assert that there is a likelihood that you need an operating model that is more dynamic and adaptable, and that's what HR 3.0 is intended to be. Not a prescriptive 'lift and shift' but a contextualized navigation tool rather than a precise series of driving instructions.

HR3.0 is a compass tool, wherein you – contextually – can build the map, the territories, the pitstops and the precise conditions for the journey and the desired outcomes and impact.

WHAT WE'VE COVERED IN THIS CHAPTER

In this chapter, we explored real-world applications of HR 3.0, showcasing how organizations across industries – both private and nonprofit – are evolving their HR functions to be more agile, data-driven, people-centric and technologically enabled. These case studies provide tangible examples of the principles underpinning HR 3.0 in action, even if they were not explicitly designed within this model.

- **Key themes and lessons**

  1. **Diverse industry applications:** Case studies from Barnardo's, Collinson, Reward Gateway, Jaguar Land Rover, The Children's Society, Santander, Novartis and NatWest demonstrated how HR transformations are driving workforce agility, digital adoption and employee experience.

  2. **Agility in HR:** Barnardo's, Collinson and Santander implemented cross-functional HR teams, iterative ways of working and adaptive workforce planning to meet evolving business needs.

  3. **Data and analytics:** Collinson and Santander leveraged digitized and AI-driven workforce insights to enhance talent management and workforce skills.

  4. **Technology and automation:** NatWest and Jaguar Land Rover modernized HR systems, integrating automation and AI-powered employee support tools.

  5. **People-centric approaches:** The Children's Society and Reward Gateway focused on employee experience, well-being and engagement, demonstrating HR's role in fostering culture and inclusion.

  6. **Innovative talent models:** Novartis and Jaguar Land Rover embraced skills-based workforce planning, moving away from rigid job structures to flexible capability development.

- **Implications for HR 3.0**

  o These case studies do not stem from HR 3.0 explicitly – the model is still forming – but they reflect (and have shaped) its principles.

  o Many organizations operate implicitly within a product-oriented and systems-led HR approach, moving beyond the rigid structures of traditional HR Operating Models.

  o HR 3.0 is not a static framework but rather an adaptive and iterative shift that allows HR functions to build their own fit-for-context model and cover steady and changing states of operating.

- **Looking ahead**

This chapter highlighted that HR transformation is already happening, and HR 3.0 provides a lens to understand, shape and refine these emerging practices. The question is no longer whether HR can change, but how HR leaders can contextualize and scale this shift to best serve their organizations.

References and further reading

General HR and business transformation sources

Bersin, J (2023) Systemic HR: The Future of HR operating models, https://joshbersin.com/2023/12/introducing-the-systemic-hr-initiative/ (archived at https://perma.cc/HT9X-QRFJ)

Deloitte (2024) 2024 Global Human Capital Trends: HR's new operating model, www2.deloitte.com/content/dam/insights/articles/glob176836_global-human-capital-trends-2024/DI_Global-Human-Capital-Trends-2024.pdf (archived at https://perma.cc/KYV8-UM2A)

Hock, D (1999) *Birth of the Chaordic Age*, San Francisco: Berrett-Koehler Publishers

McKinsey & Company (2022) Generative AI and the future of HR, www.mckinsey.com/capabilities/people-and-organizational-performance/our-insights/generative-ai-and-the-future-of-hr (archived at https://perma.cc/BG9S-WCU6)

Ulrich, D (1997) *Human Resource Champions: The next agenda for adding value and delivering results*, Boston: Harvard Business School Press

Real-world examples

Barnardo's – HR transformation in the non-profit sector

Barnardo's (2023) Annual Report 2023–4 Modernising HR to serve vulnerable communities, www.barnardos.org.uk/sites/default/files/uploads/annual-report-accounts-2023-2024.pdf (archived at https://perma.cc/926M-SJRV)

Collinson – AI and data-driven HR

Tonks, B (2023) Balancing AI & human-centric leadership with Bertie Tonks, https://waldencroft.com/balancing-ai-human-centric-leadership-with-bertie-tonks/ (archived at https://perma.cc/E8RK-B3RQ)

Jaguar Land Rover (JLR) – capability-based workforce planning

JLR (2023) Reimagine strategy: Investing in culture, skills & Agile HR practices, www.jaguarlandrover.com/news/2024/05/jlr-rapidly-trains-more-20000-colleagues-and-partners-readiness-build-luxury-electric (archived at https://perma.cc/Q8LM-KR9D)

The Manufacturer (2023) JLR's workforce transformation for electric vehicle production, www.themanufacturer.com (archived at https://perma.cc/AYL8-VNE7)

NatWest – AI-driven HR automation and workforce analytics

NatWest (2023) NatWest & OpenAI collaborate to accelerate cutting-edge AI transformation in support of bank-wide simplification and enhanced customer experience, www.natwestgroup.com/news-and-insights/news-room/press-releases/ai-and-data/2025/mar/natwest-open-ai-collaborate-to-accelerate-cutting-edge-ai-transf.html (archived at https://perma.cc/WU5B-H25B)

Novartis – Skills-based workforce development and internal gig marketplaces

Blake, D (2024) How to thrive in the 'skills economy', *Harvard Business Review*, https://hbr.org/2024/02/how-to-thrive-in-the-skills-economy (archived at https://perma.cc/6SP2-8GKA)
Novartis (2023) How Novartis put skills at the center of their workforce transformation, https://gloat.com/wp-content/uploads/Novartis-case-study.pdf (archived at https://perma.cc/RRX8-S7X5)

Reward Gateway Edenred – employee engagement and digital HR

Reward Gateway (2023) Creating a culture of recognition and reward, www.rewardgateway.com/resource/creating-a-culture-of-recognition-and-reward (archived at https://perma.cc/4URX-QQTR)

Santander UK – Agile and product-based talent development

People Management (2023) How Santander is developing its managers to embed a diversity agenda across the workforce, www.peoplemanagement.co.uk/article/1861297/santander-developing-its-managers-embed-diversity-agenda-across-workforce (archived at https://perma.cc/NF85-XMZY)
Santander UK (2023) Workday: innovation to make progress in talent management, www.santander.com/en/stories/workday-innovation-to-make-progress-in-talent-management (archived at https://perma.cc/VKN8-SKDX)

The Children's Society (TCS) – People Experience and mission-driven HR

The Children's Society (2023) Talent, diversity and people-centric HR in charities, https://careers.childrenssociety.org.uk/recruitment/category/2/4899/description/ (archived at https://perma.cc/CLQ7-GVMC)

9

Overcoming challenges in HR Operating Model transformation

The greatest danger in times of turbulence is not the turbulence – it is to act with yesterday's logic.

PETER DRUCKER, THE FATHER OF MODERN MANAGEMENT

WHAT'S COVERED IN THIS CHAPTER

- **Identifying barriers:** Common obstacles organizations face when adopting new HR models.

- **Strategic solutions:** Provide strategies and solutions to overcome these challenges.

- **Leadership and culture:** Explore the role of leadership and organizational culture in successful transformation.

Introduction

For over 25 years, HR has not fundamentally shifted its operating model beyond variations of Dave Ulrich's Business Partner model. Despite vast changes in workforce dynamics, technological advancements and business expectations, HR remains largely structured the same way it was in the late 1990s – built around HR Business Partners, Centres of Excellence and Shared Services.

A hypothesis for this might well be:

'Why hasn't HR transformed in the way digital, marketing or operations have?'

And further:

> 'What is preventing the adoption of newer, more dynamic models such as Systemic HR (Josh Bersin) and the Human Capability model (Ulrich's latest iteration)?'

This chapter explores the barriers that have constrained HR's evolution, the systemic resistance to change and how HR can overcome these challenges to shift towards a modern, more dynamic, value-creating operating model.

Some might argue that with an ever-expanding and more complex 'arena' to operate in, surely the last thing HR and People teams/functions need is to create any potential confusion by shifting approach at a time when more is being bolted on and fused into HR's expanded domains (ESG, inclusion, AI-driven change, leadership dilemmas and capabilities, business model transformation and economic pressures and intensity).

Some would argue this is **precisely** when an incumbent and legacy operating model **needs** to be reimagined and reinvented to cater for such diversified, dynamic conditions.

That is the call for HR 3.0 to be considered as a starting point to shift from the legacy operations in meeting expanded, diversified demands and much-sought-after competitive and adaptive advantages. Recognizing that reality and aspirations, though, is where we need to think more strategically and tactically about how to overcome the challenges, not by 'hunkering down' but more by 'stretching up and over' those challenges.

Identifying barriers: why HR hasn't shifted its operating model in 25+ years

Despite major shifts in business models, workforce expectations and technological advancements, HR has mainly remained static in its fundamental operating structures.

In operations, many companies have had to transform to use real-time analytics, automation and predictive modelling; in marketing, which has embraced AI-driven insights and hyper-personalized engagement strategies, HR has continued to operate on a decades-old playbook. The question is: Why?

Legacy mindsets and cultural resistance

One of the most significant barriers to HR's evolution is the deeply ingrained legacy mindset in businesses and their leaders that HR should function as an administrative and compliance-driven department rather than as a strategic, business-enabling function. This manifests in several ways:

- **HR's traditional focus on process over outcomes**
  Many HR teams lead with compliance, payroll, policies and standardized performance management rather than workforce agility, adaptability and impact on business outcomes.

- **A risk-averse culture**
  HR professionals are often conditioned to avoid risk, fearing legal exposure or employee relations issues, which impairs innovation in areas like skills-based workforce models, AI-driven talent acquisition and decentralized work structures.

- **Perceived threat to existing power structures**
  Many senior HR leaders, particularly those who have built their careers within the Ulrich Business Partner model, may resist changes that undermine their established authority or require them to acquire entirely new competencies in data science, product management or workforce analytics.

- **Employee scepticism (and fear) around new ways of working**
  Employees often resist changes to traditional HR structures, especially if those changes demand more self-service engagement, AI-driven career pathing or agile workforce models where role fluidity replaces rigid job hierarchies.

Leadership hesitance and lack of strategic buy-in

HR transformation requires strong C-suite sponsorship, yet many HR leaders struggle to convince executives that HR is more than just an operational function. The lack of strategic buy-in stems from several core issues:

- **HR has historically not spoken the language of business**
  Unlike finance, which reports on cost efficiencies and revenue impact, or sales, which demonstrates customer acquisition metrics, HR often fails to tie its initiatives directly to financial performance, market competitiveness or innovation. To be fair to HR, the 'lines' are less straight in its product line and impact compared to sales, capital or assets/stock. Marketing faces similar challenges to HR, with often indirect impacts, and yet it receives attention, support, investment and decisive inputs because of its efforts and endeavours that link directly to customers, markets and product/service growth.

- **The CFO's view of HR as a cost centre**
  Many CFOs see HR as a non-revenue-generating function, focused on administrative efficiency rather than business growth. This perception limits investment in HR technology, workforce analytics or experimental operating models.

- **Fear of losing centralized control over talent decisions**
  Business leaders, particularly in hierarchical organizations, may resist a shift towards something like HR 3.0's skills-based models or a more dynamic version of HR, as these frameworks often decentralize decision making and place greater workforce autonomy in the hands of employees, teams and their direct managers.

- **HR's overall framing as a bureaucratic function rather than a growth enabler**
  In most organizations, HR has been positioned as an operational support role rather than being seen as a strategic driver of business performance, innovation and agility.

Not all of this is of HR's own doing. Some causal trails, admittedly, lie at the door of a function that accepts a more subservient role in administrative compliance as its only genuine offer. And one of the reasons for this perception and lower operating 'ceiling' is that HR suffers through either the recognition or opportunity from legacy leadership principles that prevent even the most robust case for alternatives (and willingness to be more active and accountable) from being accepted, adopted and activated. A catch-22 of sorts.

The structural stagnation of the HR Business Partner model

While the Ulrich/HR Business Partner model was groundbreaking in the 1990s, its effectiveness has diminished in today's fast-paced, technology-driven business landscape. The model's key limitations include:

- **HR business partners are often overburdened**
  Instead of serving as strategic advisors to the business, many HR business partners are bogged down with operational and transactional work, leaving little time for strategic workforce planning.

- **Centres of Excellence (CoEs) have become bureaucratic and siloed**
  Originally designed to drive expertise, CoEs in some organizations have become disconnected from business needs, focusing on policy and

programme creation rather than innovative systemic evolution, talent-based solutions and ground-breaking strategic programmes that handle change and shift performance.

- **HR Shared Services often over-standardize**
  While efficiency is critical, overly rigid HR processes limit adaptability. Employees expect personalized, consumer-grade experiences, yet HR Shared Services often struggle to deliver flexibility or customization.

- The model doesn't account for today's dynamic workforce. Skills-based talent marketplaces, AI-driven recruitment and gig workforces are increasingly stress-testing the HR structure. The silos of the Business Partner model appear to be leading to some serious challenges around capability, capacity and creativity through a lack of connectivity, convergence and collaborative working across value streams, employee lifecycle needs and overcoming leadership shortcomings.

Lack of capability in data, technology and product thinking

Modern HR Operating Models demand expertise beyond traditional HR competencies – yet many HR professionals are overloaded and have little or no capacity to increase their skills in:

- **Data analytics and evidence-based decision making**
  Without the ability to leverage workforce analytics, HR struggles to forecast talent needs, measure productivity or drive strategic workforce planning.

- **AI-driven HR solutions**
  AI and automation can revolutionize recruiting, learning and performance management, yet many HR teams lack the knowledge to implement or scale these technologies.

- **Product and service design thinking**
  Unlike marketing, which constantly iterates customer experiences, HR has been slower to apply employee experience design, A/B testing and Agile HR product development.

- **Digital literacy and fluency**
  As workforces become more remote and tech-driven, HR teams need digital-first thinking, yet many still rely on legacy systems and outdated processes.

Short-term fixes over long-term model shifts

Organizations often attempt to 'fix' HR through initiative-based projects, but these efforts rarely drive systemic change. Why? Because they:

- **Focus on org charts instead of operating models**
  Many HR transformations merely rearrange team structures without fundamentally changing how HR delivers value.

- **Are reactive rather than proactive**
  HR is called to shift in response to crises (e.g. talent shortages, remote working diktats and productivity dips) rather than through intentional, future-focused transformation.

- **Lack sustained investment**
  Leadership might approve a new HRIS or analytics platform but fail to invest in ongoing capability development, agile workforce strategies or Systemic HR redesigns.

- **Fail to work to a longer-term roadmap**
  Many HR transformations focus on immediate process improvements, but true transformation requires multi-year, iterative evolution aligned with business strategy.

Deep-seated resistance, leadership hesitance, structural stagnation and lack of capability in modern business disciplines explain why HR's Operating Model has remained largely unchanged for approaching three decades.

However, these barriers are not insurmountable, and indeed, the pressures and intensity of the 2020s alone call for HR as a profession and practice field to be stronger in something that's been talked about for decades: *HR being more strategic.*

However nebulous that is, it is worth using it as a frame for how we might shift perspectives and gain support for a new operating model for HR.

HR delivering business value and strengthening compliance

Operational compliance is one thing, and when combined with strategic impact, gives HR something more tangible to link and create a shift in its role and value within the organization.

Baseline compliance is one thing but there is a need for a stonger link to HR's work and the organization's goals and objectives.

HR's work is currently linked to compliance only, and needs to forge a greater connection to its work in compliance with the strategic impact and value creation the business exists to deliver.

If we can create a stronger frame for compliance into value creation we could shift that perspective and strengthen our impact on the latter (value creation) to the former (compliance).

Defining this beyond rhetoric and into actuality is a challenge worth looking into more through the work of those thought leaders, academics, practitioners and revered voices in the changing dynamic of work, business and the impact of people.

Strategic solutions: moving towards a new HR Operating Model

Overcoming these barriers requires bold thinking, adapted structures and capability development. Here's how HR could break free from outdated models and move towards a more dynamic, future-ready operating model.

As we emerge into the second half of the 2020s, two thinkers already mentioned – Josh Bersin and Dave Ulrich – have developed their thinking to give more power to the concept of a shifted HR Operating Model: Systemic HR (Bersin) and Human Capability (Ulrich).

Embracing Systemic HR (Josh Bersin) as a modern alternative

Josh Bersin's *Systemic HR* model provides a way forward by recognizing that HR must operate as a fully integrated system rather than as a set of defined (and somewhat disconnected) functions. It moves HR from being a service provider to an embedded, systemic force that influences the entire organization.

Key elements of Systemic HR include:

- **AI-driven workforce intelligence**
  HR functions should shift from reactive processes to predictive analytics, using AI-driven tools to assess skills gaps, workforce trends and engagement metrics in real time.
- **HR as an integrated business system**
  Rather than treating HR as a separate function, Systemic HR integrates talent, learning, technology and people analytics into business strategy.

FIGURE 9.1 Josh Bersin's Systemic HR Model©

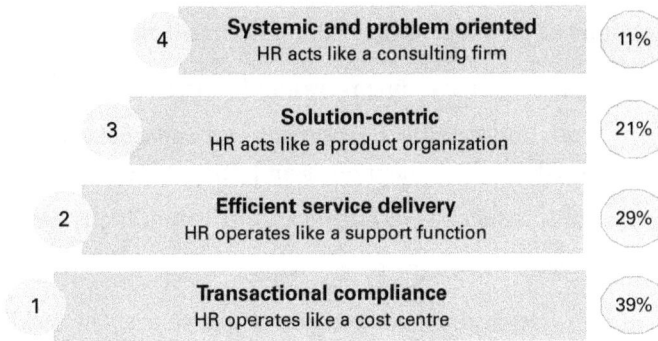

4	**Systemic and problem oriented** HR acts like a consulting firm	11%
3	**Solution-centric** HR acts like a product organization	21%
2	**Efficient service delivery** HR operates like a support function	29%
1	**Transactional compliance** HR operates like a cost centre	39%

Adapted from Josh Bersin (2023) Introducing The Systemic HR™ Initiative, https://joshbersin.com/2023/12/introducing-the-systemic-hr-initiative/

- **Workforce experience as a core product**
  The role of HR should evolve to focus on creating an employee experience ecosystem, where HR delivers services and tools designed like consumer-grade products.

- **Agile HR practices**
  HR should abandon slow-moving annual processes in favour of continuous feedback loops, iterative planning and dynamic workforce management.

Systemic HR represents a shift from a siloed, process-oriented model to a fluid, technology-enabled and insights-driven model, aligning HR operations seamlessly with business performance.

Indeed, Bersin refers to Systemic HR as an *operating system.* So, if Systemic HR is that, HR 3.0 is potentially the operating model to design and deliver the function to use such an operating system. Most crucial is the embedding and integrating of HR *functions* into a cohesive system, aligning closely with business strategies to enhance organizational adaptability and performance, from HR domains – considered somewhat adjacent to business functions – into more shared spaces of business, where HR offers considerable expertise (to use a Bersin phrase, *in the flow of work.*)

Bersin's argument is framed around the diversification of business models that are evolving to go beyond their traditional operating domains into more markets, products and service lines (often referred to as business transformation).

With this being the case, traditional HR compliance and development activities call for more systemic approaches (over specific initiatives) to tackle this cluster of more *interdependent* than *independent* challenges, such as:

- cost of living crises yet avoiding recession frames;
- culture at work and employee sentiment and engagement flatlined and backlashes to DEI amid a talent crisis and skills demands;
- ageing lifespans, reductions in birthrates, changes in lifestyle choices;
- the climate crisis and new forms of energy.

Having HR in three distinct domains does not sit well in tackling such multifaceted demands and opportunities. There can be confusion on ownership of solutions, limited application of the broad range of skills, intellect and capabilities that sit in People professionals, and systems and workflows that aren't as fluid as, say, R&D in Pharma or Product Development in Tech.

Systemic HR is a perfect mindset, paradigm and frame of reference for what HR should 'be' and HR 3.0 is a way to 'do' things in service of a bigger, more strategic impact.

Bersin admits that he's not an HR practitioner, but his research and analysis work is based on the intersection of people, skills, technologies and data. And HR is an intersectional model of science, systems, processes and products – Bersin himself and his work, and HR 3.0, are indeed very complementary and even stack on top of one another.

Leveraging Dave Ulrich's Human Capability Model for business alignment

Ulrich's latest Human Capability Model builds on his foundational work by shifting the focus from HR's efficiency to its impact on **business value creation**. The key principles of this model include:

- **Human, organizational and leadership capabilities as business enablers**
  HR must develop workforce capabilities that directly impact business outcomes such as innovation, agility and customer experience (CX).
- **HR as an orchestrator, not a gatekeeper**
  Instead of serving as a control mechanism, HR should function as a strategic partner that facilitates business growth.
- **Embedding workforce agility into HR strategy**
  HR's role isn't just to fill vacancies but to ensure continuous workforce adaptability, upskilling employees to meet evolving business demands.

- **Breaking down silos between HR, finance and operations**
  HR should integrate financial and operational data to create workforce strategies that are grounded in business metrics.

By adopting the Human Capability Model, HR shifts from being a support function to a business enabler, ensuring that workforce strategies are deeply connected to enterprise success.

Adopting HR 3.0: a product-led, Agile HR model

HR 3.0, as outlined in this book, represents the next evolution of HR Operating Models, focusing on agility, Systems Thinking and product-based HR services. Key principles include:

- HR as a set of products and services
  - o Instead of seeing HR as a function, organizations should treat HR as a portfolio of workforce products, such as internal talent marketplaces, performance enablement platforms and AI-driven hiring solutions.
- Agile methodologies applied to HR
  - o HR should adopt Scrum, Kanban and lean startup methodologies to rapidly iterate on policies, workforce solutions and employee experiences.
- Rearchitecting HR roles into cross-functional capabilities – traditional HR roles should evolve into multi-disciplinary capabilities, such as:
  - o People and Performance Analysts – using data and analytics to measure HR impact.
  - o HR Product Managers – managing HR services as iterative, user-focused experiences.
  - o Systems designers – optimizing HR processes through automation and technology.
  - o Workforce experience architects – creating personalized, digital-first HR experiences.
- Employee-centric workforce planning
  - o HR 3.0 places employees at the centre of workforce planning, leveraging AI-driven skills mapping, digital learning platforms and intelligent career pathing.

HR 3.0 bridges the gap between Systemic HR's technology-driven approach and Ulrich's capability-focused model, ensuring that HR operates as a high-impact, business-aligned function.

FIGURE 9.2 Dave Ulrich's Human Capability Model

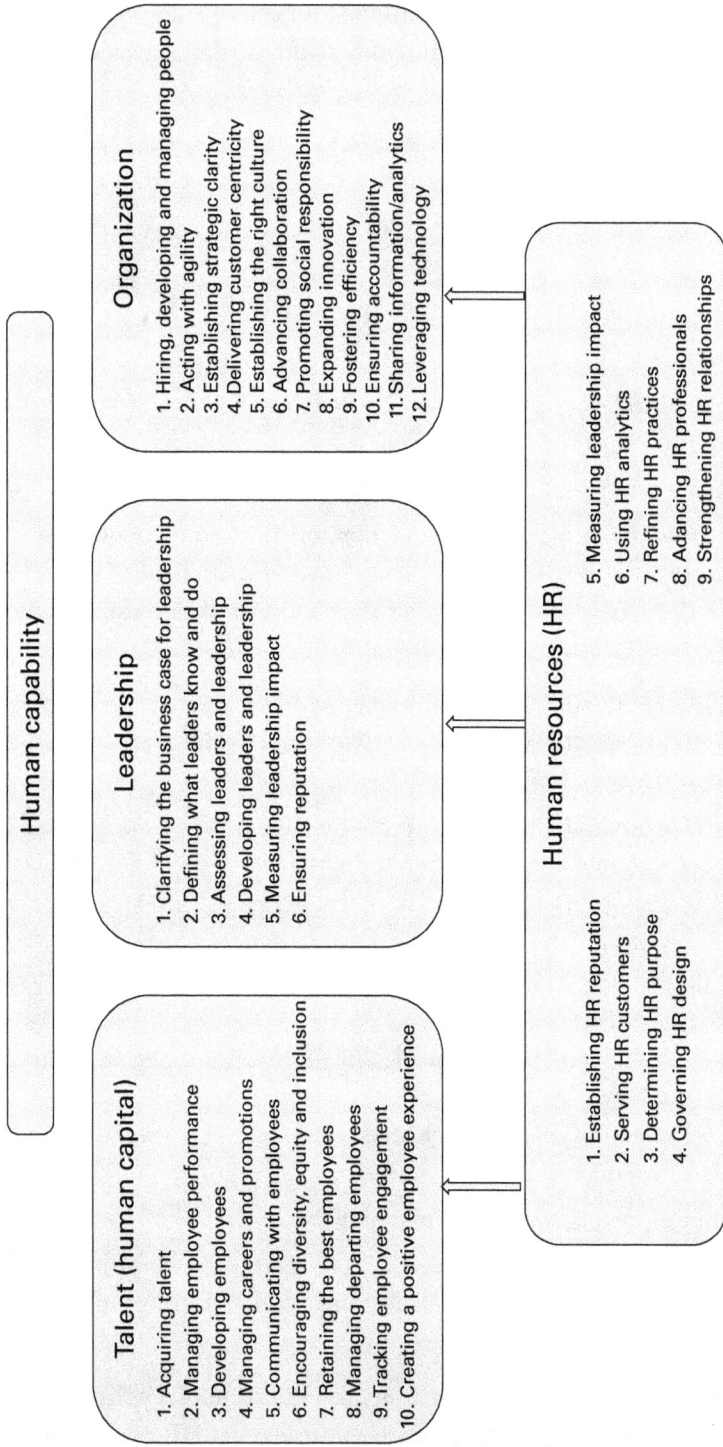

Human capability

Talent (human capital)

1. Acquiring talent
2. Managing employee performance
3. Developing employees
4. Managing careers and promotions
5. Communicating with employees
6. Encouraging diversity, equity and inclusion
7. Retaining the best employees
8. Managing departing employees
9. Tracking employee engagement
10. Creating a positive employee experience

Leadership

1. Clarifying the business case for leadership
2. Defining what leaders know and do
3. Assessing leaders and leadership
4. Developing leaders and leadership
5. Measuring leadership impact
6. Ensuring reputation

Organization

1. Hiring, developing and managing people
2. Acting with agility
3. Establishing strategic clarity
4. Delivering customer centricity
5. Establishing the right culture
6. Advancing collaboration
7. Promoting social responsibility
8. Expanding innovation
9. Fostering efficiency
10. Ensuring accountability
11. Sharing information/analytics
12. Leveraging technology

Human resources (HR)

1. Establishing HR reputation
2. Serving HR customers
3. Determining HR purpose
4. Governing HR design
5. Measuring leadership impact
6. Using HR analytics
7. Refining HR practices
8. Advancing HR professionals
9. Strengthening HR relationships

Developing new HR capabilities in systems, products, analytics, digital and science

For HR to function effectively in these new models, HR professionals must upskill and reskill in areas beyond traditional HR expertise. The most critical new capabilities are outlined in Table 9.1.

TABLE 9.1 New HR capabilities

Data fluency	Every HR leader must understand how to use workforce analytics to make strategic decisions.
AI – augmentation and automation	HR should lead in leveraging AI-powered talent acquisition, internal mobility platforms and personalized learning.
Digital-first thinking	HR services should be designed with a consumer-grade digital experience, using tools like chatbots, self-service dashboards and digital collaboration platforms.
Behavioural science and human-centred design	HR teams should incorporate psychological insights and user experience design into performance management, engagement strategies and learning ecosystems.
Product Management expertise	HR professionals should adopt agile product development approaches, designing HR services with A/B testing, iterative feedback and user personas.
Systems Thinking	How to analyse, understand, navigate, shape and utilize complex adaptive systems in creating value for people and the business (and all the stakeholders engaged or impacted upon the work of HR).
Value creation	Understanding and using a broader range of value creation methods and measures and being able to report and present HR's value through data and evidence-based appraisals and decisions.
Innovation and creative thinking	As a repeat critical skill in things like the World Economic Forum's reports, novel circumstances and unprecedented change and incidents require creative and adaptive thinking and application of solutions.

Reimagining HR roles from their traditional job brackets to more dynamic role frames

For the HR function to truly embed these principles they will need to pioneer a detachment from fixed 'vessels' of the job traditions, towards more adaptable roles that morph and flex to the demands of the work and impacts necessary to create human and business value.

- From roles cast in the three pillars of the Business Partner model to working as problem-solving, professional services roles that operate in cross-functional teams – assembling, disassembling and reassembling into 'networks of excellence', not centres of excellence.

- We can frame our roles to mean more to our business colleagues, so we have distinct specialities and proficiencies: People Analyst, Performance Architect, Systems Designer, People Scientist, Product Manager, Academy Faculty and Workforce Planning Consultant.

- Moving our mental models from fixed to fluid but having a clear belonging to professional disciplines – from ER Advisor to Employment Law Practice Lead – showing it is still important for us to have professional 'anchoring' without it feeling obtuse to business value and strategic growth and not overly fixated on traditional structures and representation of the impact and value of our work. We should pioneer the departure from ageing job description constructs into more dynamic roles and capability pools of professional practitioners and leaders.

- Using more Agile approaches to how the HR team 'swarms' to providing solutions to problems and creating strategic impact in pursuit of human and business value creation.

And there is a double gain in HR realigning itself to more fluidity and measurable impact through the *disaggregation* of jobs into capability pools, responsive teams and shorter maturity curves on value creation and learning, to use their own operating model shift then to influence more widely across other business areas still acting in rigid verticals. What better way to bring in more dynamic forms of Organization Design than to have tested, learned and embedded that in your own function?

If anything, HR Centres of Excellence in Organization Design and Development are often so fixated on doing that work across the business, there's some short-sightedness on HR as a function to have a pioneering and experimental version of OD/D for itself.

HR 3.0 addresses this by being a function that pioneers itself before it can be truly confident in delivering that transformation for its business colleagues and functions.

To do that, HR will have become comfortable and confident in expunging traditional jobs and creating more dynamic and proficient skills-based, diversified and adaptive roles.

Reframing HR as a strategic growth function

HR has an opportunity to reposition itself as a business growth driver by:

- aligning HR directly with financial performance, innovation cycles and customer outcomes;
- shifting from one-size-fits-all policies to flexible, personalized workforce solutions;
- embedding continuous iteration into HR strategy, moving away from static annual processes;
- partnering with finance, governance and operations to integrate real-time workforce insights into business decision making;
- creating a culture of workforce experimentation, where HR prototypes solutions before scaling them.

Conclusion – Systemic HR and the Human Capability Model

Both Bersin and Ulrich recognize that through their distinct but related work, the HR Operating Model and professional capabilities within the field are expanding, adapting and strengthening.

Potential business resistance to HR 3.0: organizational barriers to transformation

Let's be realistic about all of this: even if HR leaders are prepared to drive transformation, the wider business environment can be a major obstacle to adopting a more progressive HR Operating Model like HR 3.0. Many of the challenges HR faces are not internal but stem from the legacy structures, leadership mindsets and operational constraints of the businesses they support and enable.

Leadership and executive reluctance

Many business leaders still view HR through a traditional compliance and cost-control lens rather than as a strategic function. Key reasons for their reluctance include:

- **Fear of decentralizing control**
  HR 3.0 shifts decision-making power to employees and managers through self-service tools, skills-based talent models and AI-driven workforce planning, which can make executives uncomfortable as they lose direct oversight of people decisions.

- **A focus on short-term financial goals**
  Many businesses prioritize quarterly results over long-term workforce transformation. Investing in HR 3.0's data-driven, product-led approach requires time and financial commitment that some executives are unwilling to make.

- **Limited understanding of HR's strategic impact**
  Business leaders who lack exposure to modern HR models may not see the value in moving away from static, process-driven HR functions.

- **HR seen as an innovation stifler, not a leading light**
  HR has often been asked to play a governance role and therefore adopt risk-management approaches to corporate initiatives and change programmes. However, this is not a paradigm HR needs to stay in. Some of the most innovative organizations adopt more flexible and experimental people practices: Menlo Innovations, Spotify and HubSpot in digital tech; Novartis, Roche and Bayer in pharma; NatWest, Atom Bank and Raiffeisen Bank in finance; and Lego, Unilever and Ikea in FMCG. All of these organizations need progressive HR, and experimentation and creativity are key.

Resistance from middle management

The most entrenched resistance may come from middle management. These leaders are often the ones most impacted by HR model changes yet are rarely included as co-creators in transformation efforts. Their resistance stems from:

- **Fear of job role changes or eliminations**
  With HR 3.0 emphasizing skills-based hiring, agile teams and automation, middle managers may feel their traditional hierarchical authority is diminished.

- **Lack of capability to manage talent in new ways**
  Many managers are not trained or strongly capable in data-driven people management, coaching-based leadership or agile workforce planning.

- **Increased accountability for employee experience**
  HR 3.0 shifts responsibility for performance enablement, career development, a culture of inclusion and well-being closer to the business, requiring managers to take a more active and strategic role in talent development.

Siloed business functions and legacy processes

Many businesses are structured around rigid functional silos, making cross-functional collaboration difficult. This has continually limited HR's ability to implement integrated, enterprise-wide workforce strategies. Challenges include:

- **HR's reliance on orthodox business processes**
  Many HR functions are forced to work within legacy ERP systems, finance-driven headcount controls and slow-moving approval hierarchies that stifle agility.

- **Fragmented people data**
  HR analytics in many companies are siloed between finance, operations and IT, preventing real-time workforce decision making.

- **Lack of alignment between HR and business goals**
  HR transformation efforts often compete with or are deprioritized in favour of more immediate business priorities such as market expansion, digital transformation or cost-cutting measures.

Organizational risk aversion and compliance-driven mindsets

HR 3.0 requires organizations to be more comfortable with experimentation, adaptive workforce models and AI-driven decision making. However, many companies operate within highly regulated environments or compliance-heavy industries that resist these changes. Common concerns include:

- **Legal and compliance fears**
  Companies in banking, healthcare and government sectors may hesitate to introduce AI-powered hiring, gig-based workforce strategies or new performance models due to legal scrutiny and regulatory risks.

- **Fear of cultural disruption**
  Businesses with strong legacy cultures may resist the greater transparency, continuous feedback loops and flexible working structures that HR 3.0 promotes.

- **Data privacy and ethics concerns**
  As HR increasingly relies on people analytics, sentiment analysis and AI-driven talent insights, organizations worry about GDPR compliance, algorithmic bias and workforce surveillance risks.

Investment challenges and competing priorities

HR 3.0 is not necessarily a cost-free, incremental shift – it likely requires investment in technology, upskilling and cultural change. Many businesses struggle to justify the cost when faced with other pressing investment priorities such as:

- **Digital transformation in other areas**
  Many organizations prioritize customer experience (CX) innovation, IT modernization or supply chain automation over HR technology investment.

- **Short-term ROI expectations**
  Business leaders often look for immediate returns, but HR 3.0 requires long-term capability building before yielding measurable results.

- **HR's limited influence over capital allocation**
  Unlike IT or operations, HR often lacks the budgetary 'clout' and executive advocacy needed to drive substantial investment.

Workforce expectations and employee adaptability

While HR 3.0 is designed to create a more personalized and empowering employee experience, workforce adaptation can be a major challenge. Employees may resist:

- **Greater self-service and digital HR tools**
  Some employees prefer traditional HR support models and may struggle with AI-driven career management or self-directed learning.

- **Shifts towards skills-based work over job titles**
  Employees used to linear career paths and hierarchical promotions may resist the dynamic, skills-based work models that HR 3.0 promotes.

- **Continuous feedback and performance transparency**
Many employees are unaccustomed to real-time performance tracking, open feedback loops and AI-driven assessments.

Addressing these business-driven obstacles requires HR to strengthen alliances with executive leadership, middle management and employees to create a shared vision for HR transformation. The next section will explore practical strategies for overcoming these external barriers and embedding HR 3.0 principles into the broader business landscape.

Overcoming barriers: experimentation, iteration and adaptive change

Addressing resistance to HR 3.0 requires a structured yet adaptive approach that prioritizes experimentation, rapid learning loops and iterative design over rigid, one-time transformation programmes. Instead of attempting an all-at-once revolution, HR must work within organizations' constraints, test new models incrementally and use evidence-based insights to refine and scale successful initiatives.

Using test-and-learn strategies for HR model evolution

HR must adopt agile, experimental approaches that mirror lean product development and iterative problem-solving methodologies. Instead of imposing change, HR should:

- **Run controlled HR pilots with real business units**
Rather than rolling out sweeping transformations, HR should prototype small-scale changes in willing teams, test impact and refine approaches before enterprise-wide adoption.

- **Implement 'minimum viable HR solutions'**
Borrowing from lean start-up thinking, HR should develop simple, low-risk versions of new models, gather feedback and evolve them based on data-driven insights rather than assumptions.

- **Use A/B testing for HR programmes**
Pilot different iterations of HR policies (e.g. traditional performance reviews vs continuous feedback models) and analyse what actually improves workforce engagement, performance and retention.

- **Adopt data-backed iteration cycles**
  Set fixed cycles (e.g. quarterly) for evaluating, refining and scaling HR transformation efforts based on business and employee response.

Embedding an experimentation culture in workforce strategy

HR can only succeed in modernizing its model if business leaders and managers actively participate. To achieve this, HR should:

- **Introduce 'HR Innovation Labs' within organizations**
  Establish dedicated teams responsible for testing, measuring and iterating new HR initiatives in collaboration with employees and leadership.
- **Reward participation in workforce experiments**
  Encourage employees and managers to engage in testing HR 3.0 initiatives by offering incentives such as leadership visibility, upskilling credits or internal recognition.
- **Establish rapid debrief loops for failures**
  Instead of treating failed initiatives as setbacks, HR should embed structured retrospective analysis that captures learnings and quickly applies them to next iterations.

Reframing leadership buy-in through data and proof of concept

One of the biggest obstacles to HR transformation is executive scepticism. To mitigate this, HR should:

- **Start with small, high-impact workforce interventions**
  For example, replacing annual engagement surveys with real-time sentiment tracking demonstrates value without requiring systemic overhauls.
- **Use business-relevant KPIs rather than traditional HR metrics**
  Instead of measuring HR's success through process efficiency (e.g. time-to-hire), HR should frame success using revenue-per-employee, productivity gains or retention of top talent.
- **Create rapid leadership engagement cycles**
  HR must present real-time workforce insights to executives monthly or quarterly, showing how iterative HR changes impact business strategy, rather than relying on static annual reports.

- **Showcase external benchmarks**
  Business leaders trust data based on comparisons before feeling comfortable and confident to adopt something new themselves. HR should compare their organization's talent agility, reskilling rates or engagement scores to industry leaders to build urgency for transformation.

Embedding HR technology with a focus on adaptability and value creation

Technology is a key enabler of HR 3.0, but many organizations struggle with rigid legacy systems. To address this:

- Deploy flexible, modular HR technology: instead of overhauling entire systems, HR should introduce API-driven, adaptable solutions that can evolve over time (e.g. integrating AI-powered talent tools into existing HCM systems).
- Pilot AI-driven workforce planning tools: experiment with AI models that predict skill gaps, internal mobility trends and attrition risks, allowing for data-driven workforce agility.
- Use low-code/no-code HR tools to empower business teams.
- Providing managers with easy-to-use workforce analytics dashboards can decentralize decision making and increase HR adoption rates.

Scaling what works: adaptive growth of HR 3.0

Once HR experiments prove successful, the challenge becomes scaling change sustainably. This requires:

- **Gradual expansion of successful pilots**
  If HR product ownership models or agile talent mobility frameworks succeed in certain units, they should be refined and expanded rather than rushed into company-wide adoption.
- **Leveraging internal HR champions**
  HR should build an advocate network of early adopters who help embed new models peer-to-peer rather than relying on top-down enforcement.
- **Embedding iteration into HR governance**
  HR transformation should never be seen as a one-time project but as a continuous evolution, with built-in reflection points to ensure constant model refinement.

The future of HR's Operating Model: sustaining long-term evolution

Moving HR beyond legacy constraints and towards a continuously evolving, adaptive model requires more than just initial transformation efforts – it requires a long-term commitment to sustained innovation, cultural embedding and systemic reinforcement. The following approaches will ensure HR 3.0 is not just a fleeting initiative but an ongoing driver of workforce agility and business success.

Embedding continuous adaptation into HR strategy

HR transformation should never be treated as a one-off project; instead, it must be built on continuous iteration cycles. Organizations can sustain HR 3.0 by:

- **Creating an HR transformation roadmap with rolling iterations**
  Instead of planning for a single large-scale change, organizations should implement a three–five-year roadmap that prioritizes incremental improvements based on data-driven insights.

- **Establishing an HR evolution council**
  A dedicated team within HR should be responsible for ongoing evaluation, testing and enhancement of HR products and services, ensuring that models remain aligned with business needs.

- **Building transformation KPIs into HR performance metrics**
  HR's effectiveness should not only be measured by cost efficiency or compliance but also by workforce agility, talent mobility and the adoption rate of new HR services.

Shaping a workforce-centric culture that embraces change

One of the biggest risks in HR transformation is cultural inertia. To prevent regression into old ways of working, organizations must:

- **Promote workforce co-creation**
  Employees should not just be passive recipients of HR services; instead, they should be actively involved in designing HR policies, feedback loops and career development programmes.

- **Use behaviour change methodologies**
  Applying nudge theory, gamification and behavioural economics can encourage employees and leaders to gradually adopt and sustain new HR models.

- **Encourage cross-functional HR experiments**
  Embedding HR transformation within business operations, not just HR functions, ensures that it is deeply integrated into how work gets done across the organization.

Leveraging technology as a scalable enabler

Technology must be viewed as an adaptive enabler of HR 3.0, not just a one-time implementation project. HR can sustain its transformation by:

- **Moving towards an HR ecosystem approach**
  Rather than relying on a single HRIS or monolithic platform, HR should adopt modular, API-driven technologies that evolve with organizational needs.
- **Implementing AI-driven talent marketplaces**
  Internal talent platforms and gig-style project marketplaces allow organizations to match employees to dynamic work opportunities based on real-time skill data.
- **Using AI-powered workforce analytics for ongoing decision making**
  HR should leverage predictive workforce insights to make adaptive, real-time adjustments to talent strategy, compensation models and succession planning.

Building HR's influence as a business function

To sustain long-term transformation, HR must be perceived as an indispensable strategic function, not just an administrative department. This requires:

- **Integrating HR into revenue-impacting strategies**
  HR should co-lead business initiatives such as workforce planning for new markets, leadership development for innovation and talent strategies for digital transformation.
- **Partnering with finance and operations leaders**
  Aligning HR investments with business growth objectives ensures continued budget prioritization and executive support.
- **Educating the C-suite on HR 3.0's business impact**
  HR leaders must proactively demonstrate how workforce agility, skills-based models and talent optimization directly improve financial outcomes.

Ensuring HR 3.0 remains agile and responsive to business evolution

Sustained transformation depends on HR's ability to stay ahead of workforce and business trends. HR should:

- **Monitor external market trends continuously**
  Understanding future skills demand, automation impacts and global workforce shifts allows HR to adapt before disruption happens.

- **Conduct quarterly HR retrospectives**
  Regularly revisiting what's working, what's failing and what needs adjusting keeps HR agile and prevents stagnation.

- **Develop an 'HR Beta' mindset**
  Just as technology companies launch beta versions before full product releases, HR should treat new initiatives as ongoing pilots, always open to refinement.

Conclusion: HR as a constantly evolving function

The shift to HR 3.0, Systemic HR and capability-based models is no longer optional – it is imperative for HR's relevance and enhanced business, operational, people, culture and intellectual value. To succeed, HR must:

- embrace an iterative, agile approach to transformation rather than a rigid, one-time change;
- continuously refine its role as a driver of workforce and business success;
- position itself as a future-ready, technology-enabled function that drives measurable impact.

By embedding experimentation, co-creation and real-time workforce analytics into its DNA, HR can finally become an adaptive, business-aligned function that continuously evolves alongside the organization it serves: HR as a true enabler of workforce agility, innovation and organizational success.

WHAT WE'VE COVERED IN THIS CHAPTER

This chapter has explored why HR's Operating Model has remained stagnant for decades, the organizational resistance that holds transformation back and the strategic solutions needed to drive HR 3.0 forward. HR 3.0 has been designed to capitalize on what key leading analysts in the industry (particularly Josh

Bersin and Dave Ulrich) are already predicting and sensing, exploring and researching, working in pockets with advanced practices in some HR teams and functions.

Key takeaways include:

1   **HR has struggled to shift from its legacy structures due to cultural inertia, leadership hesitance and lack of digital and data-driven capabilities.**

2   **Organizational barriers such as middle management resistance, siloed business processes and risk aversion have made transformation difficult.**

3   **Experimentation, iteration and test-and-learn approaches are crucial – HR cannot afford to take an 'all-or-nothing' approach to change.**

4   **Embedding HR 3.0 requires sustained effort, leadership advocacy and data-backed decision making, ensuring that HR is seen as a strategic, business-critical function.**

As HR professionals and business leaders look ahead, the focus should be on continuous adaptation, leveraging AI-driven insights and aligning HR with core business strategy. Transformation is no longer an option – it is an imperative. The next step is not to ask whether HR can change, but how quickly and effectively HR can embed these principles into their own value creation and across their entire organization.

References and further reading

Bersin, J (2023) Introducing The Systemic HR™ Initiative, https://joshbersin. com/2023/12/introducing-the-systemic-hr-initiative/ (archived at https://perma. cc/8WCD-UR5X)

Deloitte (2024) 2024 Global Human Capital Trends: HR 3.0 and workforce agility, www2.deloitte.com/content/dam/insights/articles/glob176836_global-human-capital-trends-2024/DI_Global-Human-Capital-Trends-2024.pdf (archived at https://perma.cc/Y9Y7-TD4N)

Drucker, P (1980) *Managing in Turbulent Times*, New York: Harper & Row

Lewin, K (1951) *Field Theory in Social Science: Selected theoretical papers*, New York: Harper & Row

McKinsey & Company (2022) HR's new operating model, www.mckinsey.com/ capabilities/people-and-organizational-performance/our-insights/hrs-new-operating-model (archived at https://perma.cc/D22G-VYGU)

Mintzberg, H (1979) *The Structuring of Organizations: A synthesis of the research*, Englewood Cliffs, NJ: Prentice-Hall

Ulrich, D (2024) Update on HR Business Partner model continuing evolution and relevance, www.linkedin.com/pulse/update-hr-business-partner-model-continuing-evolution-dave-ulrich-vqwoc/ (archived at https://perma.cc/P7RC-SGC8)

World Economic Forum (2023) The Future of Jobs Report 2020: Workforce trends for the 2020s, www3.weforum.org/docs/WEF_Future_of_Jobs_2020.pdf (archived at https://perma.cc/F83W-R5NW)

10

Insights from thought leaders

For good ideas and true innovation, you need human interaction, conflict, argument, debate.

MARGARET HEFFERNAN, CEO, ENTREPRENEUR AND AUTHOR

WHAT'S COVERED IN THIS CHAPTER

- **Perspectives:** What HR leaders, business executives and futurists believe is ahead of us.

- **Diverse views:** A range of perspectives on the future of HR and the role of HR 3.0.

- **Future vision:** A compilation of how thought leaders envision even further evolution of HR.

- **Practices**.

Introduction: the new frontiers of HR

HR 3.0 is not about incremental improvements – it represents a paradigm shift in how HR operates. No longer a support function focused on policies and compliance, HR must evolve into a strategic business enabler that integrates agility, workforce adaptability, Systems Thinking, product innovation and behavioural science to shape the future of work.

This chapter curates the insights of leading HR thinkers, futurists and practitioners who have challenged traditional models, paving the way for HR 3.0. Their work is not just theoretical but deeply practical, guiding HR leaders to reinvent how organizations attract, develop, engage and deploy talent.

Rethinking HR's role: from support function to business engine

For decades, HR has oscillated between operational execution and strategic aspiration. Dave Ulrich's HR Business Partner model helped shift HR towards business strategy, but its execution often fell short, leaving many HR teams caught between outdated administrative tasks and a struggle for executive influence.

> HR leaders are business builders, not just business partners. – Josh Bersin

HR 3.0 goes beyond strategy alignment – it fully integrates HR into the business ecosystem. It moves from a reactive, policy-driven function to a proactive, value-generating system that anticipates and adapts to business needs.

THE CALL FOR A NEW HR OPERATING MODEL
HR 3.0 is shaped by four major forces:

1 **Workforce fluidity.** Traditional job structures are fading. Organizations must dynamically match skills to business needs.
2 **Technological acceleration.** AI, automation and predictive analytics reshape how HR operates.
3 **Human-centric expectations and design.** People seek purpose, fulfilment, well-being, autonomy and continuous learning from their work.
4 **Business agility.** Markets shift fast; HR must move even faster.

HR 3.0's mission is clear: create adaptable organizations where talent, culture and leadership drive business success.

Theories 'lying around': building on existing thought leadership

Rutger Bregman noted that every major economic transformation builds on existing ideas. HR 3.0 is no different – it consolidates progressive thinking from multiple disciplines (Cann, 2019).

This chapter synthesises insights from:

- **Katarina Berg** – Spotify CHRO and Agile HR, data-driven employee experience.
- **Josh Bersin** – Systemic HR, digital transformation.

- **John Boudreau and Ravin Jesuthasan** – Skills-based organizations, dynamic workforce models.
- **Rob Briner** – Championing evidence-based HR practice and dispelling corporate mythologies.
- **Tomas Chamorro-Premuzic** – AI in hiring, leadership assessment.
- **Richard Claydon** – Complexity, adaptive leadership, high-performance psychology.
- **Adam Grant** – Motivation, workplace culture and rethinking leadership.
- **Margaret Heffernan** – Psychological safety and the power of dissent.
- **Linda Hill** – Innovation through collective genius.
- **Heather McGowan** – Adaptive learning and continuous workforce transformation.
- **Nathalie Nahai** – Digital ethics and behavioural science in HR.
- **Fons Trompenaars** – Cross-cultural leadership, complexity.

Key components of HR 3.0 as a progressive operating model: HR's shift to dynamic, iterative ways of working

The need for change and moving from process-driven to adaptive HR

Traditional HR functions were built around static processes, structured around annual cycles, rigid policies and hierarchical decision making. Talent acquisition followed fixed job descriptions, performance management revolved around annual reviews, and learning and development was often a one-size-fits-all approach.

However, in a world of continuous disruption, automation and evolving workforce expectations, these models no longer suffice. Organizations that thrive are those that embrace fluidity rather than efficiency – adapting rapidly to change rather than enforcing rigid systems.

> The organizations that thrive in the future will be the ones that embrace fluidity, not just efficiency. – Ravin Jesuthasan

HR must evolve from being a gatekeeper of processes to an adaptive enabler of change – a function that constantly iterates, experiments and evolves to meet shifting business and workforce needs.

Agile principles in HR: from fixed structures to continuous experimentation

HR 3.0 draws inspiration from Agile methodologies – a concept pioneered in software development but increasingly applied to business functions, including HR:

- Iteration over perfection – instead of waiting for a fully polished HR strategy, HR 3.0 focuses on small, continuous improvements driven by employee feedback and business needs.
- Cross-functional collaboration – HR cannot operate in a silo. It must integrate with business strategy, technology and operations, much like Agile teams that blend disciplines to drive innovation.
- Rapid experimentation – HR initiatives should be tested, measured and refined in real time rather than being rolled out as static, long-term programmes.
- Feedback loops and adaptation – instead of annual employee surveys, organizations should continuously gather and act upon employee sentiment, ensuring workplace policies, leadership models and talent strategies evolve in real time.

> HR should function like a product team – constantly testing and refining solutions rather than enforcing static policies. – Josh Bersin

Spotify's Agile HR model: a blueprint for adaptive HR

One of the most successful examples of Agile HR in practice is Spotify's model, led by Katarina Berg, their Chief HR Officer.

Spotify reorganized its HR function around small, cross-functional squads rather than traditional HR departments. Each squad works autonomously, focusing on a specific aspect of employee experience, talent management or leadership development.

> We don't just design HR policies and roll them out. We design, test, iterate and improve in real time. – Katarina Berg

Spotify's pioneering work in HR includes:

- Continuous employee feedback – instead of annual performance reviews, Spotify uses regular check-ins and employee sentiment tracking, ensuring managers and teams adjust in real time.

- Decentralized decision making – each squad operates independently and is empowered to experiment with new HR initiatives, whether related to hiring, L&D or employee well-being.
- Flexibility over standardization – there are no rigid HR structures. Instead, HR services are adapted based on what works best for different teams rather than a top-down, one-size-fits-all approach.

This highly adaptive HR model has allowed Spotify to scale globally while maintaining a strong, people-centric culture that attracts top talent.

Beyond jobs: the shift to skills-based talent allocation

Another fundamental transformation in HR 3.0 is the shift from job-based talent management to skills-based workforce models.

For decades, organizations have structured their workforce around fixed job roles, each with a predefined set of responsibilities and competencies. However, as work becomes more fluid and interdisciplinary, rigid job descriptions no longer align with business needs.

Instead, organizations must match talent dynamically to projects and opportunities based on skills, learning agility and emerging business needs.

From rigid career paths to skills-based talent marketplaces

> The best HR models are built on skills, not jobs. Work should be deconstructed into tasks and reconfigured dynamically. – John Boudreau

John Boudreau and Ravin Jesuthasan advocate for deconstructing traditional jobs into discrete tasks, skills and projects. In this model:

- Employees are not locked into rigid career ladders – they move between projects and roles based on evolving capabilities.
- Work is unbundled – tasks are allocated to those best suited for them, whether internal employees, gig workers or AI-driven automation.
- Organizations build internal talent marketplaces, where skills are dynamically matched to emerging opportunities, similar to how freelance platforms connect experts to short-term projects.

> Instead of designing career ladders, we must build career highways – where talent moves laterally, diagonally and fluidly based on skills and aspirations. – Ravin Jesuthasan

Practical applications of skills-based HR 3.0 models

Several forward-thinking organizations are already implementing skills-based workforce models:

- **Unilever's internal talent marketplace** – employees bid for projects internally, gaining experience across functions rather than staying in a single department.

- **Schneider Electric's AI-powered talent matching** – uses AI to predict employee skills gaps and dynamically match talent with strategic business initiatives.

- **AT&T's reskilling initiatives** – instead of hiring externally, AT&T upskills existing employees for emerging roles, saving millions in talent acquisition costs.

These organizations no longer consider work as fixed jobs but as a constantly shifting set of tasks and challenges, requiring a fluid, adaptable HR function to manage this transformation.

The psychological shift: HR as an adaptive function

For HR to truly embrace agility, it must undergo a psychological shift – moving away from control-based policies towards enabling adaptability.

> HR's biggest challenge isnt technology—it's mindset. We must unlearn traditional HR thinking and reimagine our role as enablers of change. – Heather McGowan

- HR must learn to thrive in ambiguity – traditional HR models focus on compliance and standardization, but HR 3.0 requires comfort with experimentation, ambiguity and change.

- HR teams must adopt a growth mindset – HR professionals must continuously learn and iterate, just like employees are expected to.

- HR should become a strategic learning function – L&D must be designed as an ongoing, embedded practice, not a one-time training event.

Conclusion: HR as the engine of organizational adaptability

Agility and adaptability are not just HR priorities – they are business imperatives. In a world where technology, skills and industries evolve faster than ever, HR must become the orchestrator of continuous change.

By embracing Agile methodologies, skills-based workforce models and decentralized decision making, HR can transform from a process-driven function into an adaptive powerhouse – a function that not only reacts to disruption but anticipates and thrives in it.

> HR must move beyond policy enforcement to become the enabler of business agility. – Josh Bersin

The HR teams that succeed in the future will be those that:

- embrace agility as a core HR function, moving from fixed plans to continuous iterations;
- break free from rigid job roles, shifting to skills-based talent marketplaces;
- continuously measure and refine HR strategies using real-time employee feedback loops;
- think like product designers, not policy enforcers, focusing on workforce experience over rigid HR frameworks.

HR's future is not static – it is adaptive, experimental and continuously evolving. The only question is: how quickly will organizations make the shift?

Science and data-driven HR: transforming HR into an evidence-based discipline

From intuition to evidence: the new HR imperative

For decades, HR has often relied on *gut instincts*, experience and *best practices* to make decisions about talent, leadership and workforce engagement. While intuition and human judgment remain valuable, they are insufficient in a world where organizations must make complex, high-stakes decisions about people, skills and work design.

In contrast, finance, operations and marketing have long leveraged rigorous data analysis to drive decisions. HR must now adopt the same analytical discipline to remain credible, impactful and aligned with business strategy.

> HR must adopt the same analytical rigour as finance and operations. – Rob Briner

The shift to evidence-based HR (EBHR) means making decisions based on:

- behavioral science – applying psychology, neuroscience and cognitive research to optimize HR strategies;
- people analytics – using data to measure, predict and improve workforce performance;
- AI and predictive insights – leveraging automation to reduce bias and enhance decision making;
- continuous feedback and testing – iterating and refining HR interventions in real time.

This transformation moves HR away from static policies and broad assumptions towards dynamic, data-driven workforce solutions.

Behavioural science in leadership: measuring what matters

Historically, leadership selection has been based on seniority, charisma and subjective assessments. However, research shows that many of these traits have little correlation with leadership effectiveness.

> We still select leaders based on confidence, not competence – this must change.
> – Tomas Chamorro-Premuzic

Chamorro-Premuzic, a leading organizational psychologist, argues that organizations must move from charisma-based leadership to science-backed leadership selection and development.

How AI and behavioural science improve leadership selection

AI and people analytics can:

- assess leadership potential based on objective traits, not personal biases;
- identify high-potential employees early, rather than waiting for them to rise through hierarchy;
- eliminate gender and racial bias in hiring by using algorithm-driven assessments instead of gut instinct.

For example, Unilever's AI-powered hiring process:

- uses video analytics to assess candidates' cognitive abilities and emotional intelligence;

- reduces bias by anonymizing applications, ensuring talent is evaluated on potential rather than pedigree;
- increases hiring accuracy by 25 per cent, reducing turnover among new hires.

AI-driven leadership assessment tools, like those developed by Chamorro-Premuzic's Meta Profiling, offer predictive insights into a candidate's ability to lead based on real data, not just gut feelings.

Psychological insights and employee engagement

HR has traditionally measured engagement through annual surveys, assuming that salaries, perks and promotions drive performance. However, psychological research contradicts these assumptions.

> Intrinsic motivation – purpose, autonomy and mastery – drives engagement more than financial rewards. – Adam Grant

Adam Grant's work on workplace motivation demonstrates that employees are not just motivated by external rewards but by internal fulfilment. This is famously articulated by analyst Dan Pink in his work in *Drive: The surprising truth about what motivates us.*

- **Purpose** – employees perform best when they understand how their work contributes to a greater goal.
- **Autonomy** – giving people ownership over their work increases innovation and commitment.
- **Mastery** – employees thrive when they are challenged to develop new skills and expertise.

Companies that embed psychological insights into HR strategies see higher retention, engagement, and productivity.

REAL-WORLD EXAMPLE
How Google used psychological science to drive engagement

Google's famous *Project Aristotle* – a research study on what makes teams effective – revealed that:

- **psychological safety** – the ability to speak up without fear of punishment – was the number one driver of high-performing teams;

- **collaboration and trust** mattered more than individual intelligence;
- **structured but flexible team norms** fostered the highest productivity levels.

This research influenced Google's leadership training, shifting focus from hierarchical control to coaching, trust-building and psychological safety.

People analytics: predicting workforce trends before they happen

People analytics allows HR teams to move from lagging indicators (reacting to problems) to leading indicators (predicting and preventing them).

Katarina Berg, Spotify's Chief HR Officer, has pioneered a real-time people analytics system that tracks employee sentiment daily, not yearly.

> We don't wait for an annual engagement survey to understand our people. We track and act on feedback continuously. – Katarina Berg

---

REAL-WORLD EXAMPLE
How Spotify uses people analytics

- **Real-time sentiment analysis** – Spotify continuously tracks employee mood, productivity and engagement.
- **Predicting attrition** – using AI models, Spotify can spot early warning signs of burnout, disengagement or potential turnover.
- **Data-driven HR interventions** – if engagement levels dip, HR teams immediately adjust leadership support, training or work structures.

This real-time approach to workforce analytics has allowed Spotify to:

- reduce employee turnover significantly;
- improve team productivity by aligning management style with employee needs;
- scale its workforce globally while maintaining a unified culture.

Other organizations applying real-time people analytics include:

- **Microsoft** – uses workplace analytics to track collaboration patterns and reduce burnout risk.
- **LinkedIn** – uses AI to identify top talent within the organization and redeploy them to new projects.

- **Walmart** – uses predictive analytics to improve scheduling and reduce turnover among frontline workers.

The ethics of data-driven HR: balancing insights with trust

While AI, people analytics and behavioural science unlock incredible potential, they also raise ethical concerns about privacy, bias and decision-making transparency.

> The power of AI in HR comes with responsibility – how we use it determines whether it helps or harms employees. – Nathalie Nahai

HR 3.0 must ensure that AI-driven workforce decisions are:

- transparent – employees must understand how data is collected and used;
- bias-free – algorithms must be audited to prevent discrimination;
- consent-driven – employees must have a say in how their personal data is analysed.

Companies like IBM and Salesforce are leading the charge in ethical AI for HR, ensuring that:

- AI-driven hiring systems are regularly audited for bias;
- employee data is anonymized to protect privacy;
- decision-making algorithms are explainable, so employees trust the insights provided.

HR must balance data-driven decision making with ethical responsibility, ensuring that technology empowers, rather than exploits, employees.

Conclusion: science-led HR is the future

HR 3.0 is not about gut feeling – it's about evidence, experimentation and iteration.

By embracing behavioural science, AI-driven leadership selection, real-time people analytics and ethical workforce data, HR can:

- improve decision-making accuracy;
- enhance engagement and performance;
- predict and prevent workforce challenges before they escalate;
- build a fairer, more inclusive and data-driven HR function.

> The future of HR belongs to those who embrace evidence over intuition. – Rob Briner

The challenge for HR leaders is clear: will we adapt to an evidence-based future or will we cling to outdated assumptions?

The smartest organizations are already making the shift – the question is, how can we make this our norm and help our evolution as key business value creators?

Systems Thinking and organizational complexity: rethinking HR as an adaptive system

From linear thinking to Systems Thinking: why HR has to adapt

For much of its history, HR has operated under linear, mechanistic models – a hangover from the Industrial Era, perhaps – handling organizations as predictable systems where inputs (policies, processes) directly lead to outputs (performance, engagement, retention). These models assume that HR can design perfect structures, optimize workflows and drive performance through rules, incentives and training.

However, today's organizations are not predictable machines – they are complex, adaptive systems.

> Organizations thrive when they embrace interconnectivity and emergent change. – Fons Trompenaars

This means that:

- Small changes can have outsized, unintended effects – a new HR policy can either boost morale or inadvertently create resistance.
- Solutions that worked in one part of the business may not work in another – HR strategies must be contextual, not one-size-fits-all.
- Culture, leadership and talent are interconnected – fixing engagement issues requires more than perks or policies, it demands a holistic redesign of how work happens.

HR's tendency has been to design (often) isolated, top-down programmes and in the Information/Intelligence/Creative Age has to start building interconnected, adaptive *talent ecosystems*.

Breaking down silos: HR as an integrated system

For years, HR functions have been divided into rigid silos:

- Talent acquisition – focused on hiring the best talent.
- Learning and development – separate from hiring, often disconnected from actual skills needs.
- Performance management – reviews held in isolation from employee development.
- Engagement and culture – measured annually with little real-time intervention.

However, this siloed approach creates fragmented workforce experiences, where:

- L&D doesn't strongly align with real business needs;
- recruitment is based on outdated job descriptions rather than emerging skills;
- engagement efforts focus on measuring sentiment rather than improving working conditions.

Josh Bersin argues that HR must function as a fully integrated ecosystem where:

- talent, culture, leadership and operations are interconnected;
- skills development is continuous and aligned with real business demands;
- employee engagement is measured in real time and directly linked to work design.

> HR must stop functioning as a set of disconnected departments and start operating as a dynamic ecosystem. – Josh Bersin

Complexity thinking in HR: moving beyond 'engagement scores'

For years, HR has relied on simple engagement metrics – yearly surveys, pulse checks and satisfaction scores. However, these fail to capture the deeper, more complex reality of employee experience.

> Engagement is not a number – it's an emergent property of how work is designed, how teams interact and how leadership fosters trust. – Richard Claydon

Claydon's work in organizational complexity challenges HR to move beyond:

- treating engagement as an isolated metric – real engagement is about how work is structured, not just how people feel about it;
- linear cause-and-effect models – just because perks or bonuses increase engagement temporarily doesn't mean they solve deeper workplace issues;
- annual surveys as the main engagement measure – engagement changes daily, not yearly and organizations need continuous, adaptive listening.

Instead, HR must adopt a real-time, behaviourally informed model of engagement, where:

- HR continuously analyses work patterns, collaboration networks and leadership behaviours to understand what's really driving engagement;
- leaders focus on psychological safety, autonomy and learning, rather than just providing incentives;
- technology enables real-time feedback, helping teams dynamically adjust instead of waiting for an annual review.

Systems Thinking in HR: learning from other disciplines

To understand why organizations function the way they do, HR must borrow principles from other complex systems – including biology, urban planning and network theory.

ORGANIZATIONS AS LIVING SYSTEMS (BIOLOGY AND ECOLOGY)

> HR must design organizations like living systems – where adaptability, growth and evolution are built-in. – Margaret Heffernan

In biology, complex systems adapt and evolve through constant feedback loops. Organizations work the same way:

- Companies that embrace agility (like Spotify and ING Bank) continuously evolve, while rigid, bureaucratic organizations struggle to respond to change.
- Teams function like ecosystems – where collaboration, competition and knowledge-sharing create emergent outcomes rather than predictable outputs.

- Diversity strengthens adaptability – just like ecosystems thrive on biodiversity, organizations thrive on cognitive diversity, skills variation and diverse perspectives.

This biological model of organizations suggests that HR should not try to control everything – instead, it should create the right conditions for adaptation and innovation.

ORGANIZATIONS AS NETWORKS (URBAN PLANNING AND COMPLEXITY SCIENCE)

> HR should stop designing rigid structures and start designing for emergence – where networks, not hierarchies, define success. – Fons Trompenaars

In urban planning, the best-designed cities are not rigid grids but organic, evolving networks. Cities that thrive:

- allow for self-organization – rather than dictating every street and building, they let people and businesses shape the environment;
- foster connectedness – great cities maximize *cross-pollination* of ideas, people and industries;
- enable adaptation – instead of forcing a one-size-fits-all approach, they allow different neighbourhoods to develop in their own way.

The same principles apply to HR 3.0:

- HR should enable rather than control – creating a flexible, decentralized workforce model.
- Cross-functional teams should replace traditional hierarchies, ensuring knowledge flows freely across the organization.
- Collaboration tools should create networked intelligence, rather than siloed departments.

The HR 3.0 mindset: leading with systems awareness

For HR to fully embrace Systems Thinking, it requires a mindset shift:

Traditional HR thinking (linear model):

- HR designs policies and expects compliance.
- Engagement is measured yearly and assumed to be stable.
- Leadership development happens in programmes, not in real work.
- Employees are expected to work to rigid job roles.

HR 3.0 thinking (systems model):

- HR designs systems where great culture and engagement emerge naturally.
- Workforce health is continuously measured and adjusted in real time.
- Leadership is developed through networks, mentorship and adaptive learning.
- Employees move fluidly between projects based on skills and interests.

> HR's job is to create the conditions for great work to emerge – not to dictate how it happens. – Richard Claydon

Practical actions: how HR can implement Systems Thinking

For HR leaders looking to apply Systems Thinking, here are three immediate steps:

1 Adopt real-time feedback and analytics:

   o shift from annual engagement surveys to continuous feedback loops;

   o use AI-driven tools to spot patterns and adjust interventions dynamically.

2 Rethink leadership development:

   o move from formal programmes to peer learning, coaching networks and self-directed development;

   o identify leadership potential through behavioural data, not just career progression.

3 Enable adaptive workforce design:

   o replace fixed job descriptions with skills-based talent marketplaces;

   o encourage cross-functional movement and experimentation, allowing employees to shift roles based on interests and skills.

Conclusion: HR as the architect of adaptive organizations

HR has a real chance to help organizations stop managing people as if they were static assets – instead, HR can drive the design organizations as dynamic, evolving systems, where:

- HR is not a *control* function – it is an *enabler* of adaptability that *drives* sustainable performance and *fulfilment* for people;

- the best HR leaders understand complexity, emergence and networked intelligence;
- organizations that embrace Systems Thinking will outpace those stuck in rigid structures.

The real question is: can HR catalyse organizations to evolve fast enough to lead this transformation?

> The future belongs to organizations that can sense, adapt and evolve in real time. HR must be the engine that makes this happen. – Josh Bersin

Process and product mindset: reimagining HR as a design-driven discipline

Moving from policy enforcement to workforce experience design

For decades, HR work has been felt and been seen as that of policy creator and enforcer – creating rules, procedures and governance structures (driven by a raft of employment law changes) that dictate how work should be done. Indeed, many leaders have become the drivers of their companies, insisting on a policy for every conceivable eventuality – sometimes resulting in hundreds of policies – a baffling array of acute definitions, from using company resources to comfort breaks and use of social media.

While compliance remains essential, this rigid approach to HR design no longer serves modern organizations. Today's workforce expects flexibility, personalization and a frictionless employee experience – HR must transition from rule-maker to experience architect.

> HR should be thought of as a product team – building, testing and iterating solutions for employees. – Josh Bersin

Rather than designing policies and expecting compliance, HR must:

- understand the end-user experience – employees, managers and teams are HR's 'customers' and their needs should drive HR solutions;
- use iterative design methods – HR processes should be continuously refined through experiments, user feedback and real-world testing;
- think like product managers – instead of assuming policies will work, HR must test, adapt and optimize based on data.

This shift mirrors the transformation seen in customer experience (CX) and product design. Just as companies create seamless customer experiences, HR must now build seamless workforce experiences – ones that are engaging, efficient and adaptive.

Agile methods in HR: continuous experimentation over standardization

Traditional HR follows a waterfall approach – long planning cycles, rigid structures and slow implementation. In contrast, HR 3.0 embraces Agile methodologies, ensuring that HR practices evolve continuously based on real-time feedback.

> HR needs to operate like a startup – constantly testing new ideas, refining processes and responding to workforce changes in real time. – Heather McGowan

In Agile HR, processes such as onboarding, learning and development (L&D), and performance management are:

- continuously tested and optimized – instead of launching large-scale HR initiatives, organizations roll out small, testable improvements based on employee feedback;
- adaptive to business and workforce needs – HR doesn't wait a year to adjust a policy – it iterates constantly, making incremental improvements;
- built for real-time engagement – performance feedback isn't an annual process but a continuous conversation integrated into daily work.

How Agile HR works in practice

ONBOARDING AS A PRODUCT

- Traditional onboarding is a fixed, 90-day process – in contrast, Airbnb and Google treat onboarding as an evolving experience.
- Employees provide weekly feedback on the onboarding process, allowing HR teams to adjust content and support in real time.
- HR product teams experiment with different ways to improve first-week experiences, mentoring and team integration, treating onboarding as a dynamic product, not a checklist.

L&D AS A CONTINUOUS LEARNING JOURNEY

- Old L&D models rely on formal training sessions delivered once or twice a year.
- Spotify and Microsoft have replaced this with self-directed, always-available learning ecosystems.
- Employees choose micro-learning paths that adapt to their career progression, using AI-powered content recommendations to personalize training.

PERFORMANCE MANAGEMENT AS AN ITERATIVE PROCESS

- Annual reviews are slow, biased and disconnected from real work.
- Agile HR replaces this with quarterly check-ins, ongoing feedback and peer coaching.
- Companies like Netflix and Google use continuous feedback tools, allowing managers and employees to adjust goals, skills and projects dynamically.

This approach treats every HR process like a product – always in beta, always improving.

The end of static careers: reskilling and redeployment as the new normal

The idea of linear career progression is disappearing. Employees are no longer spending decades climbing a single corporate ladder – instead, they expect fluid, evolving career paths where they:

- continuously develop new skills;
- move between roles based on emerging business needs;
- shift across industries and career functions multiple times.

> Workforce transformation is no longer an event – it's a continuous, lifelong process. – Heather McGowan

HR 3.0 gives us a chance to design careers with flexibility built in, ensuring that employees:

- acquire new skills through adaptive learning platforms;
- are redeployed into new roles as jobs evolve;
- have access to career pathways that are nonlinear, skill-based and opportunity-driven.

REAL-WORLD EXAMPLE

How AT&T future-proofed its workforce

Faced with massive technological disruption, AT&T recognized that half of its employees lacked the skills needed for future jobs. Instead of replacing workers, they:

- invested $1 billion in reskilling initiatives;
- created a digital learning platform to continuously upskill employees in AI, cybersecurity and data science;
- allowed employees to redeploy into new roles based on skills development, rather than forcing rigid career ladders.

The result?

- Forty per cent of AT&T's workforce transitioned to new digital jobs.
- Employee retention improved because workers saw growth opportunities within the company.
- AT&T built an internal talent pipeline instead of relying on external hiring.

HR leaders must design organizations where reskilling and internal mobility are the norm, rather than waiting for employees to become obsolete.

The HR 3.0 mindset: from process execution to experience design

To succeed, HR must adopt the mindset of product designers

TRADITIONAL HR THINKING (PROCESS-DRIVEN)

- HR designs policies and managers and HR enforces them.
- Employees must conform to rigid job structures.
- Career progression follows a fixed, predefined path.
- Training is delivered through standardized programmes, not personalized experiences.

HR 3.0 THINKING (PRODUCT-DRIVEN)

- HR designs experiences based on user needs (employees, managers, leaders).
- Workforce processes are tested, refined and adapted via continuously rolling *feedback loops*.

- Employees move between roles to the work, dynamically, based on evolving business needs.
- Learning and development is embedded in the *flow of work* – not a separate, scheduled series of events.

This mindset ensures that HR doesn't just manage processes – it creates adaptive, employee-centric workforce systems.

> HR should operate like a customer experience team – every touchpoint matters, and every process should be optimized for the best possible employee experience. – Josh Bersin

Practical actions: how HR can implement a product mindset

For HR leaders ready to embrace this shift, here are three immediate actions:

1 Redesign HR processes with employee experience in mind:
   o use journey mapping to analyse every HR interaction (hiring, onboarding, feedback, promotion);
   o identify friction points and bottlenecks – then experiment with small changes to improve them.
2 Apply Agile HR practices:
   o replace long HR policy documents with modular, adaptable frameworks;
   o use pilot programmes to test new talent strategies before full implementation.
3 Embed continuous learning and redeployment:
   o build AI-powered learning platforms that recommend skills training in real time;
   o create internal talent marketplaces where employees apply for new projects or roles based on evolving skills.

Conclusion: HR as the architect of workforce agility

HR 3.0 is no longer about purely process execution – it is about processes that optimize performance *whilst* using experience design to enhance the connection of people, skills and their impact/results linking to the purpose of the enterprise:

- HR functions as a continuous, iterative system – always evolving.

- Talent mobility and learning agility must be core business priorities.
- HR builds organizations where adaptability and innovation are embedded in culture.

> HR is no longer just about policies – it is about creating the conditions for human potential to thrive. – Heather McGowan

The most enduring organizations are shifting to operate this way. The question for HR leaders is: *How will you lead this transformation and evolve to create value for your organization?*

Cultural sensitivity, inclusion and intersectionality as strategic imperatives

Moving beyond DEI compliance to participatory competitive advantage

As this book is written, diversity, equity and inclusion (DEI) is 'under siege'. From seemingly every angle – political, social, operational and societal – there is an attack on DEI initiatives and activities as counter-productive, inefficient and biased in themselves, and are demonized by agendas that are used in election campaigns and in corporate priority setting.

What remains clear though, is at the heart of DEI is **fairness, participation and cultural sensitivity**. Whatever some people would have you believe, equity has *not* been fully achieved; diversity is *still* a winning formula for creativity and balance; and inclusion is just that – *inclusive of all*, no matter who you are, what you believe in and how you go about life.

What is apparent is that some people wish to force their perspectives, opinions and diktats on others. Perhaps because they are feeling affronted, threatened or marginalized by DEI approaches – which is an ironic twist. Ironic because this is *precisely* how people who originate from the Global Majority (aka Global South), women, carers, LGBTQ+, older and younger people in society, those of defined faiths, those living with disabilities and of certain socio-demographic groups, have felt for decades.

What remains once the DEI directions, policies, training and general representations have evolved is still something I would call **cultural sensitivity** – understanding, respecting and appreciating the cultures of different people. Not just customs, labels, practices and vantage points on the world – how people live in a sense of cultural 'make-up'. And within that, inclusivity and intersectionality are still relevant.

I can be both marginalized and in the majority at the same time – I am a European, Caucasian male of a certain age, demographic categorization, chosen style of life, beliefs and values. I would appreciate others to be culturally sensitive to the fact that I happen to be an adult carer for a life partner who has a chronic disease; that I choose not to consume meat of any sort; that I have come to believe in more equitable distribution of wealth and the three pillars of life as health, education and justice for all.

So is DEI dead? The answer is no. It will never be right that people have inequity of opportunity because of some aspects of who they are. *How* they are counts for more.

So, here we look at HR 3.0 as a new vehicle and a way to usher in the evolution of whatever DEI becomes. Fairer, more accessible, inclusive and participatory ways to shape the world for the better can become part of what an HR Operating Model exists to deliver. Else, it's all efficiency and profit and no lasting soul. Combined efficiency of operation, effectiveness of performance, soulful connection to work as a force for good and a sense of prosperity for all is not an ideology; it's the best way to do work and business, and create organizational purpose and a balanced life.

From diversity to inclusion: why it's more than an ethical imperative

For years though, some organizations have treated DEI as a compliance requirement – a box to tick rather than a strategic performance driver. HR teams have had to focus on hiring quotas, unconscious bias training and policies against discrimination, but many of these surface-level initiatives fail to create truly inclusive, high-performing workplaces.

The problem? Diversity alone doesn't drive better outcomes – organizations must actively be it and fully utilize it in that participatory way mentioned already.

> The best organizations don't just tolerate difference – they leverage it. –
> Margaret Heffernan

It has often been said that – putting the furore about 'anti-wokeness' to one side for now as a sensationalist backlash – that DEI is explained thus:

- Diversity is about representation – who is in the room.
- Inclusion is about participation – whose voices are heard.
- Equity is about fairness – who has access to opportunities.

And in looking to bring the best of formal legislative, anti-discriminatory approaches and the more ethical, participative ways to show respect and utilize differences, HR 3.0 can help reframe DEI as a core driver of business success. Not just something HR does, but a systemic way of working that fuels innovation, decision making and growth through cultural sensitivity, inclusion and intersectionality – the complex mosaic of us as individuals, groups, teams and, ultimately, organizations.

The business case for inclusion and participation: why inclusive organizations outperform

Companies with strong inclusion strategies build better workplaces and achieve stronger financial performance, innovation and customer alignment:

- Diverse teams make better decisions 87 per cent of the time (Cloverpop, n.d.).
- Companies with above-average diversity at senior levels outperform competitors by 36 per cent (McKinsey, 2020).
- Inclusive teams are 35 per cent more innovative because they pull from a broader set of perspectives (Rock and Grant, 2016).

Why?

- More perspectives lead to better problem solving – homogeneous teams default to groupthink, whereas diverse teams challenge assumptions and generate stronger insights.
- Employees feel safer to contribute ideas – when organizations actively design for inclusion, employees take more creative risks, leading to better innovation and engagement.
- Companies better reflect the customers they serve – organizations that embrace cultural intelligence are more aligned with global and diverse consumer bases.

Diversity of thought is one of the biggest untapped competitive advantages in business today. – Josh Bersin

Cultural intelligence: moving beyond compliance to strategy

Many organizations approach DEI with static, compliance-driven models, focusing on representation metrics without addressing deeper cultural factors.

> Diversity initiatives must be baked into business strategy, not compliance exercises. – Fons Trompenaars

Trompenaars, a leading expert in cross-cultural leadership, argues that real inclusion requires organizations to integrate cultural intelligence into everyday business operations.

WHAT IS CULTURAL INTELLIGENCE (CQ)?

Cultural Intelligence (CQ) is the ability to work effectively across different cultural contexts, both within teams and across global markets. It goes beyond basic diversity training by embedding inclusion into leadership, decision making and business models.

Companies with high CQ outperform competitors in global markets because they understand and integrate different cultural viewpoints. Research indicates that organizations with high levels of CQ experience significant improvements in various performance metrics:

- A study highlighted by Vorecol found that companies with high CQ experienced a 35 per cent improvement in employee engagement and a 20 per cent boost in team collaboration (Vorecol, 2024).
- Similarly, research from HumanSmart revealed that organizations with diverse and culturally intelligent teams outperform their peers by 35 per cent in terms of financial performance (HumanSmart, 2024).

These findings underscore that cultural intelligence enables companies to effectively bridge cultural gaps, facilitating smoother entry into new markets and providing a competitive edge over less culturally aware competitors.

Leaders with high CQ create more cohesive teams by recognizing and adapting to different working styles, communication norms and leadership expectations. Culturally intelligent leaders are better equipped to build inclusive teams, fostering a sense of belonging and engagement among team members (Jain, 2024).

Additionally, the Center for Creative Leadership emphasizes that leaders must be knowledgeable and open-minded about different cultures to gain a better understanding of employees from diverse backgrounds, which is essential for fostering inclusivity, promoting collaboration and maximizing productivity in teams (Center for Creative Leadership, 2023).

Inclusive design leads to better products and services, ensuring companies serve diverse customer bases more effectively. While specific studies directly linking CQ to product design are limited, the principles of cultural intelligence suggest that understanding and integrating diverse cultural perspectives can enhance product and service offerings. For instance, companies that prioritize CQ in their talent management practices are better equipped to navigate cross-cultural interactions, leading to higher levels of employee engagement and productivity (HumanSmart, 2024).

Moreover, leaders with high CQ create more cohesive teams by recognizing and adapting to different working styles, communication norms and leadership expectations, which can contribute to more innovative and effective product development processes.

In summary, CQ plays a pivotal role in enhancing organizational performance, leadership effectiveness, and the development of products and services that resonate with diverse customer bases.

Real-world examples:

- Airbnb redesigned its customer experience (CX) to reduce racial bias in bookings by implementing anonymous profiles – ensuring guests weren't discriminated against based on race or ethnicity.
- Microsoft embedded accessibility and neurodiversity into its product development process, leading to innovations like real-time captioning and adaptive controllers.

Intersectionality: how inclusion fuels innovation

The best ideas emerge from diverse, cross-functional collaboration, not isolated teams. – Linda Hill

Linda Hill, a professor at Harvard Business School and co-author of the book *Collective Genius*, found that organizations with diverse, cross-functional teams consistently outperform those with homogenous groups:

- Intersectionality refers to the way different aspects of identity (race, gender, ability, socio-economic background) interact to shape experiences in the workplace.
- Companies that fail to recognize intersectionality often create policies that only address one dimension of diversity, missing critical barriers faced by employees with overlapping identities.

WHY INTERSECTIONALITY DRIVES INNOVATION

- Combining diverse disciplines leads to breakthrough ideas – some of the world's greatest innovations come from cross-functional collaboration, where employees from different fields, backgrounds and perspectives co-create solutions.

- Psychological safety enables bolder thinking – teams where employees feel seen, valued and respected are more willing to challenge ideas, experiment and propose unconventional solutions.

- Removing invisible barriers unlocks hidden potential – organizations that intentionally design for inclusion help underrepresented talent contribute fully to the business.

REAL-WORLD EXAMPLE

How Pixar uses intersectionality to create groundbreaking films

Pixar is a masterclass in leveraging intersectionality for innovation. In 2015, the studio realized that most of its movies had male protagonists and were influenced by a narrow set of perspectives.

They restructured creative teams to ensure a wider range of cultural, gender and experiential diversity. This shift led to films like *Coco*, *Soul* and *Turning Red* – each shaped by authentic, intersectional storytelling that resonated globally.

By intentionally structuring teams to bring together diverse viewpoints, Pixar transformed not just the stories they told but how they created them.

Inclusive leadership: creating systemic change

For inclusion and cultural sensitivity to truly work, it cannot be HR's responsibility alone – it must be woven into leadership, decision making and workplace culture at every level.

> Real inclusion isn't a programme – it's leadership in action. – Margaret Heffernan

Inclusive leaders:

- listen deeply and challenge their own biases;
- make decisions with diverse input, not just top-down mandates;
- create space for dissenting perspectives;
- recognize and correct systemic barriers.

HOW TO BUILD INCLUSIVE LEADERSHIP INTO HR STRATEGY

Redesign leadership pipelines, creating a more inclusive product:

- Ensure that succession planning includes diverse talent, rather than defaulting to homogenous candidate pools.
- Use AI-driven assessment tools to reduce bias in leadership selection (Tomas Chamorro-Premuzic's research shows this is one of the biggest barriers to diverse leadership).

Make DEI a core business KPI, building more data and performance analytics:

- Instead of treating diversity as a CSR initiative, companies should tie inclusion to revenue growth, innovation metrics and customer engagement.
- Companies like Salesforce and Intel tie executive bonuses to inclusion progress, ensuring leaders are accountable for real change.

Shift from unconscious bias training to more participatory change:

- Research shows that standalone unconscious bias training rarely leads to long-term behaviour change.
- Instead, companies should focus on redesigning hiring systems, performance evaluations and workplace norms to remove systemic bias.

Conclusion: inclusion as a competitive advantage

HR 3.0 reframes inclusion and intersectionality as:

- a business imperative, not just an HR initiative;
- a driver of innovation, decision making and problem solving;
- a leadership responsibility, not a compliance requirement.

The challenge for HR leaders is no longer why inclusion matters – it's how fast they can build truly inclusive systems.

> The future of work isn't just diverse – it's equitable, inclusive and driven by intersectional intelligence. – Linda Hill

Organizations that embrace this will win on talent, performance and market leadership. The question isn't *whether* to invest in inclusive participation – it's whether you can afford *not* to.

HR 3.0 in practice: transforming the people function

HR 3.0 is not an aspiration – it is an operational shift already unfolding.

- Skills-based organizations (Boudreau and Jesuthasan) – work decomposes into skills, allowing fluid, gig-like workforce models inside organizations.
- AI and people analytics (Chamorro-Premuzic, Berg) – real-time AI-powered systems predict turnover, optimize hiring and enhance leadership selection.
- HR as an innovation engine (Hill, Grant, Heffernan) – innovation thrives when psychological safety, risk-taking and collective intelligence are fostered.

HR 3.0 enables organizations to:

- move from reactive to proactive HR – anticipate workforce trends and adapt in real time;
- leverage behavioural science and AI – make smarter, bias-free decisions;
- break down silos and integrate talent, culture and leadership;
- create human-centred workplaces where trust, inclusion and innovation thrive.

HR is not a department. It is the engine of business transformation. – Josh Bersin

---

WHAT WE'VE COVERED IN THIS CHAPTER

Throughout this chapter, we have explored the future of HR **through the insights of leading thinkers, futurists and business strategists**. The transition to HR 3.0 is not just about restructuring processes – it is about fundamentally rethinking HR's role in organizations.

HR is evolving from a policy-driven support function to a strategic business enabler – one that integrates agility, behavioural science, Systems Thinking and workforce experience design to create more adaptable, high-performing and human-centred organizations.

1. HR must be agile, adaptive and iterative:

- Traditional HR isn't known for pace, and is considered process-driven and reactive – HR 3.0 is fast, iterative and adaptive.

- Borrowing from Agile methodologies, HR should function like a product team, continuously improving workforce experience through experiments, real-time feedback and iterative design.

- Spotify's Agile HR model shows decentralized, squad-based HR teams can be far more responsive than rigid, hierarchical structures.

Key question: How can HR continuously test and refine its people strategies instead of enforcing static policies?

2. Evidence-based HR is no longer optional:

- For too long, HR has relied on intuition, experience and outdated best practices.

- HR must now operate with the same analytical rigour as finance and operations – leveraging behavioural science, AI and real-time people analytics to improve talent decisions, leadership selection and employee engagement.

- Tomas Chamorro-Premuzic's work reminds us that leadership should be measured and optimized, not assumed, and bias-free AI-driven assessments can enhance hiring decisions.

- Adam Grant's research proves that purpose, autonomy and mastery drive engagement more than financial incentives.

Key question: How can HR leaders shift from gut instinct to data-driven decision making?

3. Organizations are complex systems, not linear machines:

The old HR model assumes that input (policies) leads to predictable output (engagement, performance, retention). In reality, organizations are complex, adaptive systems.

- Josh Bersin argues that HR must operate as an interconnected ecosystem – where talent, culture, leadership and operations are not separate functions but deeply interwoven.

- Richard Claydon's research shows that engagement is not just a metric – it is an emergent property of workplace design, psychological safety and leadership behaviours.

- Systems Thinking helps HR move beyond siloed approaches to create dynamic, cross-functional talent networks.

Key question: How can HR adopt Systems Thinking to design more resilient and interconnected workforce strategies?

4. HR must shift from policy enforcement to experience design:

Employees today expect flexibility, personalization and frictionless experiences – HR must transition from rule-maker to experience architect.

- HR should function like a customer experience (CX) team, continuously improving onboarding, L&D and career progression.
- Heather McGowan emphasizes that static career paths are disappearing – HR must support continuous reskilling and redeployment, enabling employees to move fluidly between roles and projects.
- Companies are already investing in internal talent marketplaces, allowing employees to bid for projects based on skills, rather than being confined to rigid job descriptions.

Key question: How can HR design employee experiences that are dynamic, personalized and continuously evolving?

5. Inclusion and intersectionality are strategic imperatives, not compliance checkboxes:

Diversity is not enough – organizations must actively leverage it. Margaret Heffernan reminds us that the best companies don't just tolerate difference; they actively use it to drive innovation.

- Cultural Intelligence (CQ) is critical – Fons Trompenaars' research shows that companies with high CQ outperform competitors because they integrate diverse viewpoints into decision making.
- Linda Hill's work proves that cross-functional, intersectional teams generate the most innovative ideas – companies like Pixar intentionally structure teams to blend diverse perspectives.

Key question: How can HR embed inclusion and cultural intelligence into leadership, product design and business strategy?

6. The future of HR: from support function to business engine:

- HR 3.0 is about it being no longer just about HR – it is about people and business transformation.

- HR must align more strongly with prioritized business agendas, ensuring that workforce strategy is deeply integrated into how organizations scale, compete and innovate.

- HR leaders must act as business architects, not just HR specialists – fostering adaptability, learning and high-performance cultures.

   'HR is not a department. It is the engine of business transformation.' – Josh Bersin

Key question: How can HR reposition itself as a key driver of business agility, innovation and long-term success?

The call to action: HR 3.0 is here. Will you lead it?

We are at a turning point. The old ways of managing talent – rigid job structures, standardized career paths, slow decision making and gut-based leadership selection – are obsolete. The future belongs to HR leaders who embrace adaptability, Systems Thinking, behavioural science and continuous innovation.

   HR 3.0 isn't just an operating model of functional shift – it's a movement. The future of HR is already here.

The challenge for HR leaders is no longer about understanding these shifts but leading them. The organizations that succeed in the next decade will be those whose HR teams are at the forefront of agility, innovation and transformation.

References and further reading

Bersin, J (2023) Systemic HR: The future of HR operating models, www.joshbersin.com (archived at https://perma.cc/W75W-EU9E)

Boudreau, J and Jesuthasan, R. (2022) Work Without Jobs: How to reboot your organization's work operating system, Boston: Harvard Business Review Press

Brazier, J (2025) Spotify CHRO Katarina Berg on why the company has launched an HR people analytics solution, UNLEASH, www.unleash.ai/data-and-analytics/spotify-chro-katarina-berg-on-why-the-company-has-launched-a-hr-people-analytics-solution/ (archived at https://perma.cc/Z9WB-GUK7)

Briner, R (2023) Evidence-based HR and people analytics are the same, right? Afraid not, People Management, www.peoplemanagement.co.uk/article/1851101/evidence-based-hr-people-analytics-same-right-afraid-not (archived at https://perma.cc/Q5EU-LN77)

Cann, O (2019) Of course Davos should talk about taxing the rich. But there's more to solving inequality, World Economic Forum, www.weforum.org/stories/2019/02/davos-talk-taxes-inequality-rutger-bregman/ (archived at https://perma.cc/VX7X-A4CG)

Center for Creative Leadership (2023) Leading a multicultural team, www.ccl.org/articles/leading-effectively-articles/leading-a-multicultural-team/ (archived at https://perma.cc/D7EJ-6H45)

Chamorro-Premuzic, T (2017) *The Talent Delusion: Why data, not intuition, is the key to unlocking human potential*, London: Piatkus

Claydon, R (n.d.) LinkedIn post, www.linkedin.com/posts/drrichardclaydon_futureofleadership-culture-behavior-activity-7120555990432833536-Ycf3?utm_source=share&utm_medium=member_desktop&rcm=ACoAAAFOgYQBZgCKd-Kqs8wilCF6OUGTt6M22wE (archived at https://perma.cc/Q6RF-NL3C)

Cloverpop (n.d.) Hacking diversity with inclusive decision-making, www.cloverpop.com/hubfs/Whitepapers/Cloverpop_Hacking_Diversity_Inclusive_Decision_Making_White_Paper.pdf (archived at https://perma.cc/R47Z-CEC3)

CRF (n.d.) Evidence-based HR, www.crforum.co.uk/hubs/evidence-based-hr/ (archived at https://perma.cc/Z4JH-YK4R)

Deloitte (2024) 2025 Global Human Capital Trends, www2.deloitte.com (archived at https://perma.cc/7DBS-PW7J)

Google (2024). Google re:Work – Guides: Understand team effectiveness, Withgoogle.com, https://rework.withgoogle.com/en/guides/understanding-team-effectiveness#introduction (archived at https://perma.cc/2B29-JRWS)

Grant, A (2021) *Think Again: The power of knowing what you don't know*, London: WH Allen

Hamel, G (2012) *What Matters Now: How to win in a world of relentless change, ferocious competition, and unstoppable innovation*, San Francisco: Jossey-Bass

Heffernan, M (2015) *Beyond Measure: The big impact of small changes*, London: TED Books

Hill, L A (2014) *Collective Genius: The art and practice of leading innovation*, Boston: Harvard Business Review Press

HumanSmart (2024) What role does cultural intelligence play in successful international talent management strategies? https://humansmart.com.mx/en/blogs/blog-what-role-does-cultural-intelligence-play-in-successful-international-talent-management-strategies-56418 (archived at https://perma.cc/PKX4-EQXE)

Jain, A (2024) Bridging cultures: Developing cultural intelligence in leadership, Digicrusader, https://digicrusader.com/developing-cultural-intelligence-in-leadership/ (archived at https://perma.cc/E6TP-99HB)

Jesuthasan, R and Boudreau, J (2018) *Reinventing Jobs: A 4-step approach for applying automation to work*, Boston: Harvard Business Review Press

Lewin, K (1951) Field Theory in Social Science: Selected theoretical papers, New York: Harper & Row

McGowan, H and Shipley, C (2020) *The Adaptation Advantage: Let go, learn fast, and thrive in the future of work*, Hoboken, NJ: Wiley

McKinsey (2020) Diversity wins: How inclusion matters, www.mckinsey.com/featured-insights/diversity-and-inclusion/diversity-wins-how-inclusion-matters (archived at https://perma.cc/S6A3-BW4N)

McKinsey & Company (2022) *HR as an Engine of Business Transformation: Systems Thinking and workforce agility*, www.mckinsey.com (archived at https://perma.cc/65T3-6HBG)

Nahai, N (2021) *Business Unusual: Values, uncertainty and the psychology of brand resilience*, London: Kogan Page

Pink, D H (2009) *Drive: The surprising truth about what motivates us*, New York: Riverhead Books

Rock, D and Grant, H (2016) Why diverse teams are smarter, *Harvard Business Review*, https://hbr.org/2016/11/why-diverse-teams-are-smarter (archived at https://perma.cc/XK9L-E4S5)

Senge, P M (1990) *The Fifth Discipline: The art and practice of the learning organization*, New York: Doubleday

Trompenaars, F (1998) *Riding the Waves of Culture: Understanding diversity in global business*, New York: McGraw-Hill

Trompenaars, F and Hampden-Turner, C (2004) *Managing People Across Cultures*, London: Capstone

Ulrich, D (2021) *The HR Business Partner Model Revisited: The shift to human capability and business value*, www.daveulrich.com (archived at https://perma.cc/MA8M-32XR)

Vorecol (2024) How cultural intelligence shapes performance management strategies in multinational companies, https://vorecol.com/blogs/blog-how-cultural-intelligence-shapes-performance-management-strategies-in-multinational-companies-191534 (archived at https://perma.cc/8PR3-5RXF)

World Economic Forum (2023) The Future of Jobs Report: Workforce trends for the 2020s, www.weforum.org (archived at https://perma.cc/39Q8-264T)

11

HR 3.0 and organizational culture

WHAT'S COVERED IN THIS CHAPTER

- **Culture transformation:** Examining how HR 3.0 influences organizational culture and vice versa.

- **Leadership's role:** Analysing how leaders can drive cultural change in alignment with HR 3.0.

- **Engagement and performance:** Exploring the connection between culture, employee engagement and performance.

Introduction

Organizational culture has long been a determinant of business success, shaping behaviours, decision making and employee engagement. With the emergence of HR 3.0 – a model that redefines HR as an adaptive, human-centred, data-driven and Systems-Thinking function – culture transformation has taken on a new dimension. HR 3.0 not only reflects culture but also acts as a catalyst, helping organizations evolve into culture-strong entities where engagement and performance thrive. This chapter explores the interplay between HR 3.0 and organizational culture, the role of leadership in driving cultural change, and the profound link between culture, engagement and performance.

Culture transformation: HR 3.0 as a catalyst for change

The interplay of HR 3.0 and organizational culture: a systems-level transformation and understanding organizational culture: Schein's perspective and HR 3.0's influence.

Former MIT professor Edgar Schein's foundational work on organizational culture defines it as a deeply embedded system of assumptions, values and artifacts that shape how an organization functions. Culture is not just a set of beliefs – it is an invisible force that determines how people think, act and interact within a company.

Schein's model highlights three layers of organizational culture:

- **Artefacts** – the visible aspects of culture (office layout, dress code, policies, rituals).

- **Espoused values** – the stated principles and company ideals (e.g. 'We value innovation and collaboration').

- **Underlying assumptions** – the deeply ingrained, often unconscious beliefs that truly dictate behaviour (e.g. whether employees really feel psychological safety to challenge authority).

HR 3.0 fundamentally reshapes culture by changing how the HR team (and thereby their colleagues across the enterprise) experience work. By embedding agility, skills-based talent structures and a product-led approach, HR 3.0 doesn't just support culture – it actively engineers it.

Where traditional HR often reinforced bureaucratic structures and rigid hierarchies, HR 3.0 creates cultures that are adaptive, human-centred and innovation-driven.

Let's explore four ways HR 3.0 influences organizational culture.

Human-centred design: shaping culture through employee experience (EX)

In HR 3.0, employee experience (EX) is at the core of HR strategy. This shift moves beyond traditional engagement surveys and places a continuous, user-driven approach at the heart of workforce design.

> Employee experience is not a programme—it's an ecosystem. The way we design work determines whether people feel heard, valued, and empowered.
> – Josh Bersin

Comparing Traditional HR to HR 3.0:

- Traditional HR – employees adapt to rigid HR policies and structures.

- HR 3.0 – HR adapts to employee needs, ensuring work is designed for, not against, human potential.

HOW HR 3.0 TRANSFORMS CULTURE THROUGH EX

- Journey mapping and personas – just as customer experience (CX) teams use journey mapping to optimize customer interactions, HR 3.0 applies the same principles to EX.

- Real-time feedback loops – instead of one-size-fits-all engagement surveys, HR 3.0 tracks real-time sentiment data, ensuring HR interventions are continuously refined based on what employees need in the moment.

- Personalized work models – Spotify's Agile HR approach allows employees to tailor work based on personal and team needs, reinforcing a culture of flexibility and autonomy.

REAL-WORLD EXAMPLE
How Airbnb designed culture through EX

When Airbnb CEO Brian Chesky sought to define the company's culture, he didn't start with HR policies – he started with the employee experience:

- Airbnb applied design thinking to HR, mapping out every employee touchpoint – from hiring to daily work to career progression.

- The result was a culture of belonging, where HR continuously evolved to match employee expectations.

- This reinforced Airbnb's brand identity both internally and externally, making it one of the most sought-after places to work.

Key takeaway: HR is the architect of employee experience, and employee experience determines culture. By applying human-centred design principles, HR 3.0 ensures culture is designed with, not imposed upon, employees.

Adaptive Systems Thinking: from bureaucracy to continuous learning

HR 3.0 draws on Peter Senge's Learning Organization Model, which highlights that organizations must:

- continuously learn (personal mastery and team learning) and evolve rather than operate under fixed structures;

- empower individuals to challenge assumptions and question the status quo (shared vision and mental models);

- adapt and design systems processes based on a mission, and use real-time feedback that tests and develops this, not just implementing *best practice* rigid frameworks (shared vision and Systems Thinking).

> Growth and comfort do not coexist. If you want to build a learning organization, you must be willing to let go of control and embrace uncertainty. – Ricardo Semler

Comparing Traditional HR to HR 3.0:

- Traditional HR culture – bureaucracy and hierarchy slow decision making, discouraging experimentation.
- HR 3.0 culture – employees and leaders are encouraged to iterate, learn and continuously improve through structured feedback loops and a culture of psychological safety.

HOW HR 3.0 CREATES A LEARNING CULTURE

- Skill-based workforce models – John Boudreau and Ravin Jesuthasan's work emphasizes that work should be deconstructed into skills, not fixed job roles, allowing for continuous upskilling and redeployment.
- *In the flow of work* learning and digital L&D – embedding learning directly into workflows, ensuring that skill-building is ongoing and practice-based, rather than episodic events of a deluge of content.
- Fail-fast, learn-fast culture – HR 3.0 is about experimentation in HR in areas such as policies being products and use of sciences and systems in designing solutions and support.

REAL-WORLD EXAMPLE
Haier's adaptive talent ecosystem

Chinese multinational Haier has replaced traditional job structures with dynamic, skill-based talent ecosystems:

- Employees are not assigned to fixed roles – instead, they bid for projects based on real-time business needs and personal skill development goals.
- Teams function autonomously, reinforcing a culture of continuous learning and adaptability.
- This has made Haier one of the most innovative and resilient global organizations, proving that adaptive HR structures fuel adaptive cultures.

Data and science-led decision making: from intuition to insight-driven culture

> What we've learned is that intuition is the enemy of good decision making. The best HR teams use data, not hunches, to shape how people work and thrive. – Laszlo Bock, former VP of HR at Google

HR 3.0 replaces intuition-based decisions with data-driven, evidence-led workforce strategies.

HOW DATA SHAPES CULTURE

- AI and people analytics – companies like Microsoft use workplace analytics to track collaboration patterns and burnout risk, enabling HR to intervene proactively.

- Bias-free leadership selection – Tomas Chamorro-Premuzic's research shows that data-driven hiring improves leadership quality and reduces bias in promotion decisions.

- Real-time engagement and retention models – Spotify's real-time people analytics helps managers identify and address employee concerns before they escalate, reinforcing a culture of responsiveness and inclusion.

REAL-WORLD EXAMPLE
How Standard Chartered Bank uses data in HR

Standard Chartered Bank has embraced a data-centric approach across its operations, fostering a culture where analytics drives business outcomes. The bank's Data Innovation Value Engagement (DIVE) team collaborates with various divisions to implement data analytics solutions, enhancing decision-making processes:

- **Citizen Data Science training programme:** To democratize data usage, Standard Chartered launched a training programme that has certified over 500 staff members as citizen data scientists. This initiative empowers employees at all levels to leverage data in their roles, promoting a culture of continuous learning and innovation.

- **Space Planning and Optimization Tool (SPOT):** In response to evolving workplace dynamics, the bank developed SPOT using data analytics to optimize office space utilization. This tool led to a $34 million reduction in annual property costs, demonstrating how data-driven initiatives can result in significant operational efficiencies.

- **Flexible working model:** Standard Chartered implemented a flexible working model, allowing 52,000 colleagues across 44 markets to work under agreed flexible arrangements. This approach, rooted in the bank's values, led to increased employee satisfaction with work-life balance, which rose from 63 per cent in 2018 to 72 per cent in 2023.

- **Recognition and learning culture:** The bank emphasizes the power of recognition to drive a learning culture. Regular acknowledgement of top learners by leadership reinforces the importance of continuous development and contributes to a culture that values growth and adaptability.

Through these initiatives, Standard Chartered Bank exemplifies how integrating data-driven strategies can transform organizational culture, leading to enhanced employee engagement, operational efficiency and a robust learning environment.

Product-based HR: reinforcing a culture of innovation and experimentation

> Think of People Ops as a subscription product. Employees buy into it during the recruitment process, subscribe monthly, and unless they remain a part of an alumni team, they stop subscribing when they resign. People Ops teams should focus on constantly iterating this product. – Jessica Zwaan, COO at Whereby

Comparing Traditional HR to HR 3.0:

- Traditional HR culture – HR policies are fixed, rolled out top-down and rarely adjusted.

- HR 3.0 culture – HR is an iterative function where policies are treated as products, tested and refined based on user experience.

HOW PRODUCT-BASED HR REINFORCES CULTURE

- HR experiments and prototypes – organizations use pilot programmes and A/B testing instead of rigid HR rollouts.

- Continuous feedback loops – every HR intervention is tested and refined based on employee experience data.

- Innovation-friendly policies – companies like Netflix remove bureaucratic constraints, replacing them with culture-based accountability models.

REAL-WORLD EXAMPLE

Netflix's freedom and responsibility culture

- Netflix removed rigid vacation policies – employees take time off based on trust and accountability, not HR rules.

- Performance management is not a top-down rating system – it is a continuous dialogue based on real outcomes.

- By designing HR around innovation and autonomy, Netflix ensures its culture is aligned with creativity and risk-taking.

Conclusion: HR 3.0 as the architect of culture

HR is no longer just managing culture – it is actively shaping it through:

- human-centred workforce experiences;
- adaptive learning and continuous improvement;
- data-driven decision making;
- a product-based, experimental approach to HR.

Shaping culture through behaviour and mindsets

Culture transformation is about rewiring mindsets, as articulated by John Kotter's model of organizational change. The move to HR 3.0 necessitates:

- **Psychological safety:** Creating an environment where employees feel safe to experiment, share ideas and challenge norms.

- **Cultural agility:** Organizations must adopt the cultural agility framework (Caligiuri, 2012), enabling them to adapt HR practices to global and local nuances.

- **Rituals and norms:** Defining new rituals that reinforce HR 3.0's principles, such as cross-functional problem-solving sprints or skills-sharing marketplaces.

Leadership's role in cultural change

Leadership as culture architects shape culture through vision, behaviour and communication. Kotter's work on leading change underscores the importance of leadership in embedding new cultural norms. HR 3.0 provides leaders with tools to:

- Model desired behaviours: Leaders set the tone by embodying values such as transparency, agility and accountability.

- Reinforce psychological ownership: Research on psychological ownership suggests that when employees feel a sense of ownership, they are more engaged in cultural shifts. Leaders can achieve this by decentralizing decision making and increasing autonomy.

- Drive Systems Thinking: Russell Ackoff's work on Systems Thinking reminds us that leaders must view culture as an interconnected system rather than isolated initiatives.

Leadership development in HR 3.0

HR 3.0 calls for a rethink of leadership development:

- Adaptive leadership: Leaders must navigate complexity, fostering an environment where employees continuously adapt and evolve.

- Distributed leadership: Moving beyond hierarchical leadership, HR 3.0 promotes distributed leadership, where decision-making authority is shared.

- Empowering teams: Drawing on Hackman's model of team effectiveness, HR 3.0 equips leaders to create self-managed, high-performing teams aligned with cultural goals.

Engagement, performance and culture

THE CULTURAL DRIVERS OF ENGAGEMENT

Engagement is a leading indicator of business performance, as demonstrated in Gallup's extensive research. HR 3.0 enhances engagement by:

- Aligning work with purpose: Connecting individual contributions to organizational purpose, reflecting Dan Pink's motivation model of autonomy, mastery and purpose.

- Creating growth-oriented environments: Leveraging a skills-based approach to talent, HR 3.0 ensures employees have opportunities for continuous development.

- Strengthening belonging and inclusion: Ensuring inclusive workplace cultures through data-driven inclusion strategies.

Culture's impact on performance

Research by Denison (1990) and Cameron and Quinn (1999) highlights the link between strong cultures and organizational performance. HR 3.0 accelerates performance through:

- Agile performance management: Moving away from annual reviews to continuous, real-time feedback loops.
- Data-informed decision making: Using analytics to refine talent strategies and ensure alignment with cultural objectives.
- Experimentation and learning: Fostering a growth mindset culture (Dweck, 2006) where employees see challenges as opportunities to improve.

In Chapter 3, I introduced this:

Five words to frame the importance of an optimized HR Operating Model:

People. Culture. Learning. Performance. Purpose.

We have focused on Culture here but that is inextricably linked to the other four and is a crucial factor in how a new HR Operating Model sets the tone, tempo and framework for a more adaptive, dynamic and future-ready culture. As much as we extolled the virtues of engineering in Chapter 1 and Futures Thinking in Chapter 2, an important symbolic element of a new operating model like HR 3.0 is the manifestation of a strongly evolved culture.

A culture where products represent creating value for people; science is underpinning everything that becomes a product, solution or intervention that uses data psychology and robust evidence to prove the worth, merit and construct of HR deliverables. And where systems and processes are all aligned to the business goals and people's needs, and benefit the wider ecosystems of life.

Culture transformation is talked about a lot in the game of business. Having the right attitudes, belief systems, values and social 'glue' are as critical as deployed technologies, efficient protocols and great marketing.

What HR 3.0 does is set a new climate of versatility in a function long-maligned for its rigid and dogmatic sense of compliance and rules-based operating. Whilst still delivering stabilizing supportive interventions, HR has the chance to become known as the inventor and architect of agility, creativity and next-stage evolution.

Conclusion

HR 3.0 is not just a reaction to modern workplace shifts; it is an enabler of strong, adaptive and high-performing organizational cultures.

By embedding human-centred design, Systems Thinking and science-led decision making, HR 3.0 redefines how culture is shaped and sustained. Leaders play a pivotal role in this transformation, acting as culture architects who embed new ways of thinking and working.

Ultimately, the intersection of HR 3.0 and organizational culture leads to workplaces that are not just efficient but also thriving, engaged and future-ready.

WHAT WE'VE COVERED IN THIS CHAPTER

This chapter explores the interplay between HR 3.0 and organizational culture, demonstrating how HR is no longer just a steward of culture, but an architect of transformation. It examines how HR 3.0 redefines cultural norms, leadership expectations, employee engagement and organizational performance by embedding agility, Systems Thinking, data-led decision making and product-based approaches.

1 Culture transformation and HR 3.0's influence:

- o How HR 3.0 shifts from bureaucratic structures to adaptive, human-centred and innovation-driven cultures.
- o The role of employee experience (EX) design in shaping workplace culture.

2 Systems Thinking and continuous learning in culture:

- o How Peter Senge's Learning Organization model informs HR 3.0's approach to cultural agility.
- o The shift from fixed structures to real-time feedback loops and a growth mindset.

3 Data and science-led decision making in culture design:

- o How people analytics replaces intuition-based HR decisions.
- o The impact of AI, workforce analytics and evidence-based leadership selection.

4 Product-based HR: innovation and experimentation in culture:

- o The shift from rigid policies to agile, iterative HR products.

5 **Shaping culture through mindsets and behaviour:**

   o How psychological safety, rituals and cultural agility reshape workplace norms.

   o Insights from John Kotter's change model and Paula Caligiuri's cultural agility framework.

6 **Leadership's role in cultural change:**

   o Leaders as culture architects driving psychological ownership and Systems Thinking.

   o How Russell Ackoff's systems approach helps leaders sustain HR 3.0 cultures.

7 **Engagement, performance and cultural alignment:**

   o How Gallup's research on engagement proves that strong cultures drive performance.

   o The role of agile performance management and real-time feedback.

This chapter reinforces that culture isn't just about values – it's about systems, behaviours and leadership shaping how work happens. HR 3.0 provides the tools, frameworks and strategies to turn culture into a measurable driver of success.

References and further reading

Ackoff, R L (1999) *Recreating the Corporation: A design of organizations for the 21st century*, New York: Oxford University Press

Bersin, J (2023) Introducing The Systemic HR™ Initiative, https://joshbersin. com/2023/12/introducing-the-systemic-hr-initiative/ (archived at https://perma. cc/TDM4-QHMS)

Bock, L (2015) *Work Rules!: Insights from inside Google that will transform how you live and lead*, New York: Hachette

Boudreau, J and Jesuthasan, R (2022) *Work Without Jobs: How to reboot your organization's work operating system*, Boston: Harvard Business Review Press

Caligiuri, P (2012) *Cultural Agility: Building a pipeline of successful global professionals*, San Francisco: Jossey-Bass

Cameron, K S and Quinn, R E (1999) *Diagnosing and Changing Organizational Culture: Based on the competing values framework*, Reading, MA: Addison-Wesley

Chamorro-Premuzic, T (2017) *The Talent Delusion: Why data, not intuition, is the key to unlocking human potential*, London: Piatkus

Deloitte (2024) 2024 Global Human Capital Trends: HR 3.0 and the future of work www2.deloitte.com/content/dam/insights/articles/glob176836_global-human-capital-trends-2024/DI_Global-Human-Capital-Trends-2024.pdf (archived at https://perma.cc/5ZH6-LB96)

Denison, D (1990) *Corporate Culture and Organizational Effectiveness*, New York: Wiley

Dweck, C (2006) *Mindset: The new psychology of success*, New York: Random House

Gallup (2024) State of the Global Workplace: Insights into Employee Engagement and Performance, www.gallup.com/workplace/349484/state-of-the-global-workplace.aspx (archived at https://perma.cc/GF7A-BJLN)

Hackman, J R (2002) *Leading Teams: Setting the stage for great performances*, Boston: Harvard Business Review Press

Jesuthasan, R and Boudreau, J (2018) *Reinventing Jobs: A 4-step approach for applying automation to work*, Boston: Harvard Business Review Press

Kotter, J P (1996) *Leading Change*, Boston: Harvard Business Review Press

Laloux, F (2014) *Reinventing Organizations: A guide to creating organizations inspired by the next stage of human consciousness*, Brussels: Nelson Parker

Lewin, K (1951) *Field Theory in Social Science: Selected theoretical papers*, New York: Harper & Row

McKinsey & Company (2021) The impact of agility: How to shape your organization to compete,www.mckinsey.com/capabilities/people-and-organizational-performance/our-insights/the-impact-of-agility-how-to-shape-your-organization-to-compete (archived at https://perma.cc/8VLW-FDFZ)

Pink, D H (2009) *Drive: The surprising truth about what motivates us*, New York: Riverhead Books

Schein, E H (2017) *Organizational Culture and Leadership*, 5th edn. Hoboken, NJ: Wiley

Semler, R (1993) *Maverick: The success story behind the world's most unusual workplace*, London: Random House

Senge, P M (1990) *The Fifth Discipline: The art and practice of the learning organization*, New York: Doubleday

Zwaan, J (2023) People ops as a product, Medium, https://jessicamayzwaan.medium.com/people-ops-as-a-product-8976f70f025c (archived at https://perma.cc/P9R8-9RQY)

12

Conclusion and call to action

WHAT'S COVERED IN THIS CHAPTER

The HR 3.0 playbook – a narrative summary and series of factors that showcase a 'how to' guide to deliver a step-change in HR Operating Models.

Introduction

We have covered a range of factors in setting up the HR and People, Culture, Learning and Organization Design/Development functions, teams and practitioners to recast their Operating Model for the *turbulent twenties* and beyond.

With the greatest of respect to what has gone before, there is a real need to modernize, reimagine and evolve not just what HR delivers but how it operates and creates value for people and business to be more prosperous, adaptable and have a positive impact on the planet, not just markets and profits.

The crucial word as a call to action is the one that often causes a reaction: change.

HR 3.0 represents a fundamental change in how HR operates – moving from traditional, process-driven models to an adaptive, human-centred and product-led function. This chapter provides a sense of a playbook for HR teams looking to implement HR 3.0, offering a step-by-step guide, illustrative scenarios and actionable insights. By embracing this model, HR can lead cultural transformation, enhance workforce agility and drive strategic impact.

Firstly though, we need to *change change*. Particularly the practices of *change management*.

Changing change management: a theory of evolutionary change

The traditional approach to change management – structured, linear and programmatic – has become obsolete. Instead, a new **Theory of Change** advocates for **evolutionary, participatory and purpose-driven change,** where organizations work in a state of *perpetual beta*, continuously evolving through Systems Thinking, experimentation and adaptability.

Beyond traditional change management into a theory of evolution

So much work is linked to a form of change or transformation. Programmes seem abundant and everyone is 'on a journey'. The more recognizable stimulators for change – external forces, mergers and acquisitions, technological advancement/introduction – are more apparent, regularized and part of everyday work.

Many of the responses to market forces (economic downturns, introduction of legislation, competitors entering spaces) result in organizations immediately looking to cut costs, reshape the workforce, adapt practices and deploy efficiency programmes.

Increasingly, these reactions feel limp, predictable and aimed mainly at balance sheets, shareholder appeasement and short-term 'patches' rather than extensive and comprehensive 'upgrades'.

All of this leads me to theorize:

- **Restructures are redundant:** The legacy of 'restructures' has led to superficial changes that fail to drive sustainable transformation. Instead, HR must facilitate ongoing evolution.

- **Transformation needs to transform:** True transformation is irreversible, yet most transformation programmes follow outdated, programmatic models.

- **Evolution has evolved:** Change is not a destination – it's an ongoing, responsive and adaptive process embedded in the flow of work.

Using the metaphor of the *Four Horsemen*, let's look at what's going wrong with change.

THE FOUR HORSEMEN OF *APOCALYPTIC* CHANGE

The failure of traditional change management is evident in four key challenges:

1 Complacency (stagnation): Resistance to evolution leads to obsolescence.

2 **Fragmentation (disconnection):** Siloed, disjointed efforts disrupt cohesive transformation.

3 **Overload (exhaustion):** Change fatigue erodes engagement and resilience.

4 **Short-termism (myopia):** Quick wins undermine long-term impact and sustainability.

And taking a more comprehensive, systems-wide evolution frame, that should be:

THE FOUR HORSEMEN OF *EVOLUTIONARY* CHANGE

To counteract these destructive forces, HR must embrace the four enablers of evolutionary change:

1 **Vision (purpose-driven change):** An inspiring, unifying vision ensures alignment and motivation.

2 **Connectivity (collaboration and inclusion):** Breaking down silos fosters trust and systemic alignment.

3 **Fortitude (sustainable adaptation):** Supporting people and systems to evolve resiliently.

4 **Foresight (future-readiness):** Balancing agility with long-term strategic positioning.

Using a *Back to the Future* movie metaphor, *HR becomes the flux capacitor of organizational evolution.*

HR powering the possibilities of securing a better future

HR can become a more prominently utilized *power source* of transformation, bridging:

- Organization Design
- emotional responses to change and more participatory approaches to evolving;
- using people science, data-driven decision making and evidence-creating experiments;
- agile, adaptive and rapid bursts of work packages that will deliver evolutionary aspirations, opportunities and overcome problems;

- productizing the offer for leadership development, and strengthening organizational adaptability, workflow optimization and balancing intensity, pressures and demands to foster more well-being and inclusivity.

And within these deliverables, recognize that change is no longer about programmes, episodic initiatives and 'bolt-ons' to core business.

The prevailing links to Organization Design and Development activity – highlighted in Chapter 1 – used in the change arena are part of the shift to more dynamic and regularized evolution activity.

Table 12.1 highlights the shift from **static change programmes** to **continuous, embedded change as a strategic necessity**. The Heraclitus change quote 'Change is the only constant' has never been truer. Therefore this oscillation is because change is now a **core** business activity and not a programmatic change **event**. The shift from Change Management to Organizational Oscillation (OO) is where we recognize that change *has* changed and therefore needs a more integrated approach as an effective response to evolutionary needs and becomes an operationalized but strategic approach to navigate, plot and deliver.

If people are suffering from change fatigue and crave periods of stabilized operations, this may not be good news to them. However, it is potentially the best news they can have, as change is no longer attached to convulsive

TABLE 12.1 Comparing traditional change to organizational oscillation

Concept	Description
Traditional change management (BAU vs change programmes)	Historically, organizations managed change through structured programmes separate from daily operations. Change was designed then implemented almost like an 'overwrite' of the previous ways of working.
	The traditional 'Unfreeze, Change, Refreeze' model by Kurt Lewin no longer feels applicable as we are more in a constant state of liquid-like fluidity rather than frozen states of steadiness.
Organizational oscillation (OO) – the new approach	Changing change into evolution means that core business activity is constantly intertwined with operationalized change.
	Organizations, therefore, oscillate between stability and evolved states as an ongoing, strategic capability.

initiatives such as the dreaded 'R' word – restructures – nor is it potentially damaging and risk-averse *stasis*. With a new form of continuous change – subsumed within the phrase of ongoing evolution – we are in the territory described and predicated as the future operating models for Teal organizations in Frederic Laloux's epochal work and book, *Reinventing Organizations* (Laloux, 2014). That is:

- Wholeness
- Self-management, and (crucially for this declaration)
- Evolutionary purpose

What is meant by these three parameters is:

1. WHOLENESS: BRINGING THE TRUE SELF TO WORK
Traditional workplaces often encourage employees to compartmentalize their identities, suppressing emotions, personal values and non-work-related aspects of themselves in favour of a professional persona exemplified by a job description and performance objectives.

In Teal organizations, *wholeness* is about creating an environment where employees feel safe to bring their full, authentic selves to work – including their creativity, emotions and vulnerabilities. This is facilitated by:

- Psychological safety – teams cultivate openness, trust and non-judgment.
- Non-hierarchical collaboration – workplaces remove rigid status-driven behaviours.
- Workspaces and rituals – organizations design spaces and practices (e.g. mindfulness sessions, check-in rounds, peer coaching) that encourage authenticity and strengthen the awareness and use of emotional intelligence.

Real-world example: At Buurtzorg, a self-managing nursing organization in the Netherlands, team members integrate personal reflection and group dialogue into their meetings, ensuring that emotions, relationships and purpose are as valued as efficiency and outcomes.

HR 3.0 connection: HR shifts from performance policing to experience curation – designing employee-centric environments that foster engagement, trust and well-being whilst sustainably delivering effective business outcomes and the mission, purpose and vision.

2. SELF-MANAGEMENT: A RADICAL SHIFT FROM HIERARCHY TO DISTRIBUTED AUTHORITY

Self-management in Teal organizations means that employees don't need traditional managers to make decisions for them – they operate within clear frameworks, shared responsibilities and mutual accountability.

Instead of hierarchical oversight, self-management relies on:

- Decentralized decision making – employees use advice-based decision models rather than seeking managerial approval.

- Autonomous teams – work is structured around small, cross-functional groups with clear roles but no fixed authority.

- Transparent information sharing – everyone has access to financials, performance data and strategic plans, ensuring decisions are made with full context.

Real-world example: Morning Star, the world's largest tomato processor, operates without traditional managers. Employees set their objectives based on peer agreements and business needs. Performance is assessed through continuous feedback loops, not annual reviews.

HR 3.0 connection: Traditional HR functions like performance management, promotions, and workforce planning become collaborative and distributed, with HR acting as an enabler rather than a gatekeeper.

3. EVOLUTIONARY PURPOSE: ORGANIZATIONS AS LIVING SYSTEMS

Unlike traditional organizations, which operate based on fixed strategic plans, Teal organizations evolve organically – they see themselves as living systems that continuously adapt based on internal and external feedback:

- Purpose is emergent – rather than executives dictating strategy, the organization's direction evolves through collective sensing and employee input.

- Decisions align with a deeper mission – rather than chasing profits alone, the company focuses on its reason for existence – whether that's sustainability, social impact or innovation.

- Intuition, not just data, guides strategy – employees are encouraged to listen to customer needs, market shifts and internal energy to determine where the organization should go next.

Real-world example: At Patagonia, strategy is shaped by commitments to environmental activism. When the company realized excessive consumption contradicted its mission, it launched the Worn Wear programme to repair and resell used Patagonia gear – aligning its business with its more profound purpose.

HR 3.0 connection: Instead of enforcing rigid corporate objectives, HR fosters dynamic goal-setting processes, enabling employees to shape and contribute to the organization's evolving mission.

Final thought: Teal and HR 3.0 – a perfect pairing

HR 3.0 operationalizes Teal principles, helping organizations move from control-based to trust-based, inclusive and participatory cultures.

It rethinks structures, policies and leadership to enable people, decentralize authority and align work with a higher purpose.

HR no longer enforces hierarchy – it enables self-organization, wholeness and purpose-driven work.

The HR 3.0 playbook: a step-by-step guide

Having read this far, you may be convinced that HR 3.0 is worth investing time, effort, thinking and doing to move towards a more dynamic operating model. Here's the *Fast Strategy* version of how to move your HR/People function into the HR 3.0 Operating Model.

Step 1: Establish a clear vision

Why it matters: A compelling vision ensures alignment and direction for HR evolution:

- Define the purpose of HR in your organization beyond compliance and administration (importantly, this should also include ambitions, dreams, aspirations and quests).

- Engage senior stakeholders and leaders to co-create a future-focused HR vision that aligns with, strengthens and adds to any existing business evolution and prioritized strategic aims.

- Craft a compelling vision and narrative and use storytelling, science and data to substantiate the rationale for evolution of this nature.

Step 2: Redesign your HR Operating Model

Why it matters: Traditional HR structures must evolve to support business agility:

- Rally the HR team to view, reimagine and reconstruct their deliverables as products.
- Move from siloed HR functions to cross-functional, product-based HR teams.
- Capture, analyse and leverage a more skills-based workforce design to the HR function that not only brings more value-adding agility to the range of products and services HR provides, but builds the agile 'muscle' to deal with rapid, iterative and ongoing evolution.
- Create capacity – not only will adopted Agile approaches do this, and more iterative, people-centric design in products bolster take-up and realization of benefits, it will allow the HR team to adopt more digital and automated solutions for self-service, enhancing data-driven, evidence-based decision making.

Step 3: Embed Systems Thinking and enhance data-driven decision making

Why it matters: HR must operate as an interconnected system, using data to enhance employee experiences and organizational outcomes:

- Apply systems mapping to understand the impact of HR products, services and enhanced value-creation possibilities.
- Strengthen your people analytics function to inform talent strategies, performance measures and motivation/culture levers.
- Use test-and-learn, rapid and continuous feedback loops to measure and refine HR services and products, designed packages of work and the impact and value creation coming from this refreshed range of deliverables.

Step 4: Craft a culture of experimentation and agility

Why it matters: HR must mirror – and exceed – the agility of the broader organization:

- Introduce iterative approaches, such as HR sprints, for rapid problem solving.

- Encourage a fail-fast, learn-fast mindset, safely testing, adapting and delivering version-controlled products, services and value-creating interventions
- Use design thinking to co-create solutions with colleagues across the business, making HR work and projects the most desirable, impactful and learning-based experiences in the corporate arena.

Step 5: Prioritize employee experience and well-being

Why it matters: The shift to human-centred HR enhances engagement, inclusion and retention:

- Map employee journeys to identify pain points and moments that matter.
- Redesign policies as products that deliver a focused approach to flexibility and autonomy that links to increased productivity, company impact and customer value creation.
- Implement well-being *in the flow of work* that supports physical, emotional and financial health in people and enhances the balanced and sustainable levels of high performance all companies dream of.

Step 6: Build leadership capability for HR 3.0

Why it matters: Leaders must champion and role-model new ways of working:

- Engage, enlighten and skill leaders in adaptive leadership, emotional intelligence and Systems Thinking.
- Shift leadership mindsets from control to participatory enablement.
- Equip HR to act as strategic enablers, not just support functions, by tackling systemic, challenging business issues and mobilizing talent, workforce planning, more dynamic OD, evidence-based data-led decisions on people, culture, learning, performance and purpose.

Call to action: shaping the future of HR

HR 3.0 is not a theoretical framework – it is a practical, necessary evolution. HR teams have the power to lead this transformation by:

- **becoming architects of culture,** embedding agility, psychological safety and inclusivity;

- **driving business impact,** positioning HR as a value-generating function rather than a support service;
- **leveraging technology and data,** ensuring HR decisions are evidence-based and employee-centred;
- **championing skills-based models,** breaking free from outdated job descriptions and fostering continuous learning.

Final thought: the imperative for evolution

The organizations that thrive in the future will be those with HR teams willing to challenge convention, embrace adaptability and continuously innovate. HR 3.0 is the blueprint for this future, but its success depends on action. The time for transformation is now.

And HR 3.0 is unique as an Operating Model because it is *not* a prescriptive framework you must adopt, in its entirety and as it has been designed here.

For the first time perhaps, it is *our* operating model – contextualized to your size, sector and purpose, shaped as you see most fitting for that context, and brought to life in a way that you, as an HR leader, function or team, co-create and deem best.

We don't have to sit in three pillars that struggle to interact. Instead, we create spaces to operate in and bring the skills, capabilities and proficiencies that match with our determination, passion and belief that we can reshape how we do the business of HR.

So adapt or adopt the HR 3.0 model however you see fit. Think of it as a technology platform, a series of applications, and deploy and use them as you know best suits the challenges and opportunities you have and want to succeed with.

Hopefully, you've read enough and feel a calling to do HR the way it needs to be – on **People, Performance and Prosperity.** Around the sense that evolution becomes an imbued and adaptive sense of constant reinvention, recalibration and reigniting of people's passion to make a difference through their work. That drives an organization forwards into the future – whatever that may be – with a readiness, resilience and regenerative energy force, for good:

- Good for **you** as a dedicated HR practitioner.
- Good for the **People profession** and its enhanced impact in the future.

- Good for the **organization** and the people and mission it serves.
- Mostly, HR's key deliverable is that evolving into a more dynamic, adaptive and evidence-led HR Operating Model will be good for the **people** who come to work in the organization.
- And good for the **planet, society and communities** beyond direct customers, partners, employes and shareholders.

> People matter. HR will matter more if we unleash and align to what matters most.
>
> *People. Culture. Learning. Performance. Purpose.*

No part of any business gets to cover the breadth, depth and possibilities of any organization like HR does. The privilege of working within the HR and People profession is felt by many in it, alongside a raft of frustrations, blockers and challenges. It feels like time to amplify the honour, devotion and application to the HR profession and reduce and overcome the blockers, frustrations and challenges.

There is a huge opportunity for HR to show what it's really capable of. I hope that with HR 3.0, we may finally have an operating model enabling us to realize that, and evolve and continue to evolve to be the jewel in the crown of the business world.

And, in turn, create better business, for a better world.

WHAT WE'VE COVERED IN THIS CHAPTER

This final chapter serves as both a conclusion and a call to action, solidifying the role of HR 3.0 as the blueprint for the future of HR. It provides a playbook for HR teams looking to transform their operating model, reinforcing HR's role as a strategic enabler of business success, workforce adaptability and cultural evolution.

1 **The HR 3.0 playbook: a step-by-step guide:**
   o A structured approach for transitioning HR functions into an agile, product-driven and people-centric model.
   o Practical steps for redefining HR's vision, redesigning operating models, embedding Systems Thinking and prioritizing employee experience.

2 **Changing change: the shift to Organizational Oscillation (OO):**
   o Why traditional change management is outdated – and how HR 3.0 embeds continuous evolution into core business operations.

o The concept of Organizational Oscillation (OO), where change is no longer a programmatic event but a strategic, ongoing capability.

3 **The Four Horsemen of change: from apocalyptic disruption to evolutionary enablement:**

o A critique of legacy change management failures, including complacency, fragmentation, overload and short-termism.

o A new framework for sustaining transformation through vision, connectivity, fortitude and foresight.

4 **HR as the flux capacitor of organizational evolution:**

o A metaphor for how HR powers continuous reinvention by linking Organization Design, emotional adaptation to change and participatory evolution.

o The role of people science, data-driven decision making and Agile experimentation in making HR a driver of business and people success.

5 **The role of Teal organizations in HR 3.0:**

o How HR 3.0 aligns with Frederic Laloux's Teal principles:

  – Wholeness – creating environments where employees bring their authentic selves to work.

  – Self-management – replacing hierarchy with distributed authority and collaborative decision making.

  – Evolutionary purpose – allowing organizations to adapt dynamically rather than operate on fixed strategic plans.

6 **HR 3.0 as a strategic enabler of people, performance and purpose:**

o HR's role in enhancing workforce vitality, shaping cultural evolution and ensuring sustainable impact.

o Why HR is uniquely positioned to drive transformation across business, people and societal ecosystems.

7 **Final call to action: shaping the future of HR:**

o Encouraging HR professionals to adapt or adopt HR 3.0 based on their unique organizational needs.

o A rallying call for HR to unleash its full potential, break free from outdated models and embrace continuous evolution.

o The ultimate goal: better business for a better world.

This chapter is not just a conclusion – it's a launchpad for action, ensuring that HR 3.0 is not just an idea, but a lived transformation

References and further reading

Ackoff, R L (1999) *Recreating the Corporation: A design of organizations for the 21st century*, New York: Oxford University Press

Bersin, J (2023) Systemic HR: The Future of HR Operating Models, https://www.joshbersin.com (archived at https://perma.cc/A3GD-DWL7)

Boudreau, J and Jesuthasan, R (2022) *Work Without Jobs: How to reboot your organization's work operating system*, Boston: Harvard Business Review Press.

Deloitte (2024) 2025 Global Human Capital Trends: HR 3.0 and the future of work, https://www2.deloitte.com (archived at https://perma.cc/2KRY-QXU9)

Dweck, C (2006) *Mindset: The new psychology of success*, New York: Random House

Jesuthasan, R and Boudreau, J (2018) *Reinventing Jobs: A 4-step approach for applying automation to work*, Boston: Harvard Business Review Press

Kotter, J P (1996) *Leading Change*, Boston: Harvard Business Review Press

Laloux, F (2014) *Reinventing Organizations: A guide to creating organizations inspired by the next stage of human consciousness*, Brussels: Nelson Parker

Lewin, K (1951) *Field Theory in Social Science: Selected theoretical papers*, New York: Harper & Row

McKinsey & Company (2022) HR as an Engine of Business Transformation: Systems Thinking and Workforce Agility, https://www.mckinsey.com (archived at https://perma.cc/65T3-6HBG)

Schein, E H (2017) *Organizational Culture and Leadership*, 5th edn. Hoboken, NJ: Wiley

Senge, P M (1990) *The Fifth Discipline: The art and practice of the learning organization*, New York: Doubleday

Ulrich, D (2021) The HR Business Partner Model Revisited: The Shift to Human Capability and Business Value, https://www.daveulrich.com (archived at https://perma.cc/5HDE-GULR)

World Economic Forum (2023) The Future of Jobs Report: Workforce Trends for the 2020s, https://www.weforum.org (archived at https://perma.cc/39Q8-264T)

INDEX

The index is filed in alphabetical, word-by-word order. Acronyms and 'Mc' are filed as presented; HR operating model versions are filed in chronological order. Page locators in italics denote information within a figure or table.

A/B testing 127, 203
academic research 136
   see also psychology
accessibility 109–10, 236
accountability 73, 77, 103, 201
adaptability 29, 87, 91, 106–07, 116,
   216–17, 226–27, 247–48
   adaptive leadership *138*, 252
   learning 133, 142–43
adjacency 34
administration 59, 78, 79, 88, 110, 189
ageing populations 61
agentic artificial intelligence 60
agile thinking 29, 32, *37*, 63, 195, 264–65
   CIPD view 82, *84*
   cross-functional agile squads *84*, 156,
      160, 173, 198, 214–15
   cultural agility 251
   Deloitte view 73
   EY view 79, 80
   Gartner view 69–70
   McKinsey view 71
   Mercer view 78
   Mintzberg's nine design parameters *158*
   Novartis 177
   and product management 128–31,
      228–29, 231–32
   Santander UK 176–77
   Spotify 214–15
   and systems thinking 116
   Unilever 14–15
   see also adaptability; iteration; sprints
AI (artificial intelligence) 19, 38, 40, 60, 71,
   84, 85, 94, 95, 146
   adaptive learning platforms 133
   dashboards 126
   and decision making 141–42, *159*
   employee listening 132
   generative 126–27
   organizational network analysis *138*
   pilots 205
   see also automation; chatbots; predictive
      analytics; virtual global business
      services (VGBS)

Airbnb 228, 236, 247
ambiguity 22, 216
anticipatory leadership 20, 21
artefacts 246
artificial general intelligence 60
Ask Archie (NatWest) 178
assumptions 246
asymmetries 33
AT&T 216, 230
Atlassian 130, 144
augmented reality (AR) 74, 143
automation 19, 33, *37*, 38, 40, 60, *65*
   and decision making 141–42
   EY view 79, 80
   McKinsey view 71, 72
   NatWest Bank plc 178
   Talent Strategy Group view 74
   Ulrich's view 89
   workflow 144
autonomy *137*, 189, 219
   see also self-managed teams

Barnardo's 172–73
Becker, Gary 51
behavioural economics 47, 206
behavioural science 27, 61, 105, 136–37,
   139, 146, 218–19
belonging *125*, 176, 247
benchmarking 205
Bersin, Josh 93–96, 97, 192–94
bias 27, 135, *137*, 238
biofeedback 139
biological model of organizations 224–25
birthrates 61
blockchain 144–45
Bonusly 143
Boston Consulting Group 50
'boundaryless' HR 72–74, 86
business as usual 180
business models 7, 25
Buurtzorg 261

capability development 77, 89–91, 160, 175,
   190, 197–99

capability pools 62, 69, 198
care 104
'case work' approach 113–14
centralization 69, 79, 80
    see also decentralization
centre-out culture 39
centres of excellence (expertise) 58, 69, 76, 77, 189–90
challenger organizations 46
Chamorro-Premuzic, Tomas 218, 219
champions 59, 59, 88, 205, 265
change 74–77, 117, 124, 137, 180, 213
    evolutionary 258–63
    fear of 188, 200
    resistance to 92, 258
change agents 59, 69–70, 88
change fatigue 259
change management 51, 258–59
Chartered Institute of Personnel and Development (CIPD) 81–87, 97
chatbots 64, 74, 127, 142, 178
check-ins 127, 130, 157, 214, 229, 261
Chesky, Brian 247
chief human resources officers 76
chief people officers 106
Children's Society, The 175–76
chronobiology 139
circular economy 168
citizen data scientists 249
citizenship 37
clarity 103, 104, 122, 149
climate emergency 61, 100
cloud computing 82, 141, 144
co-creation 30, 111, 206
cognitive load theory 138
cognitive neuroscience 47
collaboration 77, 91, 138, 139, 220, 259, 261
    cross-functional 12, 116, 175, 195, 207, 214
collaboration tools 127, 132, 144
Collinson 173–74
competency profiles 6
compliance 123, 125, 191–92, 194, 201–02
computers 21
conflict resolution 125
contingent workforce models 61–62, 74
continuous improvement 15, 62, 91, 124
continuous learning 61, 93, 94, 159, 160, 177, 229, 231, 247–48, 252
contracts of employment 33, 35–36
corporate social responsibility 168
Covid-19 pandemic 15, 74, 82, 86, 123
creative thinking 197
cross-functional agile squads 63, 84, 156, 160, 173, 198, 214–15

cross-functional collaboration 12, 116, 129, 159, 175, 195, 207, 214
cross-functional HR teams 129, 159
cultural agility 251
cultural intelligence 139, 157, 234–36
cultural sensitivity 232–33
culture 10, 39, 41, 46, 47, 153–57, 202, 245–56
    high-performance 139
    Jaguar Land Rover 175
    performance 127
Culture Amp 143
culture in action storyboarding 155
culture spectrum mapping 155
curiosity 179, 182
customer experience 59, 61, 86, 89, 112, 126–27, 236, 262

da Vinci robots 38
dashboards 126, 134, 157, 205
data 32, 33, 136
data analysts 162
data analytics 82, 91, 94, 131–35
    see also people analytics; predictive analytics; prescriptive analytics; real-time analytics
data-driven decision making 10, 27, 85, 91, 116, 129, 173, 190, 217–22, 253
    and AI 141–42, 159
    Gartner view 70
    McKinsey view 71, 72
    Standard Chartered Bank 249–20
data fluency (literacy) 131, 197
data modelling 74
data privacy 135, 145, 202
data science 27, 146
data scientists 64, 134–35, 249
data visualization tools 144
decentralization 14, 159, 189, 200, 215, 262
    see also centralization
Degreed 143
DEI 64, 76, 85, 232–33
    see also diversity; inclusion
Deloitte 72–74
dependency 111
descriptive analytics 131
design thinking 61, 176, 247
development 103
    leadership 85, 135, 138, 140, 226, 252
    see also learning; training
dialogue 110, 117
digital assistants 142
digital integration 14, 38, 77, 78, 79, 94
digital literacy 83, 160, 190
digital resumes 145

digital transformation 41, 50, 82, *84*, 167, 176, 202
digitization *9*, 31, 37–38, 41, 75, *81*, 109–11, *197*
disruption (disruptive innovation) 8–9
distributed leadership 252
diversification 108, 193
diversity 117, 133, 144, 225, 233
Drucker, Peter 50, 52

economic context 53
ecosystems 95, *159*, 207, 224, 225
EdCast 143
Edelman Trust Barometer 54
education sector 37, 56, 62
Eglin, Sarah 173
embedded HR teams *85*
emergent strategy 153
emotional intelligence *138*, 261
empathy 110
employee engagement 53–54, 59, *84*, 95, 115–16, 123, *137*, 174, 219–20, 252
    digital tracking tools 143
    metrics 223–24
employee experience (EX) 61, *63*, 101–02, 111–12, 166–67, 195, 201, 265
    Bersin's view of 93, 95–96
    Children's Society, The 175–76
    CIPD view 83, *84*
    Collinson 173–74
    Deloitte view 73
    EY view 80
    Jaguar Land Rover 175
    McKinsey view 71
    Mercer view 78
    and organizational culture 246–47
    and product mindset *124*, 129, 227–32
    Reward Gateway Edenred 174
    and technology 142–43
employee listening 132
    see also sentiment analysis
employee personas *129*, 176, 247
employee self-service tools 141, 142, 178, 202
employee turnover (attrition) 133, 144, 220
employee value proposition 73, 168
employer brand *124*
    see also reputation
employment contracts 33, 35–36
employment endings *125*
energy 102, 140
engagement *see* employee engagement
engineering 1–5
enterprise resource planning (ERP) systems 141, 172, 201

environmental stewardship 167
equity 232, 233
ergonomic research 139
ESG 61
    see also governance; social context
espoused values 246
esteem *48*
ethical leadership 169
ethics 53, 54, 135, 146, 169, 202, 221
eudaimonia 102
evidence-based HR 105, 136
    see also data-driven decision making
evolution councils 206
evolutionary change 258–63
evolutionary purpose 262–63
EX *see* employee experience (EX)
experimentation 117, 160, 203–04, 214, 228, 248, 250–51, 253, 264–65
external trends analysis 91, 208
EY People Value Chain model 79–81, 97

family life 56
feedback 139, 226, 228
feedback loops *137*, 203, 214, 231, 247, 250, 253
Firstsource 84–87
flexibility 82, 123, *159*, 215
flexible working 37, 38, 250
    see also hybrid working
flourishing at work 101–04, 119, 128
flow *138*, 231, 248, 265
force field analysis 51
framing 123
fulfilment 104, 226
Future Skills programme (JLR) 175
futures literacy 21, 22
futures thinking 20–23, 26, 30–36, 40

Gallup 54
gamification *137*, 143
Gartner frameworks 69–70
General Electric 52
generative AI 126–27
gig economy 61–62, 74
Global Human Capital Trends Report (Deloitte) 72–74
globalization 75
Google 130, 219–20, 228, 229
governance *10*, 91, 205
    see also compliance; data-driven decision making
Graves, Professor Clare 34
green HR policies 167
gross domestic product 38
group dynamics 51
growth mindset *159*, 216, 253

Haier 248
Hawthorne Studies (Mayo) 50–51
heritage 32, 33
    see also industrial relations
hierarchical organizations 6, 34, 75–76
hierarchy of needs (Maslow) 48, 51
high-performance cultures 139
hiring *see* recruitment (hiring)
holistic (multi-disciplinary) solutions
    73, 105, 116
home life 56
Homebase 84–87
HR
    budgetary influence of 202
    and business buy-in 188–89
    as a business function 199, 207, 212
    complexity of 4–5
    as a cost centre 189
    perception of 4, 44, 52–55, 66, 189,
        200, 207
'HR Beta' mindset 208
HR business partner model 52, 58–62, 64,
    69, 82, 86, 87–93, 97, 149, 186
    and collaboration 76
    stagnation of 189–90
HR operating model 23–30
HR Operating Models Review (2024)
    (CIPD) 83–87
HR V2.0 15
HR V3.0 15–16, 99–185, 195, 211–44
human capability model 194–95, 196
human capital 51
human resource information systems 141
human resources management 49–55
hybrid working 60, 74, 138, 139, 144,
    167, 173
    see also remote working
hypothesis testing 157, 186

IBM 52, 144, 221
ideological operating conditions 25
implementation complexity 81, 148–70
inclusion 38–39, 103, 125, 133, 144, 176,
    233–35, 236, 237–38, 252
incubators 34, 36, 37
individual meaning 102
industrial relations 45, 50, 51
Industrial Revolution 2, 6, 39
influence 103
information sharing 262
ING Bank 130, 224
innovation 8–9, 33, 37, 78, 197, 200,
    236–37, 250–51
innovation labs 204
integration 71, 73
    digital 14, 38, 77, 78, 79, 94

Intel 238
internal talent marketplaces 63, 177, 207,
    215, 216
internet 8, 9
intersectionality 107, 113–14, 176, 236–37
    see also systems thinking
investment 191, 202
IPOs 75
'irresistible organization' framework 94
iteration 91, 126, 128, 129, 204, 205, 206,
    214, 229
'It's (Still) the Mortar not the Bricks' (Talent
    Strategy Group) 74–77

Jaguar Land Rover 175
job augmentation 37–38
job crafting 138
job design 138
job rotation 160
journey mapping 126, 129, 247

kanban 129
key performance indicators (KPIs) 38, 91,
    204, 206
knowledge economy 6, 62, 65

language 123
leadership 3, 28, 37, 53–55, 71, 83,
    218–19, 265
    adaptive 138, 252
    anticipatory 20, 21
    buy-in from 204–05
    and cultural change 251–52
    distributed 252
    ethical 169
    inclusive 237–38
    purpose-driven 168
    resistance from 188–89, 199–203
leadership agenda 151
leadership development 85, 135, 138, 140,
    226, 252
learning 33, 46, 47, 56, 117, 174, 180–81
    adaptive 133, 142–43
    and AI 142–43
    continuous 61, 93, 94, 159, 160, 177,
        229, 231, 247–48, 252
learning experience platforms 143
legacy mindset 187–88, 201
leisure 56
Lewin, Kurt 51
linear (traditional) HR thinking 225, 230,
    246, 248, 260
LinkedIn 220
long-termism 22, 191, 259

machine learning 60, 71

management 39, 50, 51, 53–54, 200–01
    operational 105, 142, 157–66
    see also leadership
market conditions 25
Maslow, Abraham *48*, 51
massive online open courses 143
mastery 219
McGregor, Douglas 51
McKinsey & Company 50, 70–72, 96
meaning 102, 106
meaning maker role 163–66
mental health *84*, 114
    see also well-being
mentoring 160
Mercer Target Integration Model 77–79, 96
Meta 219
metrics (measurement) *10, 15, 63, 73, 90*,
    105, 128
    culture 156
    DEI *64*
    people, planet, prosperity 169
    progressive HR analytics *132*
    prosperity 167
    value creation 150
    see also key performance indicators
        (KPIs)
Microsoft 132, 142, 144, 220, 229,
    236, 249
middle management 200–01
mindset
    growth *159*, 216, 253
    'HR Beta' 208
    legacy 187–88, 201
    science 26–30, *40, 47–49*, 118, 135–40,
        217–22
    see also product management mindset
minimum viable products *129*, 156,
    173, 203
Mintzberg, Henry 158–60
mission 25
mobile technology 9
    see also smartphones
modular technology 205
monitoring systems 135
Morning Star 262
motivation *29, 30*, 219
multi-disciplinary (holistic) solutions
    73, 105, 116

natural language processing 141
NatWest Bank plc 84–87, 177–78
Netflix 229, 250, 251
network science 139, 225
neurofeedback 139
nine parameters (Mintzberg) 158–60

norms 251
Novartis 177
nudge theory *137*

occupational psychology *27*, 105, 137–38,
    140, 146
onboarding 33, *63, 124*, 228
operating conditions 25
operating models 7, 9–15, 25, 26
operating systems 156, 193
operational management 105, 142, 157–66
organizational data 136
organizational design & development
    (OD) 6, 7, 8, *11–13*, 23–30, *45*, 55,
    61, 62, 151
organizational effectiveness 118
organizational meaning 102
organizational network analysis *138*, 144
organizational oscillation 258–63
organizational psychology *28, 47*, 105,
    137–38, 146
organizational structure *10*, 188, 225
    hierarchical 6, 34, 75–76
    restructuring 258
Østergaard, Erik Korsvik 20
outcome (results)- driven HR 89, 92, 107
outsourcing *63*

parent-child dependency 111
participatory organizations 21, *37*
    see also culture; governance;
        organizational structure
Patagonia 263
pay analytics 133
Peabody 84–87
Peakon 143
people analytics *28, 64, 85*, 144, 173, 218,
    220–21
people and organization development
    model 62
people and performance analysts
    133–35, 181
people experience *see* employee experience
    (EX)
people function 48–49, 105, 108–14,
    180, 239
people, planet and prosperity-
    centricity 166–68
people proposition 55
people science 3–4, *46–47*, 49, 107
people scientists 162–63
performance *28, 29, 46, 48*, 253
    see also metrics (measurement); people
        and performance analysts
performance culture 127

performance forecasting 133
performance linkage workshops 156–57
performance management 130, 203, 229
performance science 48, 139, 140, 146
personalization 38–39, 71, 134, 143, 174, 177, 229, 247
personnel management 45, 50, 51
pilots 127, 156, 203, 205
Pixar 237
plausible futures 21, 34–36
policies 122–23, 125, 167, 227
'polycrisis' world 19, 31, 32
population decline 61
Porter, Michael 50
positive framing 123
possible futures 21, 152–53
Power BI 144
power structures 188
practice leads 105, 113–14, 162, 182
pre-industrialized work 5–6
predictive analytics 30, 90, 131, 133, 134, 142, 144, 178, 207, 221
preferable futures 21
prescriptive analytics 131, 133, 144
principles 103
    see also trust
processes 10, 14, 78, 85, 118, 188, 201, 231
Procter & Gamble 52
product 46
product management mindset 63, 86, 105–06, 122–31, 146, 156, 163–65, 195, 197, 227–32
    and innovation 250–51
    Santander UK 177
product owners 130
productivity 38, 139
professional expertise 136
Project Aristotle 219–20
project work 37
Propel (Novartis) 177
prosperity 166, 167–68
prototyping 126, 156
    see also pilots
psychological ownership 252
psychological safety 138, 160, 219, 237, 251, 261
psychology 27, 162–63, 219–20
    occupational 105, 137–38, 140, 146
    organizational 28, 47, 105, 137–38, 146
    sports 139
    team 28
pulse surveys 63, 132, 143, 157
purpose 46, 48, 64–66, 85, 89, 94, 102, 153, 219, 252
    Children's Society 176

evolutionary 262–63
    work 55–57
purpose-driven leadership 168

quantum computing 60

real-time analytics 132, 137, 141, 204
recognition 103, 143, 174, 250
recreation 56
recruitment (hiring) 45, 63, 137, 218–219, 238
    and AI 141–42
    digital resumes 145
redeployment 229
Regenerative Era 36, 65, 100, 168
'Reimagine' strategy (JLR) 175
relationship brokers 163
remodelling risks 87
remote working 138, 144, 168
reputation 46, 89
    see also employer brand
resilience 93, 94, 116–17, 138
reskilling 83, 216, 229
    see also upskilling
responsive operating conditions 25
restructuring 258
results (outcome)-driven HR 89, 92, 107
retrospectives 204, 208
return on capital employed 150
return on capital invested (ROI) 150, 157, 202
return on total assets 150
Reward Gateway Edenred 174
reward systems 57, 76, 174, 204
    see also pay analytics
risk aversion 188, 201–02
rituals 251
roadmaps 206
robotic process automation 142
robotics 37–38, 40, 74, 142
role definition 77, 107, 252

Salesforce 132, 221, 238
Santander UK 176–77
SAP 145
scalability 25, 80, 81, 127, 179, 205, 207
scenario planning 29, 32, 33, 37, 40
scepticism 188
Schneider Electric 216
science mindset 26–30, 40, 47–49, 118, 135–40, 217–22
scrums 129, 173, 174
self-determination theory 137
self-managed teams 252, 262
self-service tools 141, 142, 178, 202

self-worth *48*
sentiment analysis 132, 142, 204, 214, 220
shared service centres 58, 60, *64*, 76, 108, 111, 113, 190
short-termism 22, 191, 198, 200, *259*
siloed functions 201, 223, *259*
skills-based operating models 61–62, 160, 167, 168, 177, 202, 215–16
skills development 31–32, 41, 61, 91, 92, 95, 175
    see also reskilling
skills forecasting dashboards 126
Slack 144
sleep 56
smart contracts 145
smartphones *9*, 21
social context 53
social identity theory 138
social science *47*, 138–39, 146
space planning and optimization tools 249
specialization 83, *158*
'spin-outs' (side hustles) 33, 34, 35–36, 74
sports psychology 139
Spotify 214–15, 220, 224, 229, 247, 249
sprints *37*, 173, 174, 175
stakeholder capitalism 89, *90*, 136, 168
standalone HR functions 108–09
Standard Chartered 249–50
'State of the Global Workplace' (Gallup) 54
strategic alignment 59, 77, 79, 80, *84*, 95, 100, 188–89, 201
strategic partnering 73, 79, 83, *84*, 88, 92
strategic workforce planning *37*, 126
strategy 25, 30, 39, 53, 116, 150, 153
supply chains 75
sustainability 36, 61, *64*, *85*, 167, 168
Sustainable Living Plan 14
systemic HR 95–96, 192–94
systems designers 105, 118, 162, 165
systems maps 161–63
systems thinking 22–26, 40, 102, 114–18, 119, 176, *197*, 222–27, 252, 264

T-shaped HR professionals *159*
Tableau 144
talent acquisition 76, 86, *124*, 141–42
talent management 55, *63*, 76, *85*, 86, 168
    marketplaces 177, 207, 215, 216
    talent matching systems 177, 216
Talent Strategy Group 74–77, 97
target integration model 77–79, *96*
target operating models *9*
Teal principles 261–63, 268
team psychology 28

Teams (Microsoft) 144
technology 9–10, 36, *64*, 72–73, 82, *84*, 86, 90–91, 94, 140–45
    embedding 205
    modular 205
    scalability 207
    see also AI (artificial intelligence); augmented reality (AR); automation; blockchain; cloud computing; collaboration tools; computers; data visualization tools; digital integration; digital literacy; digital resumes; digital transformation; digitization; enterprise resource planning (ERP) systems; gamification; internet; learning experience platforms; monitoring systems; self-service tools
Tesco 84–87
three-legged stool (HRBP) model 52, 58–62, 64, 69, 82, 86, 87–93, 97, 149, 186
    and collaboration 76
    stagnation of 189–90
tiered service models 62
toxic leadership 53, 54
traditional HR thinking 225, 230, 246, 248, *260*
training 76, 117
transactional delivery 110
transformational work 89, 206, 258
transition plans 161–63
trends analysis 91, 208
trust 54, 94, 104, 110, 220

Ulrich (HRBP) model 52, 58–62, 64, 69, 82, 86, 87–93, 97, 149, 186
    and collaboration 76
    stagnation of 189–90
Unilever 14–15, 142, 216, 218–19
'Update on the HR Business Partner model' (Ulrich) 88
upskilling 175, 177
urban planning models 225

value 25, 50, 73, 79–81, 97, 102, 153, 166, 168, 246
value creation 73, 88, *90*, 102, 129, 150, 192, 194–95, *197*
Velocity Network 145
vibrant culture 154–57
virtual assistants *64*, 175
virtual global business services (VGBS) 79, 80, *81*

virtual reality (VR) 74, 143
vision 39, 45, 151, 153, 259, 263
visualization 139
Viva Insights 142
volunteering 56, 173

Walmart 143, 221
waterfall approach 228
Web 3.0 99
well-being 93, 94, 104, 116–17, *125*, *138*,
    142, 167
white-collar automation 60
wholeness 261

work
    as a craft 40
    evolution of 34–36, 72
    future of 18–43
    purpose of 55–57
    value of 3
workflow *10*, 55, 144
workforce planning 45, *63*, *84*, 133,
    142, 144
working hours 56
working weeks 33, 34
workload balance *138*
World Economic Forum 9, 19

Looking for another book?

Explore our award-winning
books from global business
experts in Human Resources,
Learning and Development

Scan the code to browse

www.koganpage.com/hr-learning-
development

More from Kogan Page

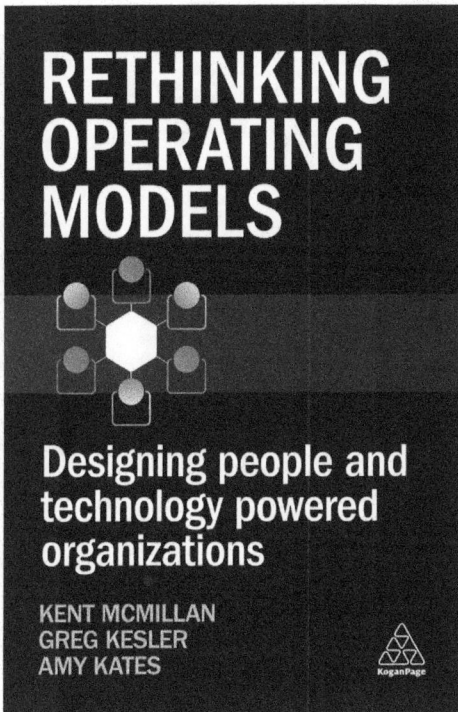

RETHINKING OPERATING MODELS

Designing people and technology powered organizations

KENT MCMILLAN
GREG KESLER
AMY KATES

ISBN: 9781398617964

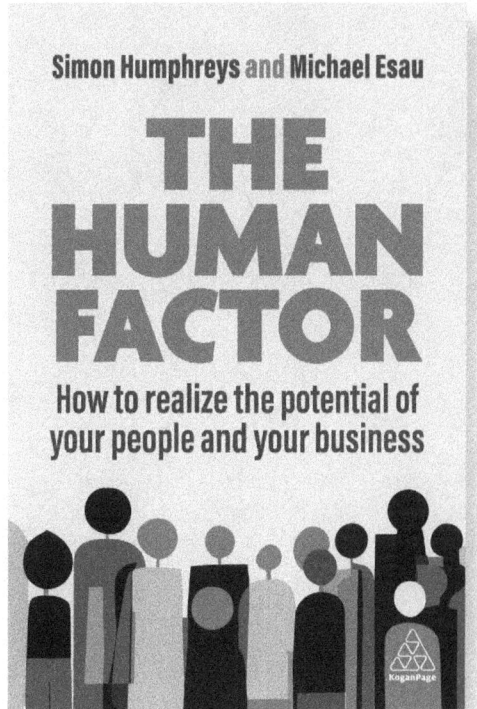

Simon Humphreys and Michael Esau

THE HUMAN FACTOR

How to realize the potential of your people and your business

ISBN: 9781398618169

www.koganpage.com

KoganPage